The languages of literature

The languages of literature

Some linguistic contributions to criticism

by

Roger Fowler

with an essay written in collaboration with Peter Mercer,
and two papers by F. W. Bateson

BARNES & NOBLE, Inc.
NEW YORK
PUBLISHERS & BOOKSELLERS SINCE 1873

First published 1971
© *Roger Fowler 1971*
First published in the United States, 1971
by Barnes & Noble, Inc.
No part of this book may be reproduced
in any form without permission from
the publisher, except for the quotation
of brief passages in criticism

ISBN 0 389 04157 2

Printed in Great Britain

Contents

Preface

In 1966 I published a collection of original essays by a number of linguists and critics, called *Essays on Style and Language*. The plan for the book was initiated four or five years earlier, at a time when many people confidently expected that a new 'linguistic stylistics' would soon become a major influence on literary criticism. But it was quite apparent to anyone who looked at the arguments carefully that the claims for linguistic criticism which were made in the fifties and early sixties were extravagant, and I attempted to collect some more modest approaches, to avoid suggesting the possibility of a sweeping programme in linguistic criticism. One or two reviewers failed to see why *Essays on Style and Language* made only very moderate claims: puzzled by the heterogeneity of the essays, they wondered why I had not assembled a collection of mutually consistent papers all agreeing to argue for and illustrate a 'linguistic approach to literature'. Of course, such a project would have been an unreasonable enterprise. I have never believed in the possibility of a coherent 'linguistic criticism'; only in a more fragmentary set of contributions to certain particular branches of literary studies and, more generally, in the educational relevance of language studies to literary students. These contributions, although short of a 'linguistic criticism', are none the less of great potential value to literary studies.

I would like to think that *Essays on Style and Language* promoted discussion in a useful way. Of particular interest was the dispute between F. W. Bateson and myself in *Essays in Criticism*; full of misunderstandings and strong language as it was, this series of articles was extremely useful to me personally in encouraging me to state my own position more clearly than I had done before. In particular, I emphasized the limitations and qualifications which have to be acknowledged by anyone proposing a linguistic contribution to literary studies. Given the framework of argument established by earlier linguists and their opponents, much of the discussion has inevitably been rather negative and thus a little unsatisfying. But it would be quite improper for me to suggest that there is such a thing as a 'linguistic criticism' which can be demonstrated by sample analyses; and the contribution is still extremely important even if it does not rise to providing a critical method as such.

In the last six or seven years I have written a number of articles on this subject expanding or clarifying material in *Essays on Style and Language*, exploring new areas, and justifying the 'interdiscipline' concerned. These have appeared in various periodicals, and since some of these journals would not normally be seen by literary critics, it may be useful to publish them together in a more accessible form. Assembled in this way, the papers provide a much more detailed and direct discussion of 'linguistics and literature' than *Essays on Style and Language* did. Although these papers do not offer one unified 'method' of linguistic criticism, they do, I think, imply the beginnings of a consistent philosophy of language and literature. Some of the papers are quite technical, but in their origins they were all related to various aspects of my teaching of literature students over the years, and cumulatively they argue and demonstrate the appropriateness of linguistic concepts to a literary education: this is the main claim. But an aesthetic also is implied: the vitality and centrality of the verbal dimension of literature, the continuity of language in literature with language outside literature; language's facility for cultural adjustment; its power to organize concepts, to make fictions. Finally, the emphasis on the plurality of languages in literature entails a rejection of normative conceptions of 'poetic language', and substitution of a principle of poetic creativity which depends on the creativity of all language: the capacity to form a discourse which is simultaneously 'new' and rhetorically decorous.

The first eight papers are polemic, historical, and theoretical. 'Linguistics, Stylistics; Criticism?' was written before *Essays on Style and Language* was published, and its negativeness stemmed from alarm at the magnitude of claims some linguists were making at the time. It was addressed to linguists, and was first delivered as a paper at a meeting of the Linguistics Association of Great Britain, under the scandalous (for that context) title 'The Inadequacy of Linguistics'. Papers 3–6 are all taken from *Essays in Criticism* and followed on the heels of *Essays on Style and Language*; they illustrate very nicely the strength of feelings entertained by participants in disputes about the application of linguistic methods to literature. The seventh paper, 'The Structure of Criticism and the Languages of

Poetry', attempts to broaden the aesthetic implications of earlier
discussions. The title is an allusion to a series of lectures by
R. S. Crane called *The Languages of Criticism and the Structure of
Poetry* (Toronto, 1953), in which a 'pluralist' criticism is defended
and a 'unified' definition of poetry is implied. My adjustment of the
title reverses this thesis, emphasizing a unified base for criticism and
the linguistic heterogeneity of literature. Because this search for a
unified concept of 'literary language' (as opposed to 'ordinary discourse' or 'scientific language' or something of the sort) has been one
of the greatest sources of confusion and error in poetic aesthetics, I
have drawn attention to the point again in the title of the present
book. The eighth paper, written in collaboration with Peter Mercer,
is historical, and concerns not merely linguistics; it delineates a
tradition of study of language in literature, and describes the critical
activities of British linguists within that tradition.

The next four papers discuss metre from a linguistic point of view.
My first paper on metre was ' "Prose Rhythm" and Metre', Ch. 5 of
Essays on Style and Language, which in its interests relates to
Seymour Chatman's famous analysis of Robert Frost's 'Mowing' and
to Wimsatt and Beardsley's 'The Concept of Meter' (for references,
see p. 172 below, note 2). 'Structural Metrics' is a review-article based
on Chatman's *A Theory of Meter,* and shows increasing distance
from Chatman's original position and the beginnings of a movement
away from his more recent theory. 'What is Metrical Analysis?'
scrutinizes the basic concepts of the major modern tradition of
linguistic metrics and proposes a reorientation and an interpretation
of fundamental terms in metrics (the terminology is developed from
Roman Jakobson). If I were writing this paper today I would
probably choose a more explicitly 'generative' approach, following
the work of Chomsky, Halle, and Keyser in phonology. The short
review which comes next is included because it sketches the application of the ideas of 'What is Metrical Analysis?' to a particular
(Anglo-Saxon) verse tradition. Next, I have included some notes on
three varieties of blank verse in an effort to balance the predominantly theoretical tone of the preceding three papers.

The final three papers also offer specific analysis: 13 and 14 both
employ a mode of description which could be labelled 'neo-Firthian',
'Hallidayan', or 'scale-and-category' analysis: this form of linguistic
description (also used by John Sinclair in Ch. 4 of *Essays on Style and
Language*) is extremely convenient for the exposition of structure in
short texts, although arguably it implies a none-too-powerful model
of syntax. The apparatus is used in Paper 14 in an attempt to
provide linguistic substantiation for a commonplace in critical
theory, the existence in lyric poems of an abstract 'pattern' or

'structure'. Readers may be especially interested in the contrast between Papers 14 and 15. The papers discuss the same poem, but use two different modes of analysis, address two quite different audiences, and focus on problems of two quite separate origins: the fourteenth considers a question formulated within critical theory, whereas the final paper is concerned with a problem formulated within transformational-generative linguistics.

The first paper could have been called, pretentiously, 'Retrospect, 1970'. It is largely a survey of ideas and techniques in 'linguistic stylistics' of the last twenty years, attempting to relate my own views to those of other linguists who have worked in this area; to state a 'position'. As I wrote this introduction, I became more and more aware that I was defining possible areas for study which had hardly been investigated at all: so the introductory paper progresses from an enumeration of past statements, attitudes, and techniques to a series of hints for future research. I would like to think that I have here indicated a prospect rather than a retrospect.

Sources and acknowledgments

The 'Introduction' and the paper 'Three Blank Verse Textures' have not been published before, but they reflect the substance of lectures delivered at universities in the Netherlands under the auspices of the British Council in 1969. I am happy to record my gratitude to the British Council for making those occasions possible, and to staff and students at the University of Amsterdam, the Free University of Amsterdam, and the Universities of Leiden, Nijmegen, and Groningen for providing responsive audiences who helped me to develop my ideas.

'Linguistics, Stylistics; Criticism?' is reprinted from *Lingua*, xvi (1966), 153–65, by permission of the North-Holland Publishing Company, Amsterdam.

'Literature and Linguistics' and 'Language and Literature' are reprinted from *Essays in Criticism*, xvii (July 1967), 322–47 and xviii (April 1968), 164–82, by permission of Mr F. W. Bateson.

'The Structure of Criticism and the Languages of Poetry' is reprinted from Malcolm Bradbury (ed.), *Contemporary Criticism* (Stratford-upon-Avon Studies, London, 1970) by permission of Malcolm Bradbury and of Edward Arnold (Publishers) Ltd.

'Criticism and the Language of Literature: some Traditions and Trends in Great Britain' was written in collaboration with Peter Mercer and is reprinted from *Style*, iii (Winter 1969), 45–72, by permission of the Editor, James R. Bennett, the University of Arkansas.

'Structural Metrics' is reprinted from *Linguistics*, xxvii (November 1966), 49–64, by permission of Mouton and Co., Publishers, The Hague.

I am grateful to Messrs Ernst Eulenberg Ltd for permission to reproduce eight bars from Miniature Score No. 55.

'What is Metrical Analysis?' and '*The Rhythm of Beowulf*—a review' are reprinted from *Anglia*, lxxxvi (1968), 280–320 and lxxxvii (1969), 444–9, by permission of Max Niemeyer Verlag, Tübingen.

'Some Stylistic Features of the *Sermo Lupi*' is reprinted from the *Journal of English and Germanic Philology*, lxv (January 1966), 1–18, by permission of The University of Illinois Press.

'Linguistics and the Analysis of Poetry' is reprinted from the *Critical Survey*, iii (Summer 1967), 78–89; the poem 'anyone lived in a pretty how town' from *Complete Poems* by e. e. cummings, quoted in this paper, is printed by permission of MacGibbon & Kee.

'On the Interpretation of "Nonsense Strings"' is reprinted from the *Journal of Linguistics*, 5 (1969), 75–83, by permission of Cambridge University Press.

Note on the text

In reprinting these papers from a variety of sources, it has been necessary to make minor changes to the format of notes and references, to ensure a homogeneous typographical style; in addition, a few printer's errors in the originals have been corrected, and some bibliographical references have been brought up to date. No alterations of substance have been made.

One

Introduction

i *Backgrounds to the linguistic study of literature*

When I read English at the University of London in the fifties, I had to make a choice between the 'literature syllabus' and the 'language syllabus'. The former entailed concentration on post-Renaissance literature; the latter reduced the literary corpus, doubled the Old and Middle English, and allowed students to study such allegedly 'linguistic' subjects as Anglo-Saxon Art and Archaeology, Old Icelandic, and Philology. This choice of alternative emphases reflected a traditional division in the field of English studies.[1] At London, Oxford, and the majority of the civic universities, English departments were staffed by people with two different kinds of training and interests. The 'language' faculty were the descendants of generations of Anglo-Saxonists in a tradition of scholarship dating back to the seventeenth century. In the nineteenth, the antiquarianism of the early Anglo-Saxonists blended with the 'scientific' spirit of the new comparative and historical philology.[2] By the close of the century there was in existence an army of scholars with advanced professional interests in the structure and early history of English and the other Germanic languages. When English was established as a university subject—effectively displacing classics as the central arts subject—philological medievalism found a prominent place in the syllabus. Regrettably, the presence of this study has been a source of continuous strife with staff on the other side of English departments: staff with predominantly 'literary' interests. In this context 'literary' came to mean 'post-medieval', and so a rather awkward division of labour was institutionalized. Literature written before about 1500 was taught by philologists; their responsibilities also included phonetics, history of the English language, etc.; they were not expected (and, in some cases, not allowed) to teach post-medieval literature, except perhaps for the occasional foray into Shakespearean or Miltonic syntax or Spenserean diction. As literary studies gained the ascendancy, 'language' was presented as an archaic irrelevance at best and an inimical source of potential contamination at worst. The position of the philologists and medievalists became an entrenched defence under constant attack. Undergraduates resented having to learn Anglo-Saxon, faculty resented staff places being taken up by Anglo-Saxonists. By the time I came into university teaching, there was a regular Berlin Wall down the middle of English studies. The flavour of the dispute between the warring factions can be sensed in the undignified squabbles which have occurred at Oxford in recent years on the question of compulsory Anglo-Saxon in the English syllabus.

One of the allegations made against philology and medieval studies was that they are irrelevant to the study of modern literature; another, that Anglo-Saxon literature is, through distance, culturally irrelevant; a third, that it maintains a study which is impertinently 'scientific'. Philology deals in 'facts' (so does editing, a necessary preoccupation of medievalists), possesses analytic 'techniques', employs 'jargon'. The study of literature entails consideration of 'values', and values are felt to be the antithesis of facts and thus unamenable to scientific study.

In short, the history of English studies in England presents the lamentable spectacle of two close neighbours jealously fencing in their own pastures and defending them at any cost, including irrational argument. I don't think that 'lettrists' and 'medievalists' have been able to see each other's concerns undistorted for many years now.

Note that this state of affairs—dispute about the place of medieval and philological studies in the English syllabus—is only indirectly related to the subject of this book: the applicability of modern linguistics to the study of literature. It is true that some linguists (including myself) started their academic careers as medievalists— but we are as well equipped as any to attest to the discontinuity between 'being a medievalist' and 'being a linguist'. Although postwar linguistics is far removed in its concepts and materials from traditional 'English language' work, the critics and literature teachers of today seem unable to distinguish these pursuits. They feel equally threatened by both, and so they dismiss the new linguistics as fervently as they condemned the old philological medievalism. It has to be said that they are in general extremely ignorant about linguistics, regarding it as an alien discipline about which they need to know nothing. It is not surprising that they fail to distinguish it from the older school of medieval textual and philological studies. To be fair, the state of ignorance is mutual. Contemporary linguistics is a demanding discipline, and few linguists have time to do more than sample the copious outpourings of the critical presses. However, it is my impression that the general level of knowledge about literature and criticism among linguists is higher than is the level of informedness about linguistics among 'lettrists'. It is a very sad fact that progress in the *rapprochement* of linguistic and literary studies has been hampered by the ignorance and prejudice of literary colleagues. I regret having to make this statement so bluntly; but it is an allegation which can easily be substantiated and is best made openly.

Because of these difficulties of communication between linguists and critics, the applicability of linguistic method and ideas has still, apparently, to be justified; this is in spite of a good deal of practical work and theoretical argument by linguists during the last twenty years. I would date the beginnings of modern interest in 'linguistic criticism' from this statement by Harold Whitehall in 1951: 'as no science can go beyond mathematics, no criticism can go beyond its linguistics.'[3] This is certainly an extravagant claim; I do not think any contemporary linguist would commit himself to such a sweeping assertion. Yet some critics evidently believe that this is the claim which linguists generally are making: the claim that criticism should be based on linguistics, and that criticism can only be as good as the linguistics which informs it. To understand why anyone should have made such an audacious statement, and why no one would maintain such a position today, it is necessary to understand that linguistics has been completely revolutionized since the early fifties: the claim arises from a style of linguistics which is almost universally condemned today. Now while the goals and practices of linguistics have changed nearly beyond recognition within twenty years, the argument about the critical relevance of linguistics has proceeded with apparent continuity and consistency. It is now necessary to moderate the excesses of the early claims, and restate as clearly as possible what critical functions it is proper for the contemporary linguist to perform.

The confidence of Whitehall's proposal stems from the mood of American linguistics at the time. In 1951 two extremely influential books were published: Z. S. Harris's *Methods in Structural Linguistics*, and *Outline of English Structure* by G. L. Trager and H. L. Smith. With the publication of these books it seemed that American structuralism, the foundations of which had been laid in the twenties and thirties, had attained methodological perfection. Harris's book, and a body of articles by authors in the same school,[4] laid out a set of efficient techniques for discovering the structure of languages;

B

Trager and Smith's monograph provided an example of a description in which the essentials of the structure of a natural language were set out symmetrically and economically. A historian of modern linguistics nicely (but without irony) captures the spirit of that time:

> With the publication of *Methods in Structural Linguistics*
> American structuralism clearly reached its majority, and could
> take its place in the world of scholarship as a mature discipline
> uncompromisingly dedicated to the scientific study of language.[5]

Descriptive linguistics was regarded as a strictly empirical science. Its data consisted of samples of speech ('texts', 'utterances'), ideally collected in accordance with certain set field-work procedures. The language corpora so built up were then subjected to a succession of analytic techniques: they were first recorded in phonetic notation, that is, transcribed as sequences of sounds. Distributional techniques could then be employed to reveal which classes of sounds ('phonemes') were used in that language to effect differentiations of meaning. Next came the discovery of syntactic units: morphemes, classes of morphemes, words, phrases, clauses, sentences, etc. These units, or classes of units, were observed to have regular privileges of occurrence relative to each other—for example, the class of articles regularly precedes the class of nouns, with adjectives optionally occurring in between. Thus the structure of sentences, texts, or languages (seen as collections of texts) could be presented in terms of the distributional privileges of units relative to each other. Structure was a generalization, or abstraction, extracted from texts by the application of techniques of *segmentation*—chopping the texts into linearly juxtaposed units—and *classification*—sorting the resulting segments into different categories according to the similarities and differences of their distributional behaviour. And it was believed that this structural analysis could be carried out in a mechanical fashion: that linguistic technicians could be trained in the methods so effectively that two separate analyses of the same data would yield the same results (the empiricist criterion of 'reproducibility of experiments'). What is more, the structuralists argued the practicality (and necessity) of conducting analysis without recourse to the *meanings* of the utterances under investigation. In theory, this condition meant only that syntactic and phonemic tests were best conducted without appeal to semantic criteria; it did not necessarily mean that no statements were to be made about the semantic dimension of language, although it was acknowledged that such statements were very difficult to make.[6] In practice, linguists had to make constant surreptitious references to meaning in order to establish their phonemic and syntactic units, while at the same time the frontal description of meaning was almost totally neglected.[7]

The general characteristics of American structural linguistics that I want to emphasize are these: the belief current among that generation of linguists that their discipline was defined by a set of analytic methods with the status of *discovery procedures*; and, relatedly, that linguistic description consisted of the induction of structure, of patterns of abstract units which were inherent in the linguistic materials under consideration. It must be stressed that this is by no means the only possible way of thinking about the nature of linguistic description; some readers may find this surprising, but they must be prepared to entertain the possibility that 'linguistic analysis' may mean any one of a range of quite distinct activities.

The next stage in the recent history of linguistics is all too familiar to a whole generation of American schoolteachers. The structuralism of the fifties was aggressively innovatory, claiming overwhelming advantages over 'traditional' or 'school' grammar. Many English teachers were persuaded to introduce the new methods into their teaching. But no sooner had they learnt the new jargon, the new styles of diagramming sentences, than they were told that they had to learn linguistics all over again. In 1957 Noam Chomsky, who had been a pupil of Z. S. Harris, published a little book called *Syntactic Structures* which heralded a new style of linguistics, *transformational-generative grammar*.[8] The repercussions of this study have literally revolutionized linguistic theory. Although the details of the approach have been hotly controversial, there is no doubt that it has completely changed our way of thinking about language; even those who do not accept Chomsky's methods would readily admit that his ideas have been a seminal influence on linguistic research in the last decade: linguistics has probably never before been such an active discipline.

Chomsky argued that structuralism was an attempt to perfect what he called a 'phrase structure grammar' (PSG). A PSG is characterized by its absolute dependence on a certain very limited range of types of linguistic rule. Every linguistic construction is seen as 'consisting of' an arrangement of other constructions at some lower level. So in a PSG a sentence such as

The dogs were chasing a cat

would be represented as a sequence of an *NP* (Noun Phrase—*the dogs*) and a *VP* (Verb Phrase—*were chasing a cat*); this information could be presented in the following rule

$$S \rightarrow NP + VP$$

where '→' means 'is' or 'consists of' or 'rewrite as'. In the same way,
a rule

$$VP \rightarrow V + NP$$

tells us that *were chasing a cat* consists of a Verb followed by an *NP*.
A third rule

$$NP \rightarrow Art + N$$

assigns the structure 'Article followed by Noun' to *the dogs, a cat*.
Other rules of the same type are necessary to explain, for example,
the internal structure of *were chasing*.

All these rules (and according to Chomsky they illustrate the only
type of rule found in a PSG) obey the two structuralist principles of
segmentation and classification. A construction is divided into
smaller sub-parts, and the sub-parts so segmented are sorted into
classes—the symbols in the rules above (*NP*, *VP*, etc.) represent
classes of linguistic units. Linguistic analysis proceeds sentence by
sentence, accepting each sentence as a linear sequence of formatives,
breaking it down progressively into its component parts and categorizing these parts. A PSG is no more than a systematization of the
traditional activity of 'parsing'.

Parsing is certainly an essential part of syntactic analysis. But
Chomsky argues that a PSG *by itself* is not adequate to the task of
describing a natural language. This is not the place to report the
argument in detail; I will content myself with giving a few examples
of some aspects of linguistic structure which a PSG is incapable of
explaining.[9] A PSG cannot account for the fact that a language is an
infinite set of sentences, i.e. that there is no longest sentence in a
language: *John eats apples, plums, pears, oranges, cheese, milk . . .* can
be extended indefinitely, as can *I believe that Chomsky alleged that
Skinner maintained that pigeons perceive that . . .* and several other
types of construction. It cannot show that many sentences are
ambiguous: *The chicken is ready to eat, I saw her in the street,* etc.—a
PSG will assign identical analyses to the different meanings which
underlie each of these sentences. A PSG is unable to show that some
sentences which appear to have different structures are in fact
synonymous: *A bus ran over him, He was run over by a bus.* It cannot
deal with discontinuous constituents, that is to say items which form
one single unit although they may be divided on the surface of a
sentence: *A bus ran him over, He took his hat off, Either John or
Peter will come.*

To remove these difficulties Chomsky proposed that a phrase
structure grammar should be supplemented by the addition of a set
of *transformational* rules. PS-rules, treat sentences as arrangements

of classes of items; transformations add *process* to *arrangement* by reordering, or adding, or deleting, items. Thus *He was run over by a bus* can be explained as a transformational reordering of *A bus ran over him*. The imperative *Eat your dinner!* is *You eat your dinner* (described by PS-rules) with *you* transformationally deleted. *A bus ran him over* is *A bus ran over him* rearranged transformationally; cf. (1) *He took off his hat*, (2) *He took his hat off*. In a sense, the transformational rule derives (2) from (1): it introduces discontinuity in one of the constituents. Whereas a PS-rule would give quite distinct analyses for (1) and (2), the transformational approach assumes that the two sentences are related, and clearly demonstrates the relationship.[10]

So far, it would seem that Chomsky has merely suggested some mechanical improvements in the technique of syntactic analysis. In fact, the consequences of his approach are much more far-reaching: the whole conception of linguistics has changed. We now no longer regard linguistics as an 'analytic' discipline in the sense proposed by the structuralists. That generation of linguists, remember, regarded the goal of linguistics as discovering structures in sentences, and listing and classifying these structures and the units which entered into them: the resulting catalogue was claimed to be the grammar of the language. Clearly, structure was felt to be somehow inherent in sentences, and this inherent structure was the subject-matter of linguistic science. This view is not obviously well-founded. It's arguable that the subject-matter of linguistics is not sentence-structure, but rather the linguistic faculties of speakers. It follows that sentences are not *subject-matter*, but *data*, interesting only in so far as they provide access to the vital, human, dimension of language: what speakers know which enables them to produce and understand sentences.

I will explain this in a little more detail. A language (*L*) may be defined as an infinite set of sentences. A language is described by a grammar. A grammar is a device which *generates* or *enumerates* the set of sentences which constitutes *L*. It does this by assigning structural descriptions to all the utterances which are grammatical sentences of *L* and to none of the ungrammatical ones. For instance, the structural description of our sample sentence *The dogs were chasing a cat* includes the information that the sentence contains two Noun Phrases, each of which is a sequence Article plus Noun. The grammar contains a rule $NP \rightarrow Art + N$. What is the status of that rule? Does it simply acknowledge the presence of sequences $Art + N$ in many English sentences? I think that, in order to be interesting, this rule has to be regarded as doing something more than noticing one regularity in English sentences. Contemporary linguists would assert that a linguistic rule has roughly the following significance. Speakers of English are observed to produce sentences which include the pattern represented by *the dogs, a cat, an apple, the books, some cheese*, etc. This patterning reflects certain knowledge speakers of English possess which is part of 'knowing English'. The rule $NP \rightarrow Art + N$ is an abstract representation of part of what a fluent, mature, speaker of English knows, which allows him to produce and understand English sentences which contain that substructure. Sentences (and, therefore, texts also) are not regarded as interesting in themselves; when we analyse them, we are asking, not What is their structure? but What does a speaker know which enables him to produce and understand sentences with these observed characteristics? A grammar is said to be a hypothesis about *linguistic competence*: about the knowledge speakers possess which makes *linguistic performance* possible. A linguist is interested in texts as samples of performance, as concrete reflections of competence.

Of course, utterances and texts reflect many factors in addition to linguistic competence.[11] By itself, linguistic competence provides no motivation for producing one sentence rather than another, one kind of structure rather than another. In ordinary discourse, the form sentences assume reflects such factors as the topic of conversation (one vocabulary rather than another); the speaker's relationship to his audience (distant or intimate); his intention (persuasion, information, etc.); the physical situation of the participants (two people face-to-face, two people on the telephone, lecturer to large audience, broadcaster to unseen audience, etc.); the mood, state of health, and so on, of the speaker. The influences on the form of linguistic performance are obviously manifold, diverse, and changeable. Consequently, there is a great range of descriptive statements that can be made about texts. But we can divide these statements into two classes. First, each sentence can be identified as a particular construction in a particular language, the reflex of a selection of rules which that language's speakers know. This is a purely grammatical description, and by itself is certainly of very little interest to criticism. Second, we can try to explain *why* the sentences have the form they do. Why does a certain text have many long, balanced sentences and a florid vocabulary? Why does a certain speaker constantly use a breathy tone? Why do some texts (e.g. newspaper advertisements) use short, verb-less sentences? Why are certain journals dense with multi-syllabic, uncommon technical terms? Why are some styles of pronunciation intonationally monotonous? The range of such questions (and, indeed, their answers) is apparently endless. And it is quite obvious that simple grammatical description goes only a short way towards answering them.

Yet it is equally obvious that they are best answered by someone who is well informed about the facts of linguistic structure—who knows fairly accurately what the phenomena are which he is asking questions about.

ii *The position of the 'linguistic critic'*

In a sense there have always been 'linguistic critics', if by that is meant students of literature who pay particular attention to the language dimension of literary texts. As far back as we have written records, there have been scholars whose linguistic and critical studies have amalgamated in their work on sacred texts, or texts which have been revered for other reasons, for instance their antiquity. Textual exegesis, and efforts to conserve ancient and honoured forms of language, have traditionally nurtured a linguistic science in intimate contact with the value and meaning of texts. The oldest, best-known and most influential example would be the work of the Sanskrit Indian grammarians in the preservation of the language of the Vedic religious texts, several centuries before Christ.[12] Much nineteenth-century philological scholarship, directly influenced by the rediscovery of the Sanskrit grammarians, carried on this spirit of enquiry: linguistics remained closely attached to textual discussion. It is only in this century that linguistics and literary studies have lost their interdependence. So, as we have seen, recent proposals to 'apply linguistics to literature' have appeared awkward and even shocking, despite the existence of a long heritage in this kind of study.

But once the proposal had been made, a steady flow of linguistic-literary analyses appeared on both sides of the Atlantic. Most of this work is discussed in other papers in the present volume, and here I will simply list some of the more significant publications. Whitehall's recommendation that the Trager-Smith mode of analysis should be applied to poetry bore fruit, especially in the field of metrics. His review was republished, in an extended form, in the 1956 *Kenyon Review*, followed by a symposium on verse structure in which Seymour Chatman made his first important contribution to metrics; in 1959 we had Epstein and Hawkes' *Linguistics and English Prosody*; in 1961, John Thompson's *The Founding of English Metre*; in 1965, Chatman's book *A Theory of Meter*.[13] Samuel R. Levin in 1962 published his monograph *Linguistic Structures in Poetry*; in the same year, papers by Levin and M. A. K. Halliday at the Ninth International Congress of Linguists attracted much discussion.[14] Already a large (and inconclusive) interdisciplinary conference on style had been held (at Indiana University, in 1958); the proceedings

were edited by Thomas A. Sebeok as *Style in Language* (M.I.T. Press,
1960), a volume which, by providing a range of theoretical discussions and models of analysis, did a great deal to promote interest in
this subject. A statement of method by British linguists is Spencer
and Gregory's *Linguistics and Style* (1964); and in 1965 the journal
A Review of English Literature devoted one issue to 'New Attitudes
to Style', in which more writings by British 'stylisticians' appeared.
One of the contributors, Geoffrey N. Leech, has now provided an
elementary textbook: *A Linguistic Guide to English Poetry* (1969).
And throughout this period there have appeared scores of specialized, popularizing or polemic articles: many of the most important
are collected in three anthologies, by Chatman and Levin, by Love
and Payne, and by Donald C. Freeman.[15] It now seems that we
have a fertile discipline of 'linguistic criticism', however controversial
the productions of that discipline might be. Reading materials—
both scholarly and pedagogic—abound.

I mentioned earlier that linguistics in literary studies still needs
to be justified; this remains true despite the productivity of the
advocates of this approach. Before proceeding further, we should
evaluate the claims that have been made for linguistics in literary
studies. We might do so by asking three questions:

Is criticism in any way dependent on linguistics?

Can linguistic analysis serve as a mode of criticism?

What specific contributions (other than under the two general
heads above) can linguistics make to literary studies?

The first two questions imply very strong claims for linguistics;
claims which are almost certainly too strong and in any case stronger
than most of the proponents of 'linguistic criticism' would put forward. As an exception, Harold Whitehall's statement, quoted on
p. 3 above, may be construed as an affirmative answer to the first
question: 'no criticism can go beyond its linguistics'. If this assertion
means that a theory and practice of criticism cannot do without an
explicit linguistic theory and methodology (rather than, more
vaguely, that criticism may be improved by some knowledge about
language), it is obviously untrue. If we can conceive of the possibility
of an adequate theory of literature, quite clearly a theory of language
can be no more than a part of that more general theory—as a theory
of language can only be a part of the theory of any specialized
variety of linguistic performance, irrespective of whether the texts
concerned are 'literary' or not. And of course the assertion is be-
haviourally untrue also: most of the world's most respected critics
haven't a clue about linguistics. Even if the claim were true, its im-

plications are impracticable. Most academics would find it impossible
to keep up the necessary reading in both subjects. It can only be true
in the sense that a precise knowledge of language is helpful to criticism; but this is a quite different admission. (I will return to it
shortly.)

To take the second question, very briefly.[16] There is a strong implication in the critical work of some linguists (notably Halliday and
Hill) that linguistic analysis is an available mode of criticism. Let it
be stated yet again that linguistic description is not critical study;
that the use of techniques or terminology drawn from linguistics is
no guarantee whatsoever of discovering, or saying, anything specially
interesting about texts as literature. Particularly, linguistic description can suggest nothing distinctive about literature: there is
no 'linguistic criticism' if by that is meant a recognizably different,
viably alternative, kind or mode of criticism.[17] As I have said before,
linguistics in this context must either serve as an ancillary apparatus
or lose some of its identity.

After we have disposed of the most ambitious proposals in this
way, what claim for linguistics in literary studies remains? I think
three areas of advantage can be asserted. The first and most important is also the humblest and simplest:

1 Some knowledge of how language works is indispensable
   basic information for the student and critic of literature.
   (An *educational* claim.)
2 Certain areas of literary study demand close engagement
   with the mechanics of language (e.g. metrics); linguistics
   provides specific information and analytic technique. (A
   technical claim.)
3 Linguistics is an advanced theoretical discipline which provides certain insights into the nature of literature and
   criticism. (A *theoretical* claim.)

My first proposal is a weakened and redirected version of Whitehall's
claim. Whereas he suggested that linguistics is the foundation of
criticism, I am maintaining that critical practice can be improved by
knowledge about language. Linguistics is a theory of how language
works: how it is acquired, how it communicates meanings, what
kinds of structure it employs, and so on. Literary criticism is an
account of the use of language in some particular types of text. It
would be surprising if knowledge of language in general did not en-
hance understanding of specific instances of language use. There is
thus a powerful *a priori* argument for critics and students knowing
about language—by knowing some general linguistics. (This assumes
that, in academic reality, linguistics is a reliable source of information

about language!) I could here list scores of cases of critical statements vitiated by linguistic ignorance, but I will restrict myself to one student example. A graduate of the English Department of one of America's largest and most prestigious universities wrote a paper on Yeats' poem 'Among Schoolchildren' in which she had a point to make about what she called the 'long stresses' in one line. (The observation concerned a presumed 'effect' of the phonological make-up of certain of the metrically 'stressed' syllables in the line.) I tried to explain why it is improper to talk about 'long' stresses: that the devices available for metrical use—specifically, for measuring out the domain of a line—depend on the phonology of the language in which verse is written; that English, like the Germanic languages generally, is indeed a 'stress' language: some syllables are felt to be more prominent than others, such syllables are regularly disposed in sentences, and the difference between 'stressed' and 'unstressed' syllables may be exploited to effect distinctions of meaning; that stress can be regarded either as an abstract linguistic formative or a perceptual phenomenon; in the latter case, perception is induced by certain phonetic features (which I specified); that many other languages did not regularize stress—some, for instance the classical languages, depended on length of syllable, and in those languages differential length was indeed a metrical device. I also mentioned how, because of a confused early history, English metrical theory had mistakenly taken over the 'long/short' distinction and used it inappropriately in the descriptive jargon for English prosody. . . .

My explanation was doubtless pedantic and boring, and perhaps wasted, but I felt that I was justified in requiring a modicum of descriptive accuracy, at least from a graduate student. Of course, I could understand what she was saying—but by the wrong routes: first, because she had been a student in one of my classes for several weeks, so that I was sensitive to her way of expressing herself; second, because I, like everyone else who teaches literature, have learnt to 'translate' students' characteristic misdescriptions into sense. Concepts like 'stress' are linguistic primitives, which anyone who talks about language (e.g. a critic) refuses to understand at his cost. The price paid is often failure to make a point clearly; or failure to make a point in terms which can actually be talked about; or simply building a fancy castle with insubstantial foundations. The most important of these sins to avoid is probably inarticulacy: here linguistic terminology can help by providing a metalanguage for critical discussion in so far as it concerns language.

A very few major critics seem to know about the nature of language by instinct, without the benefit of formal linguistics.[18] As one reads such people one learns something about language, as well as about the texts being discussed. How should a literature department educate its students to produce critics with these qualifications? It has to be admitted at once that there is no easy way to inculcate a grasp of fundamental linguistic principles. It has long been known that speakers are naturally innocent of the character of their linguistic behaviour; that consciousness of the processes of language is (where it is not a product of social confusion, and hence inhibiting) generally achieved only as a result of professional training. (It is possible that metalinguistic naïveté is a necessary condition for linguistic fluency in many people.) Now teachers of linguistics know that it is a discipline which generates great enthusiasm among students who achieve intermediate or advanced competence in it: it is an exceedingly satisfying subject once the student 'gets on top of it'—it is formally pleasing, neat, of obvious intellectual importance and social relevance. The drawback is that the concepts and techniques involved are strange at the initial level, and highly complicated and detailed once sentences above the artificially simple are to be accounted for conscientiously.[19] There seems to be no satisfactory way of introducing students to the general framework of linguistics without forbiddingly detailed specific exemplification. A further problem is that contemporary linguists are obsessed with the theoretical implications of their discipline to the extent that a large proportion of books and articles nowadays are abstrusely metatheoretical. Beginning students are likely to make little of the most important books in the field: I suppose Chomsky's *Aspects of the Theory of Syntax* (M.I.T. Press, 1965) is the classic instance: an extremely difficult (and badly written) book which is nevertheless so important that it is impossible to proceed further than a term into an introductory linguistics course without referring students to it. The difficulty of the subject is, unfortunately, compounded by the lack of suitable texts for the task I have in mind: endearing linguistic theory to students who are not going to become utter specialists and who thus ought not to be bothered by details of phonemes, morphemes, lexemes, tagmemes, sememes, kernels, double-base transformations, feature analysis, audible friction, formants, glottal plosion, arytenoid cartilages, and all the rest. This problem in elementary textbook-writing I commend to my colleagues in linguistics: it is a problem very much worth solving. If there were a contemporary equivalent of Saussure's *Course in General Linguistics* —a brilliantly penetrating yet simple book—many of the pedagogic and public-relations difficulties which an interdisciplinary linguist like myself has to face would evaporate.

My major recommendation (a difficult one to fulfil, in the light of the above observations) is that a place for general linguistics should be found in literary education. Under this recommendation, the student is supposed to have his critical statements improved by knowing about language in a profound, general, but perhaps unspecific way. Of course, he knows the language expertly;[20] but he only needs to know *about* language in rather general terms—just enough to meet the conditions of accuracy, sensitivity to linguistic functioning, and clarity of exposition. As a concrete example of what he needs to know and what he doesn't, let me again cite the case of 'stress' as an indispensable piece of knowledge; or, the student ought to know what an embedding transformation is, but he need not acquaint himself with the dispute about the validity of the notion of Verb Phrase Complementation. It is clearly possible to write interestingly and responsibly about recurrent images in Shakespeare, subculture reference in Malamud or John Braine, romantic parody in Jane Austen, or T. S. Eliot's allusions, without a very advanced linguistic apparatus. This would not seem to be the case with studies of rhythm in Hopkins, sound-texture in Keats, syntax in *Paradise Lost* or in Henry James, metaphoric structure in Wallace Stevens, ungrammaticalness in e. e. cummings, style in Flaubert. Here we move on to the second of my three claims for a linguistic contribution to literature, the *technical* claim. I would think that such studies simply cannot be undertaken except by someone with an advanced descriptive competence in the relevant dimension(s) of linguistic structure. Any worthwhile statement in any of these fields must be based on a detailed, analytic awareness of the texture of language. You cannot talk usefully about sound-structure, for instance, without knowing a lot about the acoustic and articulatory levels of speech, and a good deal about the psychology of perception. Without such special knowledge, only a meaningless impressionism is possible.[21]

At this point I would wish, ideally, to give a catalogue of linguists' successes in discussing various aspects of the linguistic structure of literary texts: triumphs in the analysis of metre, phonetic structure, metaphor, departures from grammaticalness, or whatever. As we will see from later essays in this book, good progress has been made in prosodic theory and analysis; and some of the papers in Sebeok's volume, and in Chatman and Levin's anthology, suggest the beginnings of insights into other, relatively technical areas. Again, references in the final paper in the present book suggest that linguists are starting to provide the basis for an understanding of the nature and effect of grammatical deviation in poetry. To take one more example of technical study, I can see promise of a linguistic contribution to the description of what might be called 'interlevel' effects in poetry. By this I mean concords and dissonances between different levels of linguistic structure (syntax and vocabulary, sound and semantics, etc.). In *Essays on Style and Language* Peter Wexler and I, separately, made some preliminary notes on what we called 'grammetrics', the interrelation of syntax and metre, in French and, English poetry. W. K. Wimsatt's essay 'One Relation of Rhyme to Reason' is also an exercise in interlevel theory.[22] But on the whole, the most I can do at this stage is indicate (as above) the areas in which technical contributions of linguistics to literary studies might be expected, and hope that this short paragraph may serve as an efficient plea to linguists to undertake detailed work on the verbal texture of literature.

iii *Theoretical considerations*

I want now to refer to some theoretical insights which arise from the juxtaposition of general linguistics and literary criticism, and to some theoretical problems and programmes raised by this juxta-position.

Despite I. A. Richards' efforts to place it on a scientific footing, modern literary theory remains depressingly uninformative about the nature of literature. The pronouncements of aestheticians—for example Monroe C. Beardsley[23]—are often wide of the mark because the aesthetician tends to generalize across the boundaries of differ-ent art media, neglecting the qualities which distinguish literature from, say, the visual and musical arts. If we turn from aestheticians to critics, we find that their general comments on the definition of literature are characteristically no more than apologies for their own practical methods. This is particularly true of the theoretical dis-cussions of New Critics such as Cleanth Brooks: a caveat against this style of criticism which is, I think, generally acknowledged. Aristo-telianism is apparently more abstract and more inclusive—a 'purer' theory—but more mystical also. Neither of these theories, in my opinion, is adequately 'anchored': neither makes enough reference to substantial phenomena in language, culture, or psychology. Neo-Aristotelianism seems to me to be conceptually vacuous. It has evolved (or preserved?) a descriptive metalanguage in which ordi-nary words are used in arbitrary senses—always a dangerous stra-tegy. Worse than this, however, is the way the jargon of the Chicago Critics is cut off from practical reality: if 'diction' is an attribute of 'poetry', and if 'poetry' is a thing which manifests 'diction', how much better off are we than if we had no definition of poetry at all? Aristotelianism, when it comes to theorizing, is very little more than a system of mutually interdependent terms whirling around in a vacuum. What kind of a thing *is* a lyric poem, anyway?

The isolationism of New Criticism is different. The New Critics
know what a poem is made of—language, or at least structure, ultimately linguistic. (Few of them know what it could mean to say that
a poem is made out of language, of course.) There's a damaging
romanticism about the New Critical stance: this verbal object, the
poem, is an 'urn', an 'icon', a 'monument', a thing with clear-cut
edges which you can place in front of you and admire in its self-
sufficiency. I am of course referring to the doctrine of the 'autonomy'
of the work of literature, a creed usually associated with W. K. Wimsatt but in practice a good deal more widespread. The dangerous
romanticism consists not only in believing that a particular literary
text is a separate thing (a belief which I will examine directly) but
also in believing that literature *as a whole* is a separate *kind* of thing:
belief in what Richards dismissed as 'The Phantom Aesthetic State'.
Richards' commonsense strictures should be adequate counter-
argument; here is a sample:

> When we look at a picture, or read a poem, or listen to music,
> we are not doing something quite unlike what we were doing
> on our way to the Gallery or when we dressed in the morn-
> ing. The fashion in which the experience is caused in us is
> different, and as a rule the experience is more complex and,
> if we are successful, more unified. But our activity is not of a
> fundamentally different kind. To assume that it is, puts
> difficulties in the way of describing and explaining it, which
> are unnecessary and which no one has yet succeeded in
> overcoming.[24]

In general, a view of the qualitative distinctiveness of verbal art
leads to a feeble-minded reverence in students and critics, a foolish
belief that to 'analyse' is to desecrate or destroy;[25] alternatively, it
leads to an aggressive dismissal of all 'scientific' approaches as being
irrelevant to a thing of 'value'.[26] These views are of course both
reactionary and precious; they serve only to inhibit progress in critical theory (and often, care in critical practice).

Perhaps even more unhelpful, though, is the 'tough-minded' auto-
nomism of the school of Wimsatt. In the two famous articles written
in collaboration with Beardsley,[27] Wimsatt proffers an apparently
logical demonstration of the critic's obligation to ignore all evidence
except that of the text 'itself'. Particularly, we are to reject an
author's statements about his work, not to trust them as clues or
criteria in explicating or evaluating texts; and we are to discount our
own responses to a text (*pace* Richards), preferring rather a confrontation with the objective features of the text. This is sound advice. But the argument, both in the two articles concerned and in the

injunctions of their popularizers, has run wild. Many students who have been exposed to Wimsattian doctrine are led to believe that the teaching enjoins no reference to *anything* external to 'the text'—a Calvinism which is blatantly ridiculous.[28] The theory holds that each text—poem, novel, or whatever—is unique (so that comparisons are improper) and self-sufficient: everything that can be said about it has to be learnt by concentrated study of the text itself and only the text. Criticism becomes a real voyage of discovery: you know nothing when you set out, and at the conclusion of the exercise you know just what the text has told you. But the practice of criticism proves this attitude to be unrealistic. Who can imagine a good study of Keats by someone who had not read his letters? or a critic of T. S. Eliot whose secret was that he had ignored the critical essays? an eminent Yeatsian who knew nothing of the poet's aesthetic theories? Who would regret Richard Ellman's biography of Joyce? or the existence of Hopkins' correspondence? It is of course to be admitted that 'the text' provides best evidence of its own structure; but it can't be seriously claimed that texts are utterly independent of contexts, or that their contexts are not relevant to understanding them.

These are practical considerations. There are also excellent theoretical reasons why we should refuse to regard a text as autonomous. To start from the obvious: texts may be either the same or different; when they are different, they may be closely similar or very distant; when they are closely similar, each one is nevertheless unique. By 'unique' here I mean 'having different sentences'. But a crucial point is that being unique is not equivalent to being autonomous. The uniqueness of texts derives from a natural characteristic of language: the linguistic knowledge which speakers possess enables them to produce and understand an infinite number of sentences they have never encountered before. It is likely that, when we read a poem for the first time, each of its sentences will be new to us. This does not mean that we face the poem in a state of total innocence—that the poem has no relation to any existing knowledge or experience we might have. In a sense, we know these unfamiliar sentences already: if they are grammatical sentences of English, they are wrought from materials which we and the poet share. The poem is, in a most important sense, a link between poet and audience: it derives from the linguistic knowledge that is common to both parties. In this way, a poem is neither a free creation by the poet nor his own exclusive property: it belongs to the language. With this argument in mind, we have to say that the critic is wrong who regards practical criticism as a 'from scratch' activity entailing learning, by analysis, the qualities of a brand-new creation; likewise, the linguist who claims the status of discovery procedures for his techniques is making a false assumption. In both cases, 'analysis' of the language of a text can do no more than confirm and articulate what the reader already knows. The fact is that, if a poem is read by someone who knows the same language as its author, every sentence is as much the property of the reader as of the poet: the poet does no more than exploit linguistic resources that the reader also has at his command. There is no sense in which a poem might be linguistically isolated. In fact, it is not easy to grant cultural autonomy to a poem, either, and again linguistic theory provides substantiation for this assertion.

In Papers 5 and 7 below I have begun a discussion of a linguistic theory of 'style'. (The term is in quotation marks because I do not want to suggest that I am appealing to an established, stable usage, and also because the intended sense is much more general than traditional, exclusively literary, senses.) The theory relates to the distinction between 'competence' and 'performance' referred to on p. 8 above, and it is a very simple theory. Any piece of language— informal conversation, epic poem, or newspaper article—can be viewed in two lights. On the one hand, it can be regarded as a sequence of sentences generated by a particular grammar (say, English). On this view, one would limit oneself to stating what sentences occur; to confirming that these are sentences which reflect the linguistic competence of the speaker or author and audience; to assigning structural descriptions to them. Descriptive linguistics, in its proper (and, confessedly but justifiably, limited) capacity, can do no more than state the rules by which the sentences concerned are generated: rules which, we assume, represent part of the linguistic competence of the originator of the sentences and of anyone who understands them. But such statements obviously do not exhaust the kinds of things which can be said about texts. As far as the linguist is concerned, each sentence is unmotivated: it is just an observed sentence with a certain kind of relation to the grammar of the language; he does not enquire *why* one sentence (rather than some other from the infinite set in *L*) occurs. We know, however, that sentences are indeed motivated: that one can not only describe a sentence but also try to explain why it has been chosen. Why does a sentence employ a particular structure? Why does a series of sentences repeat a particular structure? Frequencies of occurrence of, say, relative clauses, short sentences, multi-syllabic words, are of no real interest to the linguist, but to the stylistician they are vital.

What general formulation explains why texts (sequences of sentences) have the distinctive structural characteristics they do? Each text, and therefore each sentence, is a part of some definite communication situation. The needs of this situation have an influence on the form in which linguistic communication is cast: the grammar provides the materials, and these materials are put to a use appropriate to the context of utterance. This hypothesis is the basis of an extension of descriptive linguistics which has been called *sociolinguistics*, or *anthropological linguistics*, or *ethnography of communication*.[29] Less clearly formalized, this is also an assumption that the stylistician and the literary critic who seeks to account for the verbal characteristics of texts habitually make. We all acknowledge, in effect, the truth of this observation of Randolph Quirk: 'every particular *use* of English is to some extent reflected in and determines the *form* of the language that is used for that particular purpose.'[30] The sociolinguist, however, makes a stronger assumption than the critic: that the correlation of linguistic form with communicative needs is *systematic*. In modern criticism, the linked doctrines of textual autonomy and uniqueness have encouraged us to stress the idiosyncratic nature of poems-as-communicative-events. If, say, a particular metaphoric structure is discovered and accounted for in a poem of Wallace Stevens, the critic will hesitate to extend these observations to some other poem; or the syntax of *The Waves* will receive an explanation allegedly independent of that of sentence-patterning in *To the Lighthouse*. But the sociolinguist, like the structural anthropologist, takes an overview. A culture is assumed to have a vast overall pattern, a complicated network of familial, group, occupational, economic, political, sexual, linguistic, relationships. It is further assumed that cultural patterning is reflected in, and reinforced by, systematic linguistic patterning. Thus the influence of cultural context on the shape of linguistic performance in any specific instance is thought to be more profoundly understood if it is itself contextualized: if it is placed in relation to other relevant language-culture connections. This seems to me a proper and profitable approach to language and its sociocultural dimensions, and one which is adaptable to literary studies. Recognition of the general principle which is involved provides a way of integrating literature and culture in a manner which is not antagonistic to close textual criticism. It is often implied that the critic has to choose between 'textual' (i.e. verbal) and 'contextual' study. In the light of the theory sketched above, the choice seems to require a false opposition. In fact, we can quite easily envisage a linguistic study of literature which dovetails very smoothly into a study taking account of generic categories, genetic factors, or the relation of poetry to other art and non-art media.[31]

The above discussion of style concentrates on the cultural motivations for linguistic variety. It rests on a theoretical premise which seems indispensable to stylistics (though not to criticism generally): we must assume that a distinctive use of language reflects distinctive

c

extra-linguistic circumstances. There is a second assumption of
stylistics upon which linguistics can shed some light. All (strict)
stylistics apparently rests on a distinction between 'form' or 'expression' and 'content' or 'meaning': the correlation between style
and cultural context is not wholly deterministic, in the sense that it
is always assumed that a meaning 'could have been put in different
words'. Or if it is deterministic, at least it is believed that 'the same
meaning' occurring in different situations is 'expressed' in distinctive
linguistic arrangements. Of course, this supposition is very rarely
stated explicitly in stylistic studies, and is anathema to poetic
theory. New Critical doctrine asserts as a fundamental principle that
the medium is the message: that poems are definitely not paraphrasable.[32] Evidently, the kind of practical criticism which is typified by
New Criticism needs this principle; equally evidently, stylistics in
the sense intended here is committed to a quite different, and antagonistic, aesthetic—and they are independent modes of study. For
this reason, there is no point objecting to a form/content distinction
in stylistics on the grounds that poems cannot be paraphrased. By
the same token, it is confusing to apply the label 'stylistics' to just
any form of criticism which pays close attention to language—
'stylistics' ought to delimit one specific area of literary studies, and
its dependence on the form/content division will help us to define
this area.

However, the terms 'form', 'content', 'meaning', and 'expression'
are notoriously difficult to pin down and stabilize. 'Form' and 'expression' have a range of senses and additionally, in the derivatives
'formal' and 'expressive', evaluative connotations; 'content' invokes
a misleading spatial metaphor; as for 'meaning', Ogden and Richards
wrote a book on the multiplicity of its meanings nearly half a century
ago, and we are still a very long way from deciding which sense of
the term to settle for. As it happens, there is a related distinction in
recent linguistics which may help us understand the form/content
distinction more easily (though it does not cover all of the ground
which is mapped by stylistics).[33]

The major revision to transformational-generative theory since it
was first expounded in 1957 has been the formulation of a distinction
between *deep structure* and *surface structure* in syntax.[34] It is proposed
that every sentence is characterizable on both of two levels, and that
an adequate structural description *must* so characterize a sentence.
Briefly, the surface structure of a sentence consists of the 'outer'
layer of its structure: a sequence of lexical and syntactic formatives
strung together in certain structural relationships; thus:

the + new + grammar + give + s + all + the + answer + s

This surface structure may be phonetically (or graphically) represented: that is to say, it may be spoken or written down, the above sequence of elements being preserved. Notice that this sequence reflects only rather indirectly certain underlying syntactic relationships. For instance, the Noun Phrase *the new grammar* is structurally related to the sentence *the grammar is new*, but that fact is not immediately deducible from the surface structure of the longer sentence which contains the *NP*. Similarly, we have in the long sentence two affixes -*s*. Superficially, there is no way of distinguishing them; but of course we know that the first means 'verbal affix, used when Subject is singular', the second 'nominal affix, used when the noun is plural'. I have, in fact, just given information about the deep structure of the sentence: about certain aspects of the meaning of the sentence which are not clear from the surface structure. Chomsky summarizes the distinction in this way: 'The deep structure contains all the information relevant to semantic interpretation; the surface structure, all information relevant to phonetic interpretation.'[35] Now deep and surface structure are rarely isomorphic, so that we can have pairs of sentences with the same surface structure but different deep structures ('different meanings') or sentences with different surface structures but the same deep structure: respectively, examples 1 (*a*) (*b*) and 2 (*a*) (*b*) below—

1 (*a*) I saw him in the street
(*b*) I saw him in the street

(1 (*a*) means 'I saw him when I was in the street', 1 (*b*) 'I saw him when he was in the street'.)

2 (*a*) He took off his hat
(*b*) He took his hat off

With 2 (*a*) (*b*) compare 3 (*a*) (*b*):

3 (*a*) It is clear that this distinction is important
(*b*) That this distinction is important is clear

and 4 (*a*) (*b*):

4 (*a*) The prisoner who has escaped is dangerous
(*b*) The escaped prisoner is dangerous

and 5 (*a*)–(*e*):

5 (*a*) He unlocked the car and drove off
(*b*) He unlocked the car and then drove off
(*c*) When he had unlocked the car, he drove off
(*d*) After unlocking the car, he drove off

(*e*) He drove off after unlocking the car
(etc.)

In some reasonable sense,[36] the members of each of the sets 2–5 have the same meaning—are *paraphrases* of the other member(s). We can say that the same deep structure is realized in different surface structures within each set; the differences could be called 'stylistic', and a transformational grammar allows us to describe such differences as variations of 'expression' leaving 'content' intact.

I shall not state in detail the technique for this kind of description. Informally, every sentence has a deep structure comprising one or more underlying strings, each string having a determinate, unambiguous, syntactic and semantic composition. These strings could be represented as simple sentences, as long as it is remembered that they are so represented for the purpose of exposition only—they are not really fully-fledged sentences. So the deep structure of the sentence *The new grammar gives all the answers* might be shown as *The grammar gives all the answers* and *The grammar is new*. 3 is *It is clear* and *This distinction is important*; 4, *The prisoner is dangerous* and *The prisoner has escaped*. 5 consists of *He unlocked the car* and *He drove off*. The underlying strings establish the meaning of the finished sentence; the process from deep structure to surface structure involves the application of transformational rules which amalgamate the strings in various ways (see 3–5 above) or rearrange the elements in a string (see example 2) (or perform other operations) *without changing the meaning established in the deep structure*. Thus a formal linguistic definition is provided for at least one aspect of the notion of 'paraphrase'. On this basis, stylistic analysis consists of identification of the underlying strings in sentences, and a statement of the 'transformational histories' of sentences (the routes between underlying and superficial structures). Since the number of applications in a text of a particular transformation, or class of transformations, can be determined, this method is readily adaptable either to the conventional statistical approach in comparative stylistics or to the description of a 'foregrounded' syntax in one text.[37] Examples of stylistic analysis in terms of the deep structure/surface structure division are found in Richard Ohmann's article cited in note 33 (p. 30).

It is clear that the approach leaves untouched one large area of the study of stylistic paraphrase: the discussion above refers only to stylistic choices at the level of *syntactic* alternatives, and pays no attention to alternatives in *lexical* expression of 'the same meaning'. In the model of syntax preferred here, particular lexical items are chosen and inserted in the underlying strings, so that lexical choice is settled *before* the transformational processing which I have associated with stylistic choice. In view of this problem, the model obviously needs some minor adjustment. But before we can decide how to carry this out, we need to consider a very problematical issue: are there such things as synonyms? Commonsense says yes: *cat, pussy, feline quadruped; pleasant, affable, friendly, engaging; strong, powerful, tough; beautiful, attractive, handsome,* etc. But many philosophers and linguists have disputed the existence of synonyms; in general, it has been said that a word is a new word in every different context, and therefore, speaking of lexical choice, you cannot choose to say the same thing in different words—different lexical items, or different contexts, guarantee non-reproducibility of messages. (Notice the convergence of this argument with the New-Critical thesis of non-paraphrasability of poems.) I would take the view that there *are* synonyms: that some sets of words share a basic core of meaning and differ only in some secondary semantic components. These secondary components are stylistically contrastive. Now this is of course a commonplace of traditional semantic assumptions, recognized in the distinction between 'denotation' and 'connotation'. But the referential view of meaning which those terms imply is not valuable to descriptive linguistics. At present, transformational–generative grammar has no method of presenting semantic information in a form which might be assimilable to stylistic analysis on such lines. We can only look forward to a more sophisticated semantic theory than we possess at present.[38]

iv *Language of fiction*

To end this Introduction I would like to offer some speculations about a branch of literary criticism upon which linguists have, to date, had almost nothing to say: the study of fiction. Critics of the novel, under the influence of New Critical poetic theory, are now beginning to pay attention to the language of fiction. David Lodge's book *Language of Fiction* (London, 1966) is an interesting start to what may grow to be a movement in fiction-criticism: the search for a poetics of fiction. The idea of a poetics of fiction, concentrating on language and using methods well-tried in poetic criticism, is very welcome indeed; but I want to argue that the discovery of such a novel-poetics is, ultimately, of less importance than the discovery of a fiction of fiction; and here certain observations oɪ applied linguistics may be of service.

To understand what I mean by a 'fiction of fiction' we might begin by considering some critical views on the language of fiction. Lodge's first sentence indicates his orientation relative to this subject (p. ix): 'The novelist's medium is language: whatever he does, *qua* novelist, he does in and through language.' In the context of modern criticism, this assertion may appear rather ordinary. If recent criticism has agreed on anything, it has agreed that the verbal dimension of literature merits close attention. But in fact, as Lodge points out, this principle has not penetrated novel criticism as thoroughly as it has the practical criticism of poetry. As far as poems are concerned, the belief that they are in some way 'made out of language' enjoys widespread acceptance (perhaps with insufficient enquiry into what the proposition means, it has to be admitted). From this view of the poem as 'verbal object' there has sprung a series of productive metaphors for presenting the texture and shape of poems, the poem being seen as virtually tangible, made out of language as sculpture is made out of stone or bronze or wood. This is presumably what is implied by Lodge's reference to the novelist working 'in' language: and this is an uncharacteristic view of the verbal construction of novels. More typically, this quasi-physical existence is denied the language of novels; it is more often seen as a medium *through* which the novelist works: and so novel-language is valued less for denseness, concreteness of texture, than for qualities of clarity and transparency. Through language are communicated the elements from which novels are properly constructed—character, plot, etc.—language itself being subservient. Relevant here is the view, stemming from the great tradition of realism in the nineteenth-century novel, that novels are mimetic: that they should represent social and/or psychological reality with the least possible interference from mediating language. Another view, equally insistent in its refusal to grant primary importance to language, is summed up by Malcolm Bradbury: language is just 'one of a variety of elements which the writer must dispose of in producing a work'.[39] This neo-Aristotelian position sets up language as little more than an embellishing device working to relieve or heighten the 'other elements' as appropriate, or to provide a kind of separate attraction—the reader may respond to the language, or to the plot, or to the characterization. It is assumed that, in some way, the reader can discriminate these diverse elements, and that to an extent they work separately; I suppose that many of my readers will recognize the aesthetic and psycholinguistic problems associated with what I might call 'hard-core' Aristotelianism, and I will not dwell on them here.

Of the three views of the language of fiction that I have presented here (certainly with an element of caricature), Lodge subscribes to the first: but for methodological, not aesthetic-theoretical, reasons—he is concerned to justify the transfer of New Critical techniques from poetry to prose fiction. Of course, aesthetic assumptions carry over with the methods, the key words 'structure' and 'texture' having clear implications of a set of beliefs about the way the language of fiction 'works' on readers of fiction. The 'structural' approach relies on the detection and evaluation of repetition: repeated images, symbols, or lexical items from the same semantic field are held to be the basis for the reader's perception of an aesthetically relevant 'pattern' in a novel. Lodge's analysis of *Mansfield Park* is the clearest example of this approach: in the novel he detects two sets of vocabulary items—a moral vocabulary relating to conscience, spiritual duty, and so on, and a social vocabulary concerning decorum, propriety, respect, politeness, etc., in personal relationships. Lodge relates the coexistence of these two lexical streams to one prominent evaluative preoccupation of the novel: the problem its characters meet in managing what he calls 'a delicate adjustment of social and moral values'. The analysis is plausible, if incomplete. My interest in it is that it raises certain important questions in the psychology of reading. Lodge's argument is that the language of *Mansfield Park* is persuasive in that the vocabulary arrangements mentioned induce in the reader perception of an evaluative scheme, a cognitive set towards the events of the novel. Without denying that this happens, one is entitled to wonder just *how* it happens. How conscious does the reader have to be of the lexical patterns that the critic exposes? Does he arrive at the evaluative framework by the same route that the critic, by deliberate analysis, follows? Or is there some process by which we, as readers, absorb the elements of the pattern without being aware of what is happening to us? Again, what memory processes are implied by Lodge's structural method? It takes many hours to read a medium-sized novel, and it is not clear how the reader is supposed to build up the shape of the pattern through time until a moment when, retrospectively, the whole thing falls into place. Short lyrics, sonnets, and suchlike, are claimed to light up in moments of instantaneous perception, and this experience is credible with such short pieces. But many readers report analogous experiences with novels; to quote just one (David Lodge):

> It is my own experience that the moment of perceiving the
> pattern is sudden and unexpected. All the time one has been
> making the tiny provisional notes, measuring each against one's
> developing awareness of the whole, storing them up in the
> blind hope that they will prove useful, and then suddenly one
> such small local observation sends a shock like an electric
> charge through all the discrete observations heaped up on all
> sides, so that with an exciting clatter and rattle they fly
> about and arrange themselves in a certain meaningful order.
>   (*Language of Fiction*, pp. 80–1)

Such experiences need investigating with the aid of a much more sophisticated psycholinguistics than critics generally have at their disposal.

A similar comment needs to be made about the psycholinguistic implications of the 'textural' method of analysis. I assume that close analysis of fictional prose, as carried out by Lodge and others, claims to do more than reveal undiscovered structure or describe structure already discovered: that textural descriptions may duplicate, in some measure, the activities of readers engaged in the ongoing process of working through a novel's language. One supposes that, in the complete reading, the reader builds up a general view of the structure of the novel, as above; additionally, he must be continuously subjected to the processing effect of linguistic texture. I think that we are not usually aware of this continuous impact of (principally) syntax, for one of the achievements of most novels is to persuade us that the medium is normal or neutral, to convey the impression that there is a stable communicative mode holding together the universe created within the novel. Against this norm, 'specialized' language can play. But in some cases we are all too aware of the continuous demands of the texture of novel language. Reading late Henry James, everyone acknowledges that one's consciousness is forced through a highly demanding, cognitively processing, syntax: if you refuse to follow the contortions of the syntax you cannot read the book at all. Why is the reader forced into this syntactic mould, and what is the effect of the process? Ian Watt's exposition [40] of the abstractness, complexity and indirectness of James's syntax in *The Ambassadors* argues that these are the instruments of the author's tendency to 'present characters and actions on a plane of abstract categorization'. More specifically, one could add that this syntax lends itself to presenting the complicated interplay between Strether's consciousness and the narrator's interpretation which gives the whole novel its tone. But if we grant that such an interpretation of the role of syntax is illuminating, we have still left unanswered the question of the causal relation of syntax and the reader's experience.

Richard Ohmann sums up the problem very neatly. We must enquire 'just how a given literary work sifts through a reader's mind, what cognitive and emotional processes it sets in motion, and what organization of experience it encourages'.[41] As Ohmann points out, a generative grammar, by providing a powerful theory of linguistic structure, must aid investigation of this question; but the question obviously does not fall wholly within the purview of linguistics. As it happens, some linguists have speculated about certain relevant issues in the relationship of language and cognition; but these speculations have been generally on the fringes of linguistics—certainly not thought out in relation to an explicit theory of generative grammar. It would be a mistake to suggest that a linguistic science of the kind described above could directly explicate this particular question. The strategy I would recommend is to acknowledge that the question cannot be formulated *within linguistics*; that we should express it as a topic in literary theory and then see what insights of linguistics might aid its elucidation.

I have space here only to sketch very briefly and tentatively a line of approach. It is the experience of readers, and the belief of critics, that reading a novel entails being persuaded to perceive an 'imaginary world': a society with its own behaviour and values, evoked within a framework of attitudes for which the novelist, creating a pervasive voice or tone for the occasion, takes temporary responsibility. To understand this situation, we have to accept that it could not happen except through the instrumentality of language; and we must supply ourselves with workable definitions of the key concepts *fiction* and *rhetoric*. Loosely, 'fiction' refers to the reader's specific occasional conceptualization—his experience on reading the novel—and 'rhetoric' to the process of persuasion by which he is given this experience. The theory of fiction has traditionally been inhibited by mistaken notions of realistic presentation: the increasing richness and variety of subject-matter of the nineteenth-century novel (and, perhaps, the rise of photography and other allegedly representational modes) produced a belief in the possibility of depiction, through language, of 'external reality'. On this view, language depends passively on nature: it accommodates itself to an external, independent, order of things, and can thus present these things, this order, without colouring the subject-matter with any peculiarly linguistic tincture. On pp. 93 ff. below I have presented a set of counter-arguments to this view which, in the eyes of many philosophers, psychologists, and semanticists, is entirely fallacious. Rather than that language simply reflects the shape of the world, it is much more likely that the world we see has no shape without language: that the conceptual structure coded in language is used by us to project on our experience and order it so that we are not overwhelmed by a chaotic flux of impressions and ideas. As is well known, this argument, though intuitively highly reasonable, is extremely difficult to justify in any of its 'strong' forms (e.g. the Whorf hypothesis of linguistic relativity); but weaker versions are validated—for example, the fact that we are disposed to 'notice' distinctions which are enforced by the structure of our language.[42] This ('our language determines the way we see the world') is an argument about linguistic competence; there would appear to be a related argument concerning linguistic performance: that the structural characteristics of utterances may be so manipulated, or, more weakly, may so fall out, that speakers and hearers can be encouraged to adopt a particular mental set towards the subject of discourse. In other words, they see the world of the novel in a certain light, or see a certain world in the novel; a fiction. There is nothing magical in this. A literary critic such as Frank Kermode, in *The Sense of an Ending* (New York, 1967), takes as a premise of his theory that man is a fiction-making animal; the anthropologist Edmund Leach asserts, very reasonably, that the infant *must* create fictions— linguistically-stabilized cognitive organizations—in order to come to terms with the world.

Language is inherently fiction-making, and honest acknowledgment of this fact may help us to understand the not-so-special class of prose fictions which we call novels. The contribution of linguistics to the understanding of the nature of prose fiction is difficult to design, but indisputable: the relation between linguistic and cognitive structures is clearly the key to understanding how the novel works; we await a developed psycholinguistics to reveal more exactly the relation between language arrangements and fictional universes.

Notes to Paper One

1 For documentation and discussion of this division, see D. J. Palmer, *The Rise of English Studies* (London, 1965).
2 On the rise of philology in the nineteenth century, see H. Pedersen, trans. J. W. Spargo, *Linguistic Science in the Nineteenth Century* (Cambridge, Mass., 1931)—reissued as *The Discovery of Language* (Bloomington, 1962).
3 Review of G. L. Trager and H. L. Smith, *Outline of English Structure*, in *Kenyon Review*, xiii (1951), 713.
4 A representative selection is given in M. Joos (ed.), *Readings in Linguistics* (New York, 1958).
5 John T. Waterman, *Perspectives in Linguistics* (Chicago, 1963), 98.
6 See L. Bloomfield, *Language* (London, 1933), 139.
7 See R. Fowler, 'A Note on Some Uses of the Term "Meaning" in Descriptive Linguistics', *Word*, xxi (1965), 411–20.
8 *Syntactic Structures*, Janua Linguarum No. 4 (The Hague, 1957). See the review by R. B. Lees in *Language*, xxxiii (1957), 375–407.
9 For fuller discussion, see *Syntactic Structures* itself; Chomsky, *Current Issues in Linguistic Theory*, Janua Linguarum No. 38 (The Hague, 1964); Paul M. Postal, *Constituent Structure* (Bloomington, 1964).
10 The above examples are all very much simplified. For further examples consult *Syntactic Structures*;

Chomsky, 'A Transformational Approach to Syntax', in A. A. Hill (ed.), *Proceedings of the Third Texas Conference on Problems of Linguistic Analysis in English, 1958* (Austin, 1962), 124–58—reprinted in Fodor and Katz, *The Structure of Language* (Englewood Cliffs, N.J., 1964), 211–45—and an excellent modern textbook, Roderick A. Jacobs and Peter S. Rosenbaum, *English Transformational Grammar* (Waltham, Mass., 1968).

11 For more discussion of the competence/performance distinction, and of the non-grammatical factors which underlie linguistic performance, see pp. 71 and 90 ff. below and Fowler, 'Against Idealization: Some Speculations on the Theory of Linguistic Performance', *Linguistics*, lxiii (1970), 19–50.

12 See R. H. Robins, *A Short History of Linguistics* (London, 1967), Ch. 6, and references (159–60).

13 For full bibliographical details of these and other writings on metrics, see pp. 172–3, note 2.

14 See *Proceedings of the Ninth International Congress of Linguists*, ed. H. G. Lunt (The Hague, 1964).

15 Seymour B. Chatman and Samuel R. Levin, *Essays on the Language of Literature* (Boston, 1967); Glen A. Love and Michael Payne, *Contemporary Essays on Style* (Glencoe, Ill.,1969; Donald C. Freeman, *Linguistics and Literary Style* (New York, 1970).

16 I discuss it at length in Paper 2 below.

17 On 'kinds of criticism', see Paper 7 below. I suspect that, ultimately, there aren't any distinctive 'kinds' of critical study; that what appear to be different modes are merely accidents stemming from such conditions as illicit narrowing of the range of commentary, undue concentration on separate literary genres, etc.

18 William Empson is a notable example. See pp. 109–12 below.

19 An interesting example of the contrast between the neatness of problems and the complexity of their solutions is the difficulty of accounting for the distinction between phrasal conjunction and sentence conjunction in English. See Carlota S. Smith, 'Ambiguous Sentences with *and*', in David A. Reibel and Sanford A. Schane, *Modern Studies in English* (Englewood Cliffs, N.J., 1969), 75–9.

20 I apologize for not considering the problems of the student of a foreign literature, which are obviously different and much more severe; Nils-Erik Enkvist discusses the problem of style from the point of view of the non-native student in J. Spencer and M. Gregory, *Linguistics and Style* (London, 1964).

21 Let me stress once again that even here an advanced linguistic technique is not self-sufficient. For a sad illustration of this fact see the following articles, where a highly technical approach to sound-texture founders for lack of examination of the critical and aesthetic assumptions underlying the analyses: James J. Lynch, 'The Tonality of Lyric Poetry: an Experiment in Method', *Word*, ix (1953), 211–24; Dell H. Hymes, 'Phonological Aspects of Style:

Some English Sonnets', in Sebeok's *Style in Language*, 109–31.

22 *Essays on Style and Language*, Chs. 5 and 6; Wimsatt, *The Verbal Icon* (Lexington, Ky., 1954), 153–66.

23 *Aesthetics* (New York, 1958).

24 *Principles of Literary Criticism* (London, 1924, reprint of 1963), 16–17.

25 Empson disposes of this silliness in a memorable passage, quoted below, p. 110.

26 See my comments on 'art' versus 'science', pp. 68–9.

27 'The Intentional Fallacy' and 'The Affective Fallacy', *Sewanee Review*, liv (Summer, 1946) and lix (Autumn, 1951); both reprinted in *The Verbal Icon*.

28 Wimsatt and Beardsley should not receive all the blame, nor students all the ridicule. See Cleanth Brooks' analysis of Marvell's 'Horatian Ode', *English Institute Essays, 1946* (New York, 1947), 127–58, and the ensuing controversy with Douglas Bush. The articles concerned are conveniently reprinted together in W. R. Keast (ed.), *Seventeenth Century English Poetry* (New York, 1962).

29 *The Ethnography of Communication*, ed. by John J. Gumperz and Dell Hymes (Special Volume of *American Anthropologist*, 1964), is a good illustrative collection of papers in this field.

30 *The Use of English* (2nd ed., London, 1968), 21.

31 I have been arguing here that there is a viable 'general stylistics' of which the stylistics (in the technical sense) of literature is a proper sub-part. This 'general stylistics' is assumed in the sociolinguistic and linguistic–ethnographic work contained in Gumperz and Hymes (see note 29) and in the neo-Firthian school of linguistics where it relates to the concept of 'register'. I would like to say that I regard 'register' as an intuitively valuable but as yet totally ill-defined term. For some relevant neo-Firthian discussion, see M. A. K. Halliday, Angus McIntosh and Peter Strevens, *The Linguistic Sciences and Language Teaching* (London, 1964); Geoffrey N. Leech, *English in Advertising* (London, 1966) and Ch. 8 of *Essays on Style and Language*; David Crystal and Derek Davy, *Investigating English Style* (London, 1969).

32 See Cleanth Brooks, 'The Heresy of Paraphrase', in *The Well Wrought Urn* (New York, 1947), Ch. 11.

33 In the following paragraphs I elaborate a suggestion first made by Richard Ohmann in 'Literature as Sentences', *College English*, xxvii (January, 1966), 261–7—reprinted in Chatman and Levin, op. cit., 231–8 and in Love and Payne, op. cit., 149–57.

34 For historical accuracy, I should report that more recent work still hints at the necessity of rethinking this distinction. See E. Bach and R. T. Harms, *Universals in Linguistic Theory* (New York, 1968; D. Terence Langendoen, *Essentials of English Grammar* (New York, 1970).

35 'The Formal Nature of Language', Appendix A in E. H. Lenneberg, *Biological Foundations of Language* (New York, 1967),

406. (This is a readable short introduction to transformational-generative grammar.) For another exposition of the distinction between deep and surface structure, see Paul M. Postal, 'Underlying and Superficial Structure', *Harvard Educational Review* (1964), 246–66 (reprinted in R. C. Oldfield and J. C. Marshall (eds.), *Language* (Harmondsworth, 1968), 179–201). The primary sources for this distinction are J. J. Katz and P. M. Postal, *An Integrated Theory of Linguistic Descriptions* (Cambridge, Mass., 1964); N. Chomsky, *Aspects of the Theory of Syntax* (Cambridge, Mass., 1965).

36 It would be easy enough to construct contexts which would assign a different meaning to every one of these sentences; but such deliberate quibbling would deny commonsense.

37 On 'foregrounding' see Jan Mukařovsky, 'Standard Language and Poetic Language', in Chatman and Levin, op. cit., 241–9; Leech, Ch. 8 of *Essays on Style and Language*; Leech, *A Linguistic Guide to English Poetry* (London, 1969), Ch. 4.

38 For the beginnings of such a theory, see J. J. Katz and J. A. Fodor, 'The Structure of a Semantic Theory', *Language*, xxxix (1963), 170–210; U. Weinreich, 'Explorations in Semantic Theory', in T. A. Sebeok (ed.), *Current Trends in Linguistics*, iii (The Hague, 1966), 395–477; M. Bierwisch, 'Semantics', in J. Lyons (ed.), *New Horizons in Linguistics* (Harmondsworth, 1970), 166–84.

39 Malcolm Bradbury, 'Towards a Poetics of Fiction: (1) An Approach through Structure', *Novel*, i (Autumn, 1967), 50.

40 'The First Paragraph of *The Ambassadors*: an Explication', *Essays in Criticism*, x (1960), 250–74.

41 Art. cit.; in Chatman and Levin, 238.

42 For responsible discussion of these claims, see Roger Brown, *Words and Things* (Glencoe, Ill., 1958), Ch. 7; John B. Carroll, *Language and Thought* (Englewood Cliffs, N.J., 1964), Ch. 7.

Two

Linguistics, stylistics; criticism?

'. . . recently philologists have turned to the new science of linguistics to counter the Cambridge emphasis on literary appreciation'.[1]

It is no new thing for the academic linguist to turn his attention to literature. For centuries written texts were his almost exclusive concern: often, texts which were written rather than literary—any records of a directly inaccessible language community; but as often again, literary pieces, from the highly treasured sacred documents analysed and annotated by the Indian grammarians before Christ to the indisputably literary remains of the Germanic cultures of the early centuries of this era, equally treasured by nineteenth-century philologists. If all philology was not literary criticism, much of it, at least from the points of view of objects studied and motives for study, has to be granted that title.

The invention of scientific phonetics and the doctrine of the primacy of speech proved a temporary setback. Linguistics and philology drew apart, and a gulf also appeared between philology and literary studies in our universities. 'Oral linguistics' as developed in America by the followers of Leonard Bloomfield, with its demand for rigorous consistency of approach, pushed 'linguistic criticism' towards anthropology and the literatures of unlettered peoples. Paradoxically, literature had to be oral.

Significantly, linguistic criticism re-emerged as a phonetic thing. The beginning of this subject in its modern formulation can be traced to Trager and Smith's brilliant *Outline of English Structure*,[2] published in 1951. This is most compactly described as a sketch of a phonological grammar: an attempt to fuse structural, analytic, syntax and morphology with the meaningful patterns of sound found in English. Harold Whitehall, in a review of the *Outline* in *Kenyon Review* (xiii [1951], 710–14), pointed the way to the use of linguistics in criticism: 'Trager and Smith have unwittingly assembled for the critic some of the necessary linguistic tools' (713). He later expanded the implications of his comments in the same journal (xviii [1956], 411–21), heading a special section 'English verse and what it sounds like' which also contained an application of these analytic principles to Robert Frost's 'Mowing' by Seymour Chatman.[3] This, then, linguistic analysis with a strong bias towards the 'phono-grammatics' of poetry, marks the beginning of the contemporary movement to linguistic criticism.

Anyone today who reads those articles in *Kenyon Review* and *PMLA* must be struck by the narrow limitation of the position expounded there. How could this—the formal analysis of one aspect of the language of gramophone records of poetry—combine fruitfully with the new interest in literary language being shown by the exponents of Practical Criticism or by such critics as William Empson, Cleanth Brooks, and Donald Davie? These are critics with a humbling range of linguistic interest, however impressionistic their techniques may be considered. Such students of literature offered an admirable environment for the contributions of linguists; but, since the fifties, it has taken an absolute revolution in linguistics to fit us in any degree for the role of linguistic critics. And I do not believe that we will be fully fitted until we can make ourselves become, once linguists, less of linguists. Linguistics, a subject noted for its efficient handling of first principles, has reached an impasse through considering no first principles for criticism, or only its own. Blind competence has produced many a fatuous or useless analysis: technical analysis without thought or sensitivity.

I shall elaborate on two aspects of linguistic criticism: the potentiality of its methods and approaches in the service of literary studies, and the adjustment in the linguists' views of their own contribution necessary before the contribution can become really worth while.

However inadequate the analyses of Chatman and Hill may seem as an approach to poetry, however suspect in their assumptions about the oral performance of poems, their technical merit as (partial) descriptions cannot be doubted. They are founded on a powerful and productive theory of language, and by reference to this (as documented in Trager and Smith and the tradition behind them) their terms and concepts can be understood and their statements utilized. The Trager-Smith analysis of English is now viewed as outmoded (but still, I think, often useful).[4] Now we have a range of techniques for description. The precision of the early fifties can still be achieved or bettered, and the repertoire of statements we can make about the language of literature is much wider. Two chief modes of analysis are now available, and not necessarily in opposition. The *transformational-generative* mode, propounded by Noam Chomsky and all-powerful in America, has already produced some very interesting discussion of poetry.[5] Admittedly, there is a strong

suspicion that those transformationalists who have interested themselves in poetry have been using poetic utterances merely to test the
efficiency of their grammatical concepts. But in their writings there
has been a steady focus on utterances of a type highly likely to appear
in poetry: *colourless green ideas sleep furiously, seven oceans answer
from their dream, argumentative windows cook with their destinies, he
danced his did, a grief ago,* utterances on the borderlines of poetry
and nonsense, grammar and non-grammar, lexical decorum and
anarchy of diction. Here is a conscientious attempt to make a
grammar of English adequate to describe language outside normal
(colloquial, casual, common, etc.) usage, and adequate to explain the
place of *any* utterance within the corpus of possible English sentences: to state not just that an utterance is 'grammatical' or 'ungrammatical' but that it has an understandable place on the scale of
grammaticalness.

The second popular mode of analysis is the *levels-and-categories*
method, based on the thought of J. R. Firth and developed by M. A.
K. Halliday and others.[6] This operates on the basis of a model of
language which postulates the existence of the relevant levels *substance, form*, and *context*. Substance is the physical matter of speech
or writing, a 'surface' or a 'medium' without meaning. Form (linked
to substance by phonology, sound-patterning) is the level at which
meaningful patterns are found. It is the primary level for analysis,
and has two sub-levels, grammar and lexis. Here patterns are discovered and described. Context comprises all relevant things outside
language. The connexion between context and particular linguistic
forms ('contextual meaning') may be said to constitute the field for
semantic analysis. One positive assertion of the theory, however, is
that there is formal, as well as contextual, meaning. Language
functions, and its manner of functioning is significant. The implications of this theory for the study of literary language are obvious.
Linguists, when describing grammatical, lexical, or metrical patterns,
believe themselves to be making statements of meaning. Also
important is the habit of separate recognition and description of the
categories of literary language: the ability to say, for example, 'this
is a grammatical and not a lexical feature'. Needless to say, sets of
terms are available to aid analysis of features within these categories
(although lexical analysis is still at a relatively primitive stage).

We must add to these two versions of linguistic analysis the older
structural analysis associated with Bloomfield and his pupils and
followers, only recently displaced by transformational grammar. As
shown above, it first manifested itself in linguistic criticism in the
form of phonological metrics, but its range is wider than that. It can
still supply many useful and very precise analytic techniques.[7, 8]

All I have wanted to show in the brief survey above is that a range of very exact techniques for linguistic analysis is available. If one is interested in the grammar, metre, sound-structure, or vocabulary of a literary text, one has a wide choice of means to the understanding and discussion of the selected feature. Much space has been wasted by linguists justifying their methods: a necessary public-relations job that has now been done often enough. Nor is the applicability of linguistic analysis to literature a really fundamental issue worthy of discussion. Literature is (among other things, perhaps) language and evidently analysable: this is a presupposition of much modern criticism, and need not be set up as an assumption peculiar to linguistic criticism. We can say that modern descriptive linguistics is a natural companion to modern criticism because both are text-centred: both involve analysis, close reading, and both set a premium on accuracy and usefulness of description. It is arguable that explicit linguistics alone can provide a real basis for descriptive criticism, and that if descriptive criticism had succeeded in developing intelligent modes of analysis of its own, this whole problem would not exist: linguistic analysis would be detectable as a natural part of criticism.

I have affirmed the usefulness of linguistic methods as part of the critic's equipment. But is the contribution merely technical, just part of conscious method? In a publication which came into my hands during the writing of this article, Professor Jeffares asks (and I hope he knows the answer). 'How much more, in fact, does [the linguist] offer beyond a new vocabulary, a jargon which gives him that sense of exclusiveness often beloved by new groups in academic society, a new system of analysis, a new set of categories, to set against those of his rival colleagues?'[9] In fact, the linguist offers something perhaps more important than technique and terminology: a set of attitudes which are reinforcement of, not substitutes for, those of descriptive criticism. He is practised in that essential of much modern criticism, close reading; in the recognition of what is language and what is not; in seeing what are the separately analysable parts of a text; in spotting patterns and meanings. These faculties—comprising a kind of mood for analysis—are summed up in an ideal honoured by linguists since the early years of this century, 'the descriptive attitude'. The linguist focuses automatically on what is the first concern of descriptive criticism: 'what is "there" in the poem'. That phrase is from the first sentence of a book whose method demonstrates the point I am making here: that criticism can benefit from the linguistic frame of mind as well as from the techniques and jargon of the linguist.[10] 'Linguistic' criticism, as here, is often brilliant through the fact that its linguistics comes so naturally that it hardly appears at all. There are no morphemes,

D

tagmemes, sememes within sight, but just a steady focus on the form of the text. The two extremes of linguistic explicitness are well illustrated by two essays by J. M. Sinclair. In 'Taking a poem to pieces' (see note 6) he demonstrates an almost complete and very technical analysis of a poem; in 'When is a poem like a sunset?'[11] his linguistics is simply a controlled and rational handling of language: there is an implication of analysis which carries respect.

For students, the techniques of linguistics should probably be kept largely out of sight. One of my duties as a linguist teaching literature and criticism is to teach, and direct practice in, Practical Criticism. In this context I can use a linguistic approach entirely compatible with a critic's 'close reading'. The aim is to stimulate reading habits and opinions which achieve a nice balance between response and analysis—which can allow rationalization of response without its inhibition. This is met by concentration on form and by creating a mood which makes detailed linguistic analysis always possible but hardly ever practised. If I use terms like 'sentence', 'phoneme', 'lexical item' occasionally, my students will not be shocked: their class-discussion provides a sympathetic environment for formal statements, which can arise naturally and be understood easily, without the students knowing that anything as 'difficult' or 'scientific' or 'inhuman' as linguistics is in the air.

The 'public' critic ought to operate in such a state of mind; but he will also need to have explicit linguistics (of whatever sort) at his fingertips. The good Practical Critic needs to be a very good linguistician. But even the most excellent linguisticians have failed to gain respect as critics, for technical virtuosity is not a guarantee of critical success. It is not, as I think linguists have tended to believe, that critics have failed to acknowledge the efficiency of linguistic techniques. Nor, except superficially, is it a question of interdisciplinary hostility, though we linguists have given enough cause for hostility. The fault is with the linguists: to be critics, we must be competent linguists and then become less of linguists. The development of precise techniques, and theorizing in linguistic terms,[12] though essential, carry us only a short distance. A programme for linguistic criticism cannot be proposed in terms of a theory of language only. After the refinement of methods, and some thought on elementary questions (literature is basically a use of language, a literature is a part of a particular language, etc.), all remaining issues are critical problems. We should not ask 'how can linguistic criticism be established as a branch of linguistics?' More proper and rewarding is 'what is the place of objective formal description in literary studies?'

At this point there is a need for some scrutiny of our terminology. I have argued that there is an important part of criticism—and a prominent part in twentieth-century criticism—which consists of the close examination of the language of literature *qua* language before statements are made about it as literature. Differences of method of analysis are more superficial than may appear. One method is *linguistic analysis*, described in the earlier part of this article. Another is *explication de texte*, defined by H. A. Hatzfeld as

> a close analysis of . . . lexicological and syntactic features, including the so-called figures of speech and rhythmical elements.[13]

Then we have 'Practical Criticism' in the Cambridge sense—not a method, but an approach which *'involves* a minute scrutiny of the verbal detail of works of literature'.[14] The 'New Criticism' is another powerful approach which demands critical analysis or close reading.[15] At least these four historically definable phenomena—two methods and two approaches involving similar methods—can be identified. What needs to be named is the common element, focus on the text and analysis, for whatever critical uses or dependent on whatever aesthetic presuppositions. 'Critical analysis', 'practical criticism', 'close reading' are best used for whole approaches, in which verbal study is only a part; 'linguistic analysis' and 'explication de texte' have too specific connotations. I propose 'verbal analysis' as a term for the process of describing the language of literature: the analysis itself, not the criticism founded on it. I shall now consider the process of utilizing verbal analysis, and specifically that form based on linguistics, in criticism.

The aims and assumptions of criticism will determine the most important aspects of verbal analysis, irrespective of particular techniques used. There are, in a sense, two 'hows' of analysis: the 'technical', with criteria such as objectivity, precision, and flexibility of method, criteria which may select methods derived from general linguistics; the 'critical', wholly determined by questions of a critical nature, problems largely concerned with what to select for analysis and how to select it. A further question is involved in the transition from verbal analysis to critical statement: what to *add* to the verbal analysis to make complete statements about the work being discussed.

Here I would like to suggest three 'levels of achievement': description, stylistics, and criticism. This tripartite division of the field incorporates—I believe most significantly for the confrontation between linguists and critics—a value scale, with criticism (including 'evaluation', 'interpretation', etc.) at the top. Linguists have already shown themselves to be most adroit at 'mere description'. A linguistic description of any text (literary or not) is, ideally, absolutely revealing:

it can lay bare the formal structure of the language in more detail
than any critic would want. We can find out about all aspects of
grammatical structure from that of words to that of sentences;
about lexical distribution, history, and etymology; about phonological shape. The description is, in a technical sense, 'meaningful':
it reveals formal meaning, the meaning of information theory seen in
patterns, contrasts, choices.[16] Completeness and revealingness (with
simplicity and consistency) are ideals for linguistic description, and
so one can understand why linguists seem to reverse the 'scale' with
which I began this paragraph. There has been an understandable
defensive tendency to stay at the lower end of my scale, or to urge
the ideals of description passionately. So Halliday:

> In talking of 'the linguistic study' of literary texts we mean, of
> course, not 'the study of the language' but 'the study (of the
> language) by the theories and methods of linguistics'. There is a
> crucial difference between the *ad hoc*, personal and arbitrarily
> selective statements offered, frequently in support of a
> preformulated literary thesis, as 'textual' or 'linguistic'
> statements about literature, and an analysis founded on
> general linguistic theory and descriptive linguistics. It is the
> latter that may reasonably be called 'linguistic stylistics'.[17]

In fact, however linguistically wholesome these sentiments may
be, and however much apparently in accord with the views of
modern criticism in so far as they are anti-impressionistic and anti-
prejudice in spirit, the stubborn adoption of this position will be
the very thing which disqualifies linguistic description from con-
tributing significantly to literary criticism. Of course, any form of
verbal analysis must take pains to ensure the validity and meaning-
fulness of its description. But verbal analysts, to become critics,
must then renounce some part of their position. To pass on to
stylistics, we must point to patterns which are meaningful not
simply because they are efficient carriers of information, but because
they are significant in a comparative context ('Browne's style is
different from Burton's in these ways . . .'). To go further up the
scale still, we must acknowledge that the meaning of a poem is more
than the sum of its cognitive and formal meanings, and that perhaps
some of the causes of this meaning and value are inaccessible to
verbal analysis. In both cases progress involves losing some of the
description, or making it 'impure' by invoking non-linguistic
matters, or postulating the existence of an aesthetic area beyond the
linguist's power to explore.

Mere description—whether linguistic, of literary or non-literary
texts, or any kind of verbal analysis conducted for its own sake—is of

no great use, except possibly as an exercise to promote awareness of language or of method. And for a linguist to say that he will do the description, or show the critic how to do it, and leave the *using* of the description to the critic, is not constructive. It implies that description is nine-tenths of the critical task, and that interpretation has to, and can, follow directly on. No: the description itself must be purposeful. The crucial point is that linguistic study (in the sense given by Halliday) is essentially unselective. It describes everything, and all data are of equal significance. To analyse usefully (could one say 'critically'?) one must know (or have some at least marginally positive clue) *why* one is undertaking verbal analysis: and this knowledge will inevitably direct the manner of the analysis. A 'preformulated literary thesis' is essential in a very real way; to have this thesis, or hunch, or feeling, is the property of the sensitive critic or reader, and to have it is not to cheat.[18] Whether one is proceeding only to stylistics, or beyond the language to interpretative or evaluatory criticism, one must, and can without falsifying, select for description certain features which one feels to be significant.

The most obvious first use of verbal analysis is in stylistics. This is a tortured subject. The definition of 'style' is of course a sitting target for the linguist, and too often he progresses no further.[19] However one defines style, pure verbal analysis is not the same thing as stylistic description. One is concerned to *characterize* a style, not simply list all the features of the language of a text. One seeks to provide objective evidence for feelings about the distinctive linguistic character of an author or a text. A feature, or group of features, is usually isolated as a result of asking not 'what linguistic choices are made here?' but 'what *sorts of* linguistic choices are made here?' These features are characteristic—they identify a text (or author) against a norm, a norm defined by reference to the language as a whole (a difficult concept) or that of some other text or author. Stylistics is comparative, for a stylistic feature has meaning or force only against a background of usage. Granted a hunch to make him select the significant feature(s), and the patience to describe the normative background, the linguist may be an extremely revealing stylistician. He still needs an educated reader's sensitivity, of course: but there are signs that, if he has this, his equipment for handling significant variation (*deviation* in his terms[20]) can be rewardingly productive.

The linguist's 'formal meaning' perhaps provides a clue to the limits of stylistics as a branch of criticism. Stylistics examines the cause of only a narrow range of responses in the reading of literature: one's response to form and pattern. It may be a characteristic of literary expression that it draws attention to itself, is a significant artefact as well as a signifying medium: in any event, stylistics is concerned with the cause of this attention only. And for a handful of motives which are often connected with literary history rather than criticism.

To date, linguistics has tended to press no further than stylistics. A survey of the titles listed in the notes to this article reveals a limitation in labelling, if not in aim. Even the recent issue of *A Reveiw of English Literature* (vi, April 1965) calls itself 'New Attitudes to Style', although the contents are manifestly of wider critical interest than just stylistics. There is probably a feeling in both camps that the contribution of linguistics to literary studies is too limited to go beyond stylistic description. The linguist is too politically cautious to claim too much, and the critic too jealous to admit too much. Of course, there is a limitation; but not that linguistic analysis has no part to play in higher criticism. Once linguistic description has become verbal analysis (in the sense I have proposed) by being selective and purposeful, its place in criticism beyond stylistics can be challenged only by arguments which will also throw out Practical Criticism and all similar and highly-respected modern critical approaches. The limitation is that verbal analysis, though vital, is only a part of criticism: and a smaller part than of stylistics. In evaluatory and interpretative criticism verbal analysis has a basic role, because language is at once the medium and the central focus. However, criticism, acknowledging that the total meaning of a text is more than the sum of its formal and referential meanings, and probably ultimately unanalysable by objective means, must exploit all the aids it knows: verbal analysis is only the chief among many.

Notes to Paper Two

1 C. B. Cox and A. E. Dyson, *Modern Poetry, Studies in Practical Criticism* (London, 1963), 14.
2 American Council of Learned Societies, Washington, 1951. There is an important review of the book by James Sledd in *Language*, xxxi (1955), 312–35. The ultimate development of the Trager-Smith version of Bloomfieldian linguistics is A. A. Hill, *Introduction to Linguistic Structures: From Sound to Sentence in English*, New York, 1958.
3 'Robert Frost's "Mowing"': an Inquiry into Prosodic Structure', 321–38. In the same vein is A. A. Hill's 'An Analysis of *The Windhover*: an Experiment in Structural Method', *PMLA*, lxx (1955), 968–78. Structural metrics on these lines survived in Terence Hawkes, 'The Problems of Prosody', *A Review of English Literature*, iii (April 1962), 32–44. See also Chatman, *A Theory of Meter*, The Hague, 1964.

4 An interesting use of the Trager-Smith methods is John Thompson, *The Founding of English Metre*, London, 1961.

5 The classic book is N. Chomsky, *Syntactic Structures*, The Hague, 1957, and an elementary account of the method is E. Bach, *An Introduction to Transformational Grammars*, New York, 1964. S. R. Levin proposed the application of T. G. to poetry in *Linguistic Structures in Poetry*, The Hague, 1962. See also his 'Poetry and Grammaticalness', in H. G. Lunt (ed.), *Proceedings of the Ninth International Congress of Linguists*, The Hague, 1964, 308–14; J. P. Thorne, 'Stylistics and Generative Grammars', *Journal of Linguistics*, i (1965), 49–59; Richard Ohmann, 'Generative Grammars and the Concept of Literary Style', *Word*, xx (1964), 423–39.

6 See J. R. Firth, *Papers in Linguistics*, London, 1957; M. A. K. Halliday, 'Categories of the Theory of Grammar', *Word*, xvii (1961), 241–92; Halliday, Angus McIntosh and Peter Strevens, *The Linguistic Sciences and Language Teaching*, London, 1964. John Spencer and Michael J. Gregory describe the Hallidayan position and its application to stylistics in 'An Approach to the Study of Style', *Linguistics and Style*, London, 1964, 59–105. Among literary descriptions on this basis are: Halliday, 'The Linguistic Study of Literary Texts' in *Proceedings of the Ninth International Congress of Linguists*, 302–7; Geoffrey Leech, 'Language and Interpretation', *A Review of English Literature*, vi (April 1965), 66–75; J. M. Sinclair, 'Taking a Poem to Pieces', in Roger Fowler (ed.), *Essays on Style and Language*, London, 1966, 68–81.

7 'Structural' linguistics is massively documented between 1930 and 1960. The important works (apart from those cited in note 2) are: L. Bloomfield, *Language*, New York, 1933; Bloch and Trager, *Outline of Linguistic Analysis*, Baltimore, 1942; Z. S. Harris, *Methods in Structural Linguistics*, Chicago, 1951; M. Joos, *Readings in Linguistics*, New York, 1958; the journal *Language*; and a number of books by K. L. Pike and E. A. Nida.

8 Other linguistic writings relevant to literary study include the books of Stephen Ullman on semantics and stylistics; Halliday, 'The Tones of English', *Archivum Linguisticum*, xv (1963), 1–28; A. McIntosh, 'Patterns and Ranges', *Language*, xxxvii (1961), 327–37; D. Abercrombie, 'A Phonetician's View of Verse Structure', *Linguistics*, vi (June 1964), 1–13, 'Syllable-quantity and Enclitics in English', *In Honour of Daniel Jones*, London, 1964, 216–22.

9 *A Review of English Literature*, vi (April 1965), 7.

10 The book is Winifred M. T. Nowottny, *The Language Poets Use*, London, 1962.

11 *A Review of English Literature*, vi (April 1965), 76–91.

12 Aesthetic and other theory, put in terms of general linguistics, is very adequately represented in the literature of what has come to be called 'linguistic stylistics'. While much of it is essential to the adjustment of the linguists' and critics' attitudes to their

disciplines, it has hardly penetrated into profitable critical theory and practice. For some discussion see T. A. Sebeok, *Style in Language*, New York, 1960; Fowler, 'Linguistic Theory and the Study of Literature', *Essays on Style and Language*, 1–28.

13 *A Critical Bibliography of the New Stylistics Applied to the Romance Literatures, 1900–1952*, Chapel Hill, 1953, 1.

14 A. C. Spearing, *Criticism and Medieval Poetry*, London, 1964, 1 (my italics). At this point one would cite (as Spearing quotes) the writings of Empson, Leavis, and Brooks. For a clear exposition of the tenets of the Practical Criticism of today, see Cox and Dyson, op. cit. (note 1).

15 See J. C. Ransom, *The New Criticism*, Norfolk, Conn., 1941; Robert Wooster Stallman, *Critiques and Essays in Criticism, 1920–1948*, New York, 1949.

16 For linguistics as the revelation of meaning by analysis, see the items by Firth and Halliday cited in note 6, especially Firth, 190–215 ('Modes of Meaning'); Leech, *A Review of English Literature*, vi (April 1965), 66–7.

17 'The Linguistic Study of Literary Texts', *Proceedings of the Ninth International Congress of Linguists*, 302.

18 Spencer and Gregory speak of 'a response to a work of literature which is a kind of hypothesis, a basis for further observation and testing'.

19 Notable tormentors are several of the contributors to Sebeok's *Style in Language*; M. Riffaterre, 'Criteria for Style Analysis', *Word*, xv (1959), 154–74; N. E. Enkvist, 'On Defining Style', in Spencer and Gregory, *Linguistics and Style*, 3–56; M. Joos, 'The Five Clocks', *IJAL*, xxviii (April 1962).

20 Discussion of 'deviation' is to be found in Sebeok, op. cit., especially pp. 91–2, 420–2; in the article by Leech cited in note 6, and in his 'Linguistics and the Figures of Rhetoric' in *Essays on Style and Language*.

Three

Literature and linguistics

Mrs Vendler, in her review of my *Essays on Style and Language* (*Essays in Criticism*, xvi (1966), 457–63), is apparently optimistic that 'descriptive linguistics will in the end be of immense use to literary criticism'. If, however, we were to accept her generalizations about the critical attempts of linguists, we would have to doubt whether this prediction can come true; certainly, it is doubtful that she wishes it. The hostility of Mrs Vendler's voice is depressingly familiar to those of us who have suffered from an unnecessary schism between 'language' and 'literature' which has so long marred English studies. Her tone betrays the fear, common among teachers of literature although perhaps less so among the great critics, that linguists may invade and ravage precious literary territory. I shall reserve my remarks on this opposition of linguists and critics until the end of this paper, commenting at the moment only that Mrs Vendler's open invitation of confrontation in her first paragraph is a damaging strategy.

Mrs Vendler's main charge against the linguists is lack of critical achievement: 'linguistics has given us no critics comparable in literary subtlety to certain men like Richards, Spitzer, Burke, Blackmur, Empson and others, whose sense of linguistic patterning is formidably acute' (457). Here she cites the cream of critical achievement of over forty years of massive activity; obviously one grants the stature of these men. But the corpus of linguistic writings on literature is as yet minuscule and could hardly be expected to yield riches on this scale. Inevitably in the very first years of any new 'movement' there will be uncertainty, infelicity, and changes of method. Professor Hill's article on 'The Windhover' (*PMLA*, lxx (1955), 968–78) is an early and much-noticed example of 'linguistic criticism', and it would be well if critics would stop citing it as the type of current linguistic study of literature: the mode of linguistic

analysis, derived from Trager and Smith's *Outline of English Structure*, is no longer accepted by professional linguists; nor is the finite-
state grammatical model which made textual analysis of a few years
ago misleadingly easy. I acknowledge that linguistic theory is now in
a period of great crisis: witness the reorientations in the latest
writings of Noam Chomsky, modifications of a theory which even in
its early form shook linguistics to the core (see *Current Issues in
Linguistic Theory*, Janua Linguarum 38, The Hague, 1964, *Aspects
of the Theory of Syntax*, Cambridge, Mass., 1965, *Cartesian Linguistics*, New York, 1966, and compare his *Syntactic Structures*, Janua
Linguarum 4, The Hague, 1957); and we are now more conscious of
the shakiness of the neo-Firthian position, which seemed five years
ago (e.g. M. A. K. Halliday, 'Categories of the Theory of Grammar',
Word, xvii (1961), 241–92) to be clearly formulated and productive.
I hope that in these unsettled days linguists will be slow to claim too
much, and literary critics for their part more patient than Mrs
Vendler. One can agree on one level with some of her comments:
'that is what most linguists are—beginning students' (458), 'linguists . . . , who are simply under-educated in the reading of poetry,
tend to take on, without realizing it, documents whose primary
sense and value they are not equipped to absorb' (460). In so far as
this means that linguistics has only just started to attempt literary
analysis, and that linguistics has thus not yet finalized its methods,
this is a just observation. But to turn it into an unkind accusation,
as Mrs Vendler does (as if 'linguists as a species are incapable of treating literature'), is only harmful to the progress she pretends to
welcome. True, sometimes linguists have approached literature with
non-critical motives (e.g. J. P. Thorne, 'Stylistics and Generative
Grammar', *Journal of Linguistics*, i (1965), 49–59) and some work
will probably be cited more often by linguists than by critics (e.g.
S. R. Levin, *Linguistic Structures in Poetry*, Janua Linguarum 23,
The Hague, 1962). I personally see no objection to a linguist deliber-
ately advancing his *linguistic* research by the study of literary uses of
language which really put his assumptions to the test. Critics and
linguists, tired of the complacent and unadventurous linguistics of
light housekeeper v. *lighthouse-keeper*, *The sun's rays meet* v. *The sons
raise meat, white shoes* v. *why choose*, should welcome the fact that we
have at last turned to material which inevitably forces us out of our
assurance. Although the 'use' of literature is really not the issue here,
it needs comment because critics seem to consider that linguists
doing such kinds of linguistic work with literature think it is critical
work. The real allegation is that, perhaps because of their 'scientific'
education, linguists are not equipped to know the difference between
linguistic analysis and criticism, nor indeed sensitive enough to be

critics. This is nonsense. Many mathematicians and physical scientists are fine musicians and poets. There is no reason why a linguist should not be a humane, literate, sensitive person. He may write on literature purely as a linguist for linguistic ends; for critical motives, using only a selection from his linguistic apparatus; or, no differently from the non-linguist, without appeal to linguistics at all. The three separate approaches are all valuable, and I would urge non-linguists to stay their conviction that a knowledge of linguistics *must* make only the first approach possible.

The primary justification for the use of the methods of linguistics in literary study is that noted by Mrs Vendler (458): any information about language is useful in studying an art-form whose stuff is language. If linguistics is defined as 'the study of language' *tout court*, then its contribution is unchallengeable. But this bleak logic does not allow that all specific brands of linguistics are admissible. Here I must offer some disclaimers and qualifications which, Mrs Vendler may wish to note, I made elsewhere before her review was written ('Linguistics, Stylistics; Criticism?' (this volume, Paper Two). Over-simple justifications have too often been offered by linguists without considering the constraints on linguistic/literary study deriving from: the special contextual nature of the linguistic material in question; the diverse and at times inappropriate characteristics of particular linguistic models; and the very specialized (and ill-understood) demands of the various kinds and motives within literary studies. Examples of this oversimplified logic abound in Sebeok's *Style in Language*: here is just one:

> Since all metric phenomena are language phenomena, it
> follows that metrics is entirely within the competence of
> linguistics.

(John Lotz, Sebeok, p. 137); for similar sentiments, cf. David Abercrombie, 'A Phonetician's View of Verse Structure', *Linguistics*, vi (1964), 5. The apparent[1] arrogance of this assertion (which is wholly typical of much of the justificatory discussion in the early literature of 'linguistic stylistics') has understandably angered critics and literary theorists. For development of linguistic criticism, however, the serious deficiency is less the tone than the neglect of the three conditions listed above. Briefly, this means that, in the first case, although literature is language and therefore open to ordinary formal linguistic investigation (as I argued in *Essays on Style and Language*, 10–11) it has, like other formally distinctive texts, essentially distinctive contexts which the linguist no less than the critic must study. That is, the investigator must be curious about the extra-linguistic features which condition the distinctive style of a literary work. As for the applicability of different linguistic models, this is obviously variable. The old Bloomfieldian linguistics in its classic Immediate Constituent analysis phase, or Hallidayan scale-and-category grammar, both concentrating on relatively 'small' units, can have little to say about the linguistic structure of extended texts. Nor can we expect to learn much through linguistics about kinds of poetry where metaphor is dominant until we have proper tools for lexical analysis. It apparently needs repeating over and over again that there is no one linguistics providing a ready-made set of procedures or formulae perfectly apt for all kinds of texts. The appropriateness of the model is a concern for the individual analyst; just as important for this general discussion is that all those who engage in it realize that bland undefined accounts of 'linguistics' lead nowhere. There is no one linguistics except in community of certain basic and general ideals held since Saussure's time. We cannot switch on a standardized linguistic analysis machine and stand by while it puts out a definitive breakdown of a text. Doubtless the lack of such a device has its advantages.

My third prescription for a successful linguistic criticism is that it should proceed not merely from a theory of language but also from a respectful consideration of the demands and peculiarities of the many kinds of literary study. Now, the substance of this remark is addressed not only to linguists. There is no single thing 'criticism' any more than there is 'linguistics', although literary people, faced with the imagined threat of linguistics, tend to talk as if there is. (This impression is gained partly from the tendency to use 'criticism' and 'critical' as treasured value terms.) I am not talking here of diversity of critical school, the sort of thing hilariously dramatized in *The Pooh Perplex*, but of different purposes in the discussion of literature. In the real world, we are dealing with, above all, teachers of literature whose pedagogic relations with their subject-matter and with their students are much more vital than the role of the public critic. Most often literature teachers are involved in nothing more mystical than, at various degrees of sophistication, showing the ways to efficient reading of literature. Many a time literary study comprises historical, stylistic or openly technical investigation: genre description, stylistic tests of authorship, metrical analysis, for example. For some reason, 'interpretation' (an exceedingly difficult term) and 'evaluation' have come to be regarded as the only activities which are worth doing and which are actually done. Just as we need to be wary in our use of 'linguistics' as a term describing all procedures involving the study of language, so we should give careful scrutiny to terms like 'criticism', 'interpretation', 'evaluation', 'explication', 'stylistics', ensuring that we do not think that there is just one objective (of whatever kind) in studying literature, with 'linguistics' straightforwardly an alternative 'technique' for reaching that goal.[2]

I want to make reference to three more specific questions raised by Mrs Vendler's review and Mr Bateson's editorial postscript to it: the 'scientific' quality of linguistics, and the claimed 'objectivity' of its methods; the relationship between textual description and literary comment; and the implication, which critics seem to find, of a claim of 'special revealingness' by linguists.

Mr Bateson declares triumphantly: 'The essential objection is surely a very simple one: linguistics is the *science* of language.' I do not think I misrepresent my non-linguist colleagues if I guess that for them this kind of statement can be accepted as settling the issue: everyone knows that poetry is the antithesis of science (and in every way more desirable), and also Mr Richards has told us that scientific language and emotive language are polar opposites (which is neither true nor relevant, although it is often invoked to provide a characterization by contrast of poetry). Actually, it is not at all clear that linguistics *is* a science. Bloomfield and his early followers believed that linguistics could achieve the status of a science in line with the natural sciences (this approach found its most famous expression in the long-standing claim to analyse without recourse to 'meaning'). More recently, Halliday, McIntosh, and Strevens have entered a plea for the scientific study of language (*The Linguistic Sciences and Language Teaching* (London, 1964), 3–9),[3] but they appear (rightly) to be loosely concerned with the scientific attitude rather than the absolute scientific status of their subject according to all criteria (nature of subject-matter, kinds of reasoning, relationship with other disciplines, reproducibility of experiments, etc.). Perhaps the most appropriate analogy today is the social sciences, although of course their scientific status is open to argument. Even if some part of linguistics (e.g. instrumental phonetics) is scientific in its methods and data, and even if some linguists assert scientific status, it is undeniable that, overall, linguistics merely *affects scientism* in its use of, say, postulational methods of argument, statistical presentation, mathematical models, instrumentally-revealed evidence. Most terms, procedures, concepts are evaluated for practical efficiency rather than scientific wholesomeness. If a natural antipathy between science and poetry were to be demonstrated (which is doubtful), poetry would have nothing to fear on that score. Mr Bateson's charge by no means disqualifies linguistics as an aid in literary study. The whole issue of poetry *v.* science is best treated as a red herring. If this can be done, we will have fewer students vacuously objecting that any kind of close analysis necessarily destroys or is at least tangential to the sensitive, valuable, work of art.

In practice, charges of ineptness against linguistic 'science' usually narrow down to an imputation of the crudeness and irrelevance of 'objective' description when it is applied to literature. Mr Bateson writes: 'As [a science] it is dedicated to an ideal of objective description that is unsullied by the values of ordinary human experience.' *The Times Educational Supplement* reviewer (21 October 1966) puts it this way: 'All linguistics can supply is an objective account of linguistic elements. These may be as small as a phoneme or as large as a clause; but in any case they will have very little to do with literary values.' Mr Bateson's sarcasm does not encourage one to accept his characterization of linguistics as the judgment of an informed man. And our comfortably anonymous *TES* reviewer makes an assertion which would not be easy to reason out in full. I do not wish to argue *ad hominem*, but let me pose these questions: Because one phase in the history of linguistics believed that linguistic analysis could and should proceed mechanically on a textual level, does this mean that linguistics can never go beyond text? Are not the values of ordinary human experience describable and discussible? What are literary values: features of response or of literary work? If the latter, how can they be unrelated to the characteristics of the medium of that work? Is language really only a medium?

I suppose that in this context 'objectivity' relates to an account of a literary work derived from the characteristics of the object itself rather than from those of the observer of this object. 'The poem itself' is a difficult notion, but the problem is the same for the critic as for the linguist. In practical terms, surely we all wish to give an interpretation which stands open to demonstration and argument because it is based on features which can be pointed to and discussed, and because it is propounded in a descriptive terminology which is explicit as to detail and which avoids the affective fallacy. Perhaps this is all that is required by objectivity. But failure to achieve this goal has bedevilled literary criticism for generations, despite the New Criticism and its relatives. Thus we have many books like A. C. Spearing's *Criticism and Medieval Poetry* (London, 1964), which, after making great claims for close textural description, that is, practical criticism of the Cambridge sort, deals in unrealities like 'breathless short sentences' which sit neither in the critic's mind nor in the text which he is ostensibly looking at so closely. Even Donald Davie's much-praised *Articulate Energy* (London, 1955) suffers from inadequate attention to the demands of objectivity. I do not say that he should have used the term 'syntax' strictly in accordance with usage among linguists at the time, although there is of course much in favour of using words in non-idiosyncratic senses; simply, central terms with analytic pretensions should be defined more clearly and rigorously than was the case in that important book.

One has to acknowledge the impossibility of exact statement of linguistic meaning, perhaps especially so in literature, although I do not take 'ambiguity' to be absolutely defining.[4] We weigh probabilities, and linguistic analysis, far from being a key to certainty, is only one tool for helping us organize, formulate, and communicate our thoughts. The aim in descriptive criticism may be to discover and propose convincingly what one believes to be the 'correct' interpretation, but what is achieved is an interpretation, or a statement of alternatives, which through objectivity in the sense given here can provide a basis for informed argument and evaluation.

It seems that the complaint is not against objectivity in this sense but against the 'triviality', 'tediousness', 'barbarous jargon' of a full analysis. My point in *Essays on Style and Language,* repeated more than once, was that, because of the delicacy of linguistic analysis, great detail is possible—Professor Sinclair's essay demonstrated that—but may not often be required. Linguistic analysis of any school applied in totality is a kind of machine which may, one day, be able to turn up all the answers to questions about the grammatical, phonological, and lexical levels of literature. The machine needs a master; as Mrs Vendler says, 'A method is only as good as the intelligence using it . . . .' Professor Halliday condemns '*ad hoc*, personal and arbitrarily selective statements . . . in support of a preformulated literary thesis' (*Proceedings of the Ninth International Congress of Linguists,* ed. H. G. Lunt (The Hague, 1964), 302), but I consider the hunch to be essential and precipitating, and the linguistic analysis to be a subsequent process, explanatory and confirmatory. (Cf. John Spencer and Michael J. Gregory, *Linguistics and Style* (London, 1964), 61.) The relation is made between trivial details and literary values because the hunch gets values in right at the outset.

What of the place of formal description in the hierarchy of things you can do with a literary text? This was a major topic in my article in *Lingua,* and I do not want to repeat too much here. I believe that the values expressed there were not too distinct from those of critics: the chief proposition was that which underlies the paragraph above—that 'mere description', insensitive and unselective, is one way linguistic analysis manifests itself, but should rarely be the concern of the linguist *qua* critic. He must compare and evaluate and go beyond his professional techniques if he is doing anything more than practising or displaying his methods. Mrs Vendler has something to say on 'mere description', discussing my account of one feature of Bacon's 'Of Studies' (*ESL*, 18–21):

The linguist's training is in description, and Mr. Fowler, for instance, gives us an accurate description of Bacon's 'tripartite scheme in his grammatical constructions', adding that this is 'an effective but rare rhetorical scheme; compare the much greater popularity of schemes based on two- or four-fold grammatical repetition (Lyly and most other balanced or antithetical prose)'. But the *critical* act is one which goes beyond this descriptive statement and asks questions: 'What is the effect here of threes in preference to twos or fours? Are there more threes elsewhere in Bacon? Who else, like Bacon, has a liking for threes? Why?' Mr. Fowler, then, has not really been a critic here, though his analysis is useful pre-critical material.

In actuality, I was not offering the analysis as a complete linguistic treatment and certainly not as a critical statement. The analysis occurs as part of an argument about the stylistics of units larger than the sentence, and it is an example only. However, on pp. 21–2 I suggest some uses of the information provided by the analysis, rather anticipating Mrs Vendler's question in the quotation above. I do not object to the label 'pre-critical' unless it is intended to suggest that this is all that literary study by linguists can ever amount to. After all, good criticism demands good pre-criticism. *Non*-criticism (if that is what is meant) is often honourable, and in its dishonourable forms it is to be found far greater in bulk in scores of books by literature teachers, and hundreds of Ph.D.s in English every year, than in the writings of literary-minded linguists. I do object to the idea of the linguist restricted to providing pre-critical material which the more sensitive critics can use—'helping' the critics (p. 457). Linguistic analysis in literary criticism should not function as the first phase of a two-part process, the first mechanical and the second creative and valuable. I do not wish to argue for linguistic analysis as an alternative to criticism, nor for analysis as a kind of dredging for ore which is subsequently and separately transmuted to precious metal. Linguistic concepts, attitudes, and techniques may be useful *within* criticism, it is claimed. Of course, the use of these aids does not guarantee critical achievement, nor does a formal linguistic description lead directly to an evaluative statement: some other faculty assesses the significance of the data revealed by analysis, and indeed guides the process of analysis.

We come to the last of the three points. There is the constant implication in Mrs Vendler's review that linguists believe that their techniques alone can make startling discoveries barred to non-linguists' eyes:

> a complacent tone implying that the authors have come to give
> a great light to the people who walk in darkness (457)
> triumphant discoveries of obvious effects, no less obvious
> because new 'scientific' names have been attached to them
> (458)

She laments the imperceptiveness of the linguists:

> Over and over, in reading the linguistic critics on poems, one
> finds that they miss the indispensable point of grief or
> pleasure (459).

This may be a point about the thickness of practitioners to date (in which case, I say that the sample is too small for such a judgment) or, more likely, an allegation of the utter impossibility of a linguist ever being perceptive. But how could training in linguistics disable its adherents so sadly? I must confess I argue from the theoretical potential rather than the published attainment of linguistic critics but I am sure that we have not done enough to damn ourselves yet. Though we have perhaps been overly missionary, no one has suggested that linguistic analysis is an instant revelation device. Nor do we argue that linguistic analysis increases sensitivity, if that is a quality derived from intelligence or fullness of life. The closest claim is that the consciousness, concentration and fidelity to text demanded by the act of analysis may help in working out hunches about a work, and may aid in catching effects possibly missed through laziness. (I do not see why linguists should miss 'quieter foregroundings' as Mrs Vendler maintains. Everyone knows that the more complex devices and kinds of poetry encourage analysis more readily; we know it well enough, if we have understood the bias of the work of Cleanth Brooks and his associates, to avoid letting it affect our taste and vision.) The remainder of our general claim is that linguistic terminology and method will one day become more widely received and thus a very efficient means of communicating the substantial details of literary commentary and judgment in so far as these are matters of language. Mrs Vendler finds her patience exhausted by Mr Sinclair's 'unreadable and barbaric collection of symbols and words' and voices her suspicion of the magic of 'new "scientific" names'. Hopefully, the new jargon will settle down, become more standardized, appear less densely in the writings of the linguistic critics, and serve us all very well.

Finally, our claims for the contribution of linguistics are not merely general. I myself happen to believe that the general justification is the important one—that linguistics is an essential part of literary education from the earliest stages and an invaluable tool

E

for the critic, although I grant that he may rarely use it. Others would urge the practical utility of linguistic techniques in very specific areas of literary study: for example, in discussing those poets for whom phonological analysis is especially needed (and here literary critics have failed notoriously and students are abysmally incapable); in the study of metre, in which linguists have been particularly active (see Chatman's *A Theory of Meter*, cited in note 2, and, for an appraisal of 'linguistic metrics', my 'Structural Metrics' (this volume, Paper Nine)); in detailed stylistic analysis in the service of certain external problems in literary history, especially authorship problems; and in attacking knotty puzzles of meaning, where rigorous sorting of the linguistic qualifications of possible solutions is unavoidable. No doubt this list will be extended, and not spuriously, as linguists turn more to the challenge of literature.

I return to my opening complaint, that of the meaningless opposition of linguistic and literary studies. Mrs Vendler speaks of 'the current literature–language controversy' (462). I do not deny that this exists. Sometimes it is disguised as natural division of labour, but the division is attended by inevitable political hostility and, often, reciprocal lack of respect. For my part, I concede the deserved ill-repute of some of the Anglo-Saxonists many years ago, and the arrogance of some linguists of the more recent past. I invite our literary colleagues to concede, and repair, their unwillingness to consider the relevance of linguistics. Perhaps I am a renegade linguist, but nothing would make me happier than a marriage of the children of Mercury (who, Chaucer says, love 'wisdom and science') and of Venus ('riot and dispense'). We need desperately a radically modern and sympathetic linguistics for all students involved in reading the most exciting utterances in their native language, and a sufficient number of critics and teachers of literature willing to believe that linguistics is not inevitably value-destroying, and willing to seek means for the clearer articulation of their perceptions. As the literary people hold the reins of power almost everywhere in the humanities nowadays, it is first up to them to try to understand: we linguists want neither rivalry, nor a subordinated, mechanical function in literary studies, but a chance to help educate the next generation of critics in an approach indisputably relevant to their labours and to their greater pleasure.[5]

Notes to Paper Three

  1 This is, as it happens, accurate for the level of generalization at which Lotz is speaking of verse. Metric typology is founded on

recognition of only those fundamental linguistic qualities like tone and stress, and units like syllable and phoneme, which are type-characterizing for verse traditions, and ignores non-linguistic concomitants of *actual* lines of verse.

2 The variety of ways linguistics impinges on this complex which is literary study may be illustrated by these titles: S. Chatman, 'Reading Literature as Problem-solving', *The English Journal* (May 1963); Chatman, *A Theory of Meter*, Janua Linguarum 36, The Hague, 1965; Fowler, 'Some Stylistic Features of the *Sermo Lupi*' (this volume, Paper Thirteen); J. Thompson, *The Founding of English Metre*, London, 1961; A. McIntosh, '*As You Like It*: a Grammatical Clue to Character', *Review of English Literature*, iv (April 1963); J. R. Firth, 'Modes of Meaning', *Essays and Studies*, 1951; and see *Review of English Literature*, vi (April 1965), the whole issue devoted to 'New Attitudes to Style'.

3 In the course of their discussion they say, 'it is the *scientific* study of language which turns out to be most revealing. This is true even in the study of literature: the more rigorous and objective linguistic methods have become, the more they have thrown light on the literary use of language and on the patterning and impact of particular literary texts' (p. 5).

4 For an interesting discussion of the phonological implications of ambiguity in metrics, see Katherine T. Loesch, 'Literary Ambiguity and Oral Performance', *Quarterly Journal of Speech*, li (1965), 258–67; reply by Seymour B. Chatman, *QJS*, lii (1966), 283–6; rejoinder by Mrs Loesch, ibid., 286–9.

5 For a parallel argument, more specific (though not fully up-to-date) on the values of linguistics, see Eric M. Zale, 'Linguistics: an Aid to Teaching Poetry', *Journal of the Michigan Council of Teachers of English*, i (1966), 29–48. Also relevant to this general discussion is an article by Stanley B. Greenfield, 'Grammar and Meaning in Poetry', *PMLA*, lxxxii (1967), 377–87. A new collection, *Essays on the Language of Literature* (Boston, 1967), edited by Seymour Chatman and Samuel R. Levin, brings together essays by critics and linguists which demonstrate well that it is possible for the two parties to work together in harmony.

Four

Literature and linguistics: reply by F. W. Bateson

Roger Fowler is in effect proposing—both here and in the collection of essays he edited which was reviewed by Mrs Vendler—an academic alliance between post-Saussure linguistics and post-I. A. Richards criticism. And why on earth shouldn't he? *A priori*, as it were, it sounds a good idea. After all, even if a literary masterpiece is more than the sum of its words, still when the words are taken away what is left? Blank pages! To invite the reader to look hard, really hard, at the words on the page is indeed what the modern critical doctrine of close reading amounts to, when it is reduced to its simplest terms. And, since a similar concentration is the initial premise of modern descriptive linguistics, some degree of amicable co-operation between the two approaches should not be impossible.

Unfortunately it doesn't work. Or rather, when it does work, it is only at the most elementary level. In this reply to Mr Fowler I shall try to indicate rather more fully than was possible in my short postscript to Mrs Vendler's review why the sort of co-operation that Mr Fowler and his colleagues are pleading for is a vain hope.[1]

I assume as a preliminary to the argument—as Mr Fowler seems to be doing too—that the reader we are concerned with is a native speaker of the language of its literature. For a foreigner the situation is, of course, quite different, the reading of the new literature being a natural part of the process of learning the new language. I should add, in case I may seem to be initially biased against descriptive linguistics, that the old historical linguistics seems to me at least as irrelevant to the pursuit of a critical study of one's native literature. I shall be including a detailed examination of a passage from Chaucer as a guarantee of the sincerity of this disavowal.

Left to themselves general terms like *language, literature, the reader*, and so on, are slippery things to argue with. It will be better to begin with an actual contemporary example of the descriptive method applied in detail to a particular work of literature. And one such example—very well done, as far as I can see, within its self-imposed limits—is to be found in Mr Fowler's own collection. This is J. McH. Sinclair's comprehensive analysis of Larkin's 'First Sight', a short and not particularly distinguished poem (here I entirely agree with Mrs Vendler) from his *Whitsun Weddings*. Mrs Vendler's comment that Mr Sinclair uses an 'unreadable and barbaric' jargon has clearly embarrassed Mr Fowler. It need not have done so if he had accepted the definition I offered in my postscript of linguistics as the *science* of language. Why shouldn't a science evolve its own symbols and technical terms? The social sciences, with which Mr Fowler associates linguistics, have found it just as necessary to create their own jargons as the physical sciences. But Mr Fowler will not have my definition at any price—and from his own point of view he is, of course, right. This is the crux of the whole argument. If descriptive linguistics does turn out to be the science of language, the possibility of an alliance with literary criticism becomes infinitely remote. However, what Mr Fowler means when he asserts that 'linguistics merely *affects scientism*' is still a mystery to me. Surely he can't mean that linguistics is a *pseudo-science* (like graphology or palmistry)?

But to return to Mr Sinclair. The essay, which is called 'Taking a Poem to Pieces', ends with the claim that the exercise 'shows how some aspects of the meaning of the poem can be described quite independently of evaluation'. The independence can certainly be conceded to Mr Sinclair's five tables (Sentence Structure; Clause Structure; Line Boundaries; Groups; Nominal Group Structure), but outside the tables, in the long prose commentary on the poem's grammar, evaluation continually insinuates itself into the description. To me, as a non-linguist, this is perhaps the most interesting feature of the essay. The fact that Mr Sinclair is clearly unaware of the state of affairs adds a pleasant piquancy to the situation. Mrs Vendler regarded the whole essay as ludicrously irrelevant to what literary merits Larkin's poem has. But this was going much too far. What *is* paradoxical is that the accidental intrusions of evaluation are almost the only passages where Mr Sinclair appears to be concerned with the poem itself rather than with the grammatical system that it enables him to demonstrate. There is perhaps a clue here of considerable theoretical importance.

What do I mean by intrusions of evaluation? A simple example turns up on Mr Sinclair's second page. Having shown that 'each sentence-stop ends a line, each stanza ends a sentence, and sentences are as nearly uniform in length as is possible', he describes this congruence of metre and grammar as '*an exceptionally good fit*' (my italics). And by way of emphasizing this value-judgment, he adds that the congruence is unspoilt for us by 'tag-ends of sentences'. Description is also continually passing into evaluation in the account of the grammar of Larkin's poem which takes up most of the essay. Here the recurring value-terms are 'surprise', the 'unexpected', the 'unusual', the 'odd'. Surprise is, of course, one of the oldest counters in the critical game; it even turns up in Aristotle's *Poetics*. Later 'an ambiguous structure' makes its appearance, and we are explicitly told in Mr Sinclair's next paragraph that the 'poet has the advantage here also of a combination of the alternative meanings'. Later still the criterion of ambiguity is presented as the poet's ability 'to have one's cake and eat it'. *Good, surprise, advantage, one's cake!*

What is the moral of these lapses by an accomplished grammarian from the strict, lily-white integrity of description? I take it to be the self-evident fact that English, like any other language, is so full of eulogistic and dyslogistic terms that we cannot open our mouths without an evaluation popping out, however trivial the object evaluated may be. And, of course, just as evaluation seeps into description, so description oozes into evaluation. Where would literary criticism be if authors were denied names and dates?

Nevertheless, difficult though the distinction may be to adhere to in practice, the ideal of two specialized developments from the chaos of common speech—which we can agree with Mr Sinclair for the purposes of this discussion to call description and evaluation—is one that we can hardly do without. Mr Sinclair's own occasional lapses are a useful warning of the stratagems that have to be devised to preserve the purity of each of the two linguistic modes. Description is most remote from common speech in the special language of mathematics, and it is significant that Mr Sinclair's five quasi-algebraic tables are entirely free from ordinary evaluative terms. A similar absence of description, in the non-evaluative sense which the word has in modern linguistics, characterizes lyric poetry, the mode which perhaps represents the ideal form of evaluative speech. The relationship, then, between description and evaluation may be thought of as consisting of two diverging modes of verbal communication, both of which originate, for society as for the individual, in the common area of everyday speech.

No doubt, as we have seen in the case of Mr Sinclair's essay, there will always be degrees of purity or impurity. Short of the total descriptive purity of higher mathematics come such disciplines as simple arithmetic (in which 13 may still persist as an unlucky number); short of *la poésie pure* are such genres as the novel which are clearly tainted with or qualified by an element of description.

But—and this is the real point—the *direction* which the various modes of linguistic communication take cannot usually be mistaken. Descriptive linguistics is always at least headed towards total description—a detached, objective, universally available discipline (whatever the user's age, sex, nationality, or culture). Literature, on the other hand, has its ineradicable subjective core, which tends to define the range and effectiveness of its uses.[2]

The point of departure between the two specializations from the vulgar tongue can also be put in strictly linguistic terms. It is a matter either of breaking down the sentence into its separable parts—*or else* of taking the sentence as the unit and building up larger units as the sentences accumulate. The close reader, conscientiously intent on the words in front of him, can opt either way. If he is a natural grammarian he will divide and subdivide the verbal material; if he has been born a literary critic he will synthesize and amalgamate it. What is it, then, in the words of literature that encourages the literary reader to amalgamate and not to subdivide? The answer to this question is a crucial one in my argument with Mr Fowler, though to prove it as a case is proved in a court of law would require a book instead of a short article. But I can at least summarize the theoretical objections to the mating of the language of description and the language of evaluation. Grammar, for one thing, is essentially logical in its linguistic presuppositions, and as such it is governed by the principle of non-contradiction; literary criticism, on the other hand, assumes in the verbal material criticized the presence of opposite and discordant qualities whose provisional balance and reconciliation the common reader will agree under certain circumstances to accept. Those circumstances, considered linguistically, can be summed up in the word 'style'—a term that includes the whole armoury of rhetorical devices, phonetic and semantic, with their larger structural extensions such as tragedy and comedy. The function of style is to unify—or at least encourage the reader to *attempt* to unify—literature's disparate linguistic parts. As such it is the exact opposite of grammar, whose function is not primarily to unite but to divide.[3] (A sentence is grammatical when its separate parts have been found subject to classification, the 'parsing' process, and *then* shown to cohere.) Although some grammaticalness certainly survives in literature, it is as it were accidentally and incidentally, a left-over of logic from the common speech of which the language of literature is one derivative. The reader is scarcely aware of it. What he is aware of—especially in poetry but also in prose with any literary pretensions—is the style (in the wider sense already indicated). If my attention is drawn to breaches of grammar in a work of literature, I can always invoke the magic word 'ellipsis'—a term apparently invented to save grammar's face when we really ignore it.

May I offer Mr Fowler a definition of literature? A work of literature is successful linguistically, the best words in the best order, when appropriate stylistic devices co-operate to unify humane value-judgments, implicit or explicit, on some aspect of life as it is lived in the writer's own society. As for the reader of such a work, he will only be successful if he registers, consciously or at least semi-consciously, the unifying stylistic devices that enable him to respond to the human situation available to him in it. In a word, the role played by grammar in description is *comparable* to that of style in evaluation. But if comparable they are also mutually incompatible, because grammar is primarily analytic in its methods and premises, whereas style is essentially synthetic.

To Mr Fowler's optimistic escape-clause that, because 'some mathematicians and physical scientists are fine musicians and poets', *therefore* a linguistic training will sometimes be useful for the literary critic, the answer is simple and obvious: musical physicists do not improve as physicists by learning to play the piano. I am not sure who Mr Fowler's mathematicians and physicists are who are also fine poets, but these ambidextrous geniuses certainly don't grow on blackberry bushes. I can't think of *one*. On the other hand, it is common knowledge that most structural linguists don't write particularly good English prose. Why indeed should they as long as they are intelligible? The temperamental predisposition that results in Smith becoming an eminent grammarian is normally very different from that which turns Brown into a good critic. Let us agree to be different.

The argument can now be taken a step further. If the most sophisticated grammatical analysis is not going to help the reader to comprehend and respond to the particular work of literature, will 'style' (the relevant 'esemplastic', unifying feature, or cluster of features) do any better? I suggest that it does—and not merely in the complicated lyrics that have provided the Explicators with their most splendid triumphs.

I have found an unexpected ally on this issue of style versus grammar in one of the linguistic contributions to Sebeok's symposium in Professor Sol Saporta's 'The Application of Linguistics to the Study of Poetic Language'. Using Chomsky's concept of 'degrees of grammaticalness', Saporta suggests that the language of poetry is characterized by the density of its 'sequences of lower-order grammaticalness' (p. 84), rising at times to an 'optimum ungrammaticalness' (p. 92). As it happens, this is very much what Shelley said in *A Defence of Poetry*:

A poet participates in the eternal, the infinite, and the one; as far as relates to his conceptions, time and place and number are not. The grammatical forms which express the moods of time, and the difference of persons, and the distinction of place, are convertible with respect to the highest poetry without injuring it as poetry; and the choruses of Aeschylus, and the Book of Job, and Dante's Paradise, would afford, more than any other writings, examples of this fact, if the limits of this essay did not forbid citation.

No doubt Shelley exaggerated; his coyness with specific 'examples of this fact' is an amusing anticipation of the embarrassed silences of the modern linguist when asked to apply his method to literature. But the general thesis that the principles underlying poetic word-order are not those of grammar can hardly be denied. A simple example will be useful. Consider, for example, Pound's 'Papyrus' (a translation of part of a Sappho fragment that is generally recognized today to be a good English poem in its own right):[4]

> Spring . . .
> Too long . . .
> Gongula . . .

The dots at the end of each of Pound's lines invite us as grammarians to read the poem as three separate uncompleted sentences. For the reader of poetry, however, the dots act rather as a kind of visual rhyme, which is reinforced both by the actual half-rhymes (-*ing*, -*ong*, *Gong*-) and by the syllabic crescendo (one-syllable line followed by two-syllable line followed by three-syllable line). The poem's internal grammatical relationships cannot in fact be determined. In English 'Gongula' may be either the subject, the object, or the person addressed (it was apparently a pet-name for one of Sappho's girls); in the original Greek the case-ending limits the possibilities to a nominative or a vocative. The time or tense may equally be present, past, or future. In this poem therefore the word-order *has* to be ungrammatical—and yet the sequence of words undoubtedly functions as a poem. Usually, of course, a poem provides both a grammatical and a stylistic word-order, the former a relic as it were of the primitive linguistic basis in common speech, so far as that is grammatical (it often isn't), with only the latter a proper subject for literary comment. This is why—to return once again to Mr Sinclair—the tabulated analyses of the grammar of Larkin's poem leave their impression of irrelevance and futility. They have nothing to do with the poem *qua* poem.

In the archaic system of Final Examinations that we still operate

at Oxford lines 1702–15 of *Troilus and Criseyde*, Book III, were
recently part of the linguistic question in the paper called Modern
English [*sic*] that is still compulsory for all undergraduates aspiring
to 'Honours' in English literature. The rubric began: 'Comment on
and explain some major points of historical interest in the language
of *two* or *three* of the following passages. Candidates should not deal
only with stylistic features . . .'. (The examiners' dark suspicion that
the literary student might be tempted to 'deal only with stylistic
features' gives the linguistic case away.) Here at any rate is the
passage as set:

> Quod Troilus, 'Allas, now I am war
> That Pirous and tho swifte steedes thre,
> Which that drawen forth the sonnes char,
> Han gon som bi-path in dispit of me;
> That maketh it so soone day to be;
> And, for the sonne hym hasteth thus to rise,
> Ne shal I nevere don him sacrifise.'
>
> But nedes day departe hem moste soone,
> And whan hire speche don was and hire cheere,
> They twynne anon, as they were wont to doone,
> And setten tyme of metyng eft yfeere.
> And many a nyght they wroughte in this manere,
> And thus Fortune a tyme ledde in joie
> Criseyde, and ek this kynges sone of Troie.

To an Oxford linguist one of the 'major points of historical
interest in the language' here is likely, I suppose, to be 'this kynges
sone of Troie' in l. 1715. The modern group possessive ('the King of
Troy's son') was just beginning to establish itself in Chaucer's time;
I imagine the older combination survived because the *-es* in *kynges*
was still dimly felt as a genitive, as a survival, that is, from the older
inflected stage of the language, which could not be detached from its
noun. But the two forms are identical in *meaning*. What is meant by
the bailiff's daughter of Islington that is not meant by *the bailiff of
Islington's daughter*?

A descriptive linguist will probably be more interested in the distinction Chaucer seems to draw between 'Criseyde' (proper name)
and 'kynges sone of Troie' (honorific periphrasis). But again is any
difference of *meaning* involved? The literary critic will be sceptical:
Chaucer needed a rhyme and 'Troilus' did not provide one, whereas
'kynges sone of Troie' did. The 'ek' of this line can be explained away
on similar stylistic grounds. Like *ywis* (and often *and* itself) *ek* was a
'filler' in frequent use in fourteenth-century English poetry to pad

out a line with an extra syllable or stress. (But Chaucer's apparent casualness is an important part of his literary meaning.)

Another linguistic fossil in this passage is 'to doone' (l. 1711), which is, it seems, an inflected infinitive similar to the Latin gerundive. But if it is asked why Chaucer should have revived this almost obsolete form, the obvious answer is again the impudences of rhyme: 'to do' or 'to don' would not rhyme with 'soone'. The literary problem that the linguist cannot or will not explain is why Chaucer was not embarrassed or distressed by such linguistic inconsistencies and oddities. A modern poet who described Fortune as leading Criseyde for a time in joy and *also* this Prince of Troy would necessarily be implying a distinction between Criseyde's joy and Troilus's. This is what the words seem to say; why do they not in fact say this in Chaucer's hands? Such a question can only be answered in terms of the particular esemplastic mode employed.

In the first place, *Troilus and Criseyde* was written for oral delivery at the Court of Richard II: this social fact underlies all the stylistic peculiarities of the passage. Here, essentially, is an author *talking* to an audience of his social superiors; if he is to retain their attention and good will he must clearly cultivate a variety of tones of voice; above all he must avoid pretentiousness.

Chaucer's literary genius transformed a social necessity into an individual poetic style by a continuous juxtaposition of verbal units that say more than he ought to have said with those saying less than he ought to have said. (Social presumption was thus cancelled out by bourgeois clumsiness or vulgarity.) The interplay or collision between the two stylistic elements is what is meant by Chaucer's irony. At his best nothing, considered separately, carries its face meaning: plain statement does not exist and literary decorum is continuously flouted.

Thus the natural way to read l. 1703 would be to assume that 'Pirous' is the driver of the three swift horses. In fact, however, as Chaucer's source *Metamorphoses*, ii, 153 ff. makes clear, Pirous is not a charioteer but a horse, Phoebus's other three horses being Eous, Aethon, and Phlegon. But Chaucer is careful not to show off his learning too blatantly before the King and his Court, and so the three superfluous names are waived. The descent from Ovidian grandeur is even more marked in the colloquial 'bi-path' (short cut) of l. 1705. The second stanza however also begins with a line apparently in the grand style. Here the alliterating *d*s add a certain solemnity and pathos that might be thought appropriate to the introduction of the concept of necessity; no doubt it will not be long before the two lovers are parted for ever, but this is just for the interval between a sunrise and a sunset. The over-solemn tragic tone is not, of

course, maintained, and ll. 1723–5 exhibit the logical and chronological confusion of colloquial speech. Thus, if Troilus and Criseyde
'departe hem' in l. 1722 the *subsequent* chat and fun of l. 1723 is not
strictly possible; in the same way if they really 'twynne' in l. 1724
they cannot *then* arrange the time of the next meeting, as they are
said to do in l. 1725.

It would be tedious to examine the passage in greater detail. Here
is God's plenty; but the unifying verbal factor is that it is expressed
in a looser, more 'open', more elastic, more unpredictable mode of
speech than we are used to. Though superficially grammatical it
seems by its inconsistencies of accidence, word-order, and verbal
class-levels to illustrate Saporta's concept of an 'optimum ungrammaticalness' almost as conclusively as Pound's 'Papyrus'. I hope at
any rate that I have made my academic point—which is simply that
the literary student is more usefully employed in such 'esemplastic'
stylistic exercises than in memorizing the finer points of Middle
English linguistics or modern neogrammatics. Stylistic discrimina-
tion is the one indispensable prerequisite for the aesthetic appreciation of great literature. That some knowledge of linguistics,
historical and descriptive, has certain minor uses in literary studies
is not to be denied, but for the native speaker of English this additional knowledge is, as it were, supplementary—either in eking out
one's birthright by the help available in the *OED* for an unusual word
or idiom, or in saving one from incidental errors outside one's immediate range of linguistic experience. Such information may be compared to the odds and ends of social and political history with which
the scholar-critic will also have to equip himself. A little learning of
this kind will go a long way, though with none at all the reader's
fingers can sometimes be badly burnt. But for the literary beginner
the best way to acquire such information—including the sign-posts
to the topic's more sophisticated levels—is *ad hoc*; in other words,
by consulting a glossary or an editor's notes only when he needs
them. What he naturally resents is the traditional compulsory
spoon-feeding with grammar or history most of which he will never
need.[5] Of course, if he is interested in either descriptive linguistics
or the history of the language or social history for its own sake,
that is another matter. My real quarrel with Mr Fowler—or rather
with the cause for which he is pleading—is that he is presenting the
study of language as a *necessary* concomitant to the study of literature. For the native speaker, except occasionally and superficially,
this is simply not true. It is not true even for the reading of Chaucer.

This has been a fighting retort and I hope the words I have used
will not seem unnecessarily offensive. But *pace* Mr Fowler, the things
I have said do need to be said.

Notes to Paper Four

1 Mr Fowler asks us to excuse some of the follies in the excursions
 into literature by his fellow-linguists by the novelty of it all. But
 Saussure's *Cours de linguistique générale* was published in 1916,
 being based on lectures delivered at Geneva as early as 1906–11,
 and even Bloomfield's *Language* came out in 1933.

2 While anxious to disavow the objectivity of linguistics Mr Fowler
 seems equally determined to exclude the subjective element in the
 linguistic process. 'What', he asks, 'are literary values: features of
 response or of [the] literary work? If the latter, how can they be
 unrelated to the characteristics of the medium of that work?'
 (p. 328). The comment seems to dissociate 'value' from 'response' and
 to locate literary values in the 'medium'—as though a sequence of
 words can retain its quality as literature on a printed page that
 no one is reading.

3 The discomfort a linguist feels in the presence of the synthetic
 process is nicely illustrated in the discussion of 'polysemy' by
 A. E. Darbyshire in his lucid and instructive *A Description of English*
 (1967). Here we learn (p. 157) that 'a metaphor is the use of a
 word for something other than what it actually or normally
 denotes'. But in literature a good metaphor must retain its original
 meaning *at the same time* that it acquires its new or extended
 meaning. Unless both meanings are equally present the metaphor
 has failed as literature. Similar considerations apply to irony or
 even the pun.

4 The poem is discussed in some detail by G. S. Fraser in his *Ezra
 Pound* (1960), 110–11. Pound concealed the fact that he was
 translating Sappho. The source and Pound's treatment of it are
 discussed by Christopher M. Dawson, *The Explicator*, February
 1951, and N. E. Collinge, *Notes and Queries*, June 1958.

5 Mr Fowler asserts (p. 333) that 'The literary people hold the reins
 of power almost everywhere in the humanities nowadays'. This
 may be so in the United States, but in the older universities in
 Great Britain (except Cambridge) the power as between 'language'
 and 'literature' in the Departments of English is more or less
 equally divided, even if the literary teachers are generally more
 numerous than the linguists. The result is usually a kind of
 stalemate. If the compulsory 'language' papers were to be optional,
 most of the undergraduates, whose primary interest is in literature
 (especially recent literature), would tend to avoid them and the
 language professors and lecturers would find themselves with sadly
 depleted classes. Realizing this their literary colleagues find
 themselves reluctantly perpetuating the *status quo* out of a natural
 reluctance to break the hearts of old friends and acquaintances.
 Until recently, of course, 'language' meant *Beowulf* and Middle
 English sound-changes. We had hoped at first that the new
 linguistics might provide an acceptable alternative in a 'language'

more relevant to literature, but the hope, as I have shown, is not likely to be fulfilled. The undergraduate reading English ought surely to be able to study English literature and nothing else, unless he has special interests outside the subject. As a student of literature he will in fact derive far more benefit from some reading in Latin or French than from either the new or the old linguistics.

Five

Language and literature

Mr Bateson's attempt to disqualify linguistics as a discipline of relevance to literature (*Essays in Criticism*; see this volume, Paper Four) comprises a very cunning and apparently substantial argument inter-woven with a misleading line of polemic. In his usual masterly fashion, he has constructed a case against which it is very difficult to argue in an organized way. I will try to show that his argument (1) rests on premises which cannot provide an adequate aesthetic for literature, (2) is ineffective as a disqualification of linguistics because of misconceptions about the nature of linguistics, (3) is motivated by a set of prejudices which inhibit constructive discussion of the present issue.

(1) Habitual readers of *Essays in Criticism* will have noticed that Mr Bateson's case is basically a somewhat complicated version of ideas he has offered linguists and medievalists for at least the last ten years (see especially viii, 76–8, 335–6; ix, 238; xi, 255–63; xii, 107–8; xvi, 226–8, 464–5). He compounds (*a*) Coleridge's 'homely definition' of poetry as 'the best words in the best order'; (*b*) Coleridge's 'esemplastic', unifying power of Imagination; (*c*) I. A. Richards' distinction between scientific and emotive language; (*d*) de Saussure's distinction between *langue* and *parole*. These formulae are jumbled together to support an assertion of a unique and exclusive aesthetic so constructed as apparently to make literature inaccessible to objective study:

> My point of departure is Saussure's distinction between *langue* (the language-system) and *parole* (the particular language-occasion). Projected into the sphere of literature *langue* becomes 'style' (with its subdivisions of *genres*, 'topoi', figures of speech, poetic diction, etc.), and *parole* becomes the particular artifact in the context of its original audience . . . (xii, 107).

The function of style is to unify—or at least encourage the
reader to attempt to unify—literature's disparate linguistic
parts (xvii, 339).
A work of literature is successful linguistically, the best words
in the best order, when appropriate stylistic devices cooperate
to unify humane value-judgments, implicit or explicit, on
some aspect of life as it is lived in the writer's own society
(xvii, 339–40).

(*a*) 'The best words in the best order' is, except in Mr Bateson's
first book, an empty catch-phrase. Coleridge used it to distinguish
verse from prose, and his requirement that 'the words, the *media*,
must be beautiful, and ought to attract your notice' becomes impertinent when the phrase is employed to mark off literature from non-
literature, as Mr Bateson uses it currently. It is obviously at best
incomplete when applied to most kinds of poetry, and quite wrong
for narrative verse and for drama and the novel. (A hint of how Mr
Bateson is able to countenance this generalization of the definition is
his opinion, expressed in 1934 (p. 13) and again in 1967 (p. 338),
that everything which is not *la poésie pure* is tainted poetry (e.g.
novels).)

In *English Poetry* (2nd ed., 1966), p. 18 he tries another characterization of 'the best words'. Citing Jespersen, he offers a scale of
values for speech: 'merely comprehensible', 'entirely correct',
'good' (the last like Dr Johnson's conversation); corresponding to
'good' for speech is 'best' for literature. The contrast between
'entirely correct' and 'best' appears to be connected with the distinction between 'a grammatical and a stylistic word-order' (xvii,
339–42). 'Common speech' is just words and just word-order, subject
only to the judgment of correctness. In literature style transcends
the demands of grammar and survives, even welcomes, ungrammaticalness. The point seems to be that of non-literary language
(whatever that is) one can say whether it is or is not grammatical,
and what the grammatical structure is; these considerations are
irrelevant to literary language: 'the best words' obey principles
which are not those of mere grammar. Unfortunately Mr Bateson
takes this argument in a direction in which he should not want to go,
and the quotation from Shelley (p. 341) cannot save him: the equation
of style with ungrammaticalness and with it the unhappy elevation
of e. e. cummings and Dylan Thomas as the normative models of
literary language.[1] He has spoiled his argument by confusing 'ungrammatical' ('employing structures which break the rules of the
grammar') with 'non-grammatical' ('employing structures additional
to the structures of the grammar') and by equating 'non-grammati-

cal' (his 'ungrammatical') with 'literary' and 'grammatical' with 'non-literary'.

(*b*) Since Mr Bateson borrows Coleridge's 'synthetic and magical power' without naming it I shall not appeal to Coleridge for a clarification of the concept of poetic synthesis. In any event, Mr Bateson makes no use of Imagination; it is 'style' which is said to synthesize and fuse. In so far as 'style' means 'the best words' it is insubstantial; but if, as seems likely, it means only rhetoric and diction—the poetic givens of a certain tradition at a certain time—it is no mystery. It unifies 'literature's disparate linguistic parts', and there is no mystery here either. Textual criticism can easily be equipped to specify the linguistic parts and to recognize schemes such as larger-than-sentence patterns (p. 338, bottom) and discords such as metaphor, irony, etc. (p. 346, note 3).

(*c*) I. A. Richards' distinction between emotive and scientific language is generally agreed to be without reasonable foundation: it is much too simple to serve as a linguistic theory or to provide an isolation of the characteristics of 'literary language'. Obviously, certain uses of language must strain towards the pole of neutral objectivity, as Mr Bateson says. But the overall state of affairs is that natural languages develop thousands of varieties specialized to the needs of topic, function, situation, etc.[2] Geoffrey Leech and I argued this view in *Essays on Style and Language*; it is a commonplace view and does literature no disservice.

Mr Bateson words this spurious distinction as 'description' *v.* 'evaluation'. Description comprises all that is undesirable and inhuman: linguistics, analysis, science, technical terminology. Evaluation is everything that is the antithesis of description. Ambiguously, it is somehow a characteristic of *both* literature (e.g. lyric poetry is 'the mode which perhaps represents the ideal form of evaluative speech') *and* literary criticism. In order to 'preserve the purity of each of the two linguistic modes' we must resist 'the mating of the language of description with the language of evaluation' (pp. 338, 339). It is really too bad that Mr Bateson has to resort to this kind of sexual-xenophobic insult ('Linguists have their good points—but would you let your sister marry one?') in this important debate; but the inadequacy of his argument is more damaging than his tone here. Since the premise is untenable and the arguments illogical,[3] the statement is meaningless. As a literary aesthetic it is either too vague or too crude, whatever we make of 'evaluative lyric poetry'; as a guide-line for criticism it is too destructive, since it appears unsympathetic to any objective criticism without making it clear why objective criticism is wrong.

(*d*) I do not think the reference to de Saussure is merely a sop to

F

the linguists. Unfortunately, taken as a serious proposal it doesn't make sense. *Langue* and *parole* together, according to de Saussure, make up the *faculté du langage*. *Langue* is the abstract system of rules which enables a speaker to communicate with others. *Parole* is a particular concrete act of speech, or a corpus collected from many such acts. Chomsky has recently revived and adapted the distinction using the terms *competence* and *performance*. Mr Bateson, like de Saussure and Chomsky, says that linguists study *langue*, which is true in so far as linguists write grammars of languages and enquire into the linguistic mental capabilities of speakers. But, Mr Bateson says, literature 'is' *parole* (xii, 227)—or rather, 'is a kind of' *parole* (xvi, 465); the study of literature is the study of *parole*—or rather, the study of a special kind of *parole* of which the *langue* is not *langue* but 'style'; schematically:

Nonliterature	*Literature*
Parole = speech	Parole = literary text
Langue = grammar	Langue$_1$ = style
	Langue$_2$ = grammar

For literature, he says, linguists can talk about *langue$_2$* only, and since this is merely 'a relic . . . of the primitive linguistic basis in common speech' (xvii, 342) of which readers of literature are 'scarcely aware' (339), what linguists can do in this way is not worth doing. This is an illegitimate and meaningless adaptation of de Saussure. It is illegitimate because the original scheme works only if it applies in the same way for all uses of language; it is meaningless because of the poverty of Mr Bateson's definition of the linguistic components of style and because of his misunderstanding of the interests and procedures of grammatical study in relation to *langue* and *parole*.

(2) Richards' dichotomy appears most often as an opposition between 'science' and 'values'. A typical statement is this by David Lodge:

> It is the essential characteristic of modern linguistics that it claims to be a science. It is the essential characteristic of literature that it concerns values. And values are not amenable to scientific method. (*Language of Fiction*, p. 57)

Mr Bateson asserts that linguistics *is* a science (xvi, 464). I astonished him (xvii, 327; cf. 336) by alleging that linguistics 'affects scientism' (not a very good phrase, I now see). There is some difference between claiming to be a science and being a science. I think these observations would be generally accepted by contemporary linguists: (1) using 'objective', 'rigorous' methods does not by itself constitute being scientific; (2) Bloomfieldian linguistics, and allied approaches, are not scientific in any real sense; (3) Chomskyan (transformational-generative) linguistics, which is oriented towards the theory of *langue* rather than the inventorizing of *parole*, may be truly scientific by design;[4] if it is so in practice, this does not prejudice the stylistic description of texts. It is difficult to present these arguments briefly without distortion, but the substance is as follows: Bloomfieldian, *alias* 'structural', *alias* 'descriptive' linguistics held that linguistic analysis is the application of an efficient methodology to samples of speech in order to discover and classify units smaller than the sentence. Chomsky and his associates have argued that this approach—which they call 'taxonomic linguistics'—is inadequate in two ways.[5] It is mechanically inadequate because it cannot, unequipped with the notions of deep structure and transformation, account for all the linguistic relations found in sentences. It is psychologically inadequate because it bears no significant relation to the human activities of speaking and understanding language—only to the unreal situation of the analyst listening to an informant producing 'data' in a language the analyst pretends he does not understand.

Thus we should not regard the linguistic description of a text as the discovery of structure. A linguist ought only to claim to make articulate what a native speaker tacitly knows about a text he understands. In this way, linguistic description is a representation of (part of) the process of understanding: it shows how a native speaker encounters and interprets sentences generated by the grammar (*langue*) that he knows. The 'linguistic analysis' of literature is an attempt to make explicit part of the process of reading by the use of terms and concepts which have psychological reality (are humane even if they are scientific) through being appropriate to the reader's individually internalized yet culturally shared grammar of the language.[6] Some such description is necessary because speakers do not *know about* their language anything like as efficiently as they *know* it. I see no reason derived from either the supposed opposition of science and literature, or the theoretical potential of linguistics (as distinct from the claims of many linguists and some linguist–critics), why such a linguistics should be intrinsically alien to certain parts of literary study.

(3) The 'misleading line of polemic' derives from Mr Bateson's feelings about the old and disgraceful 'language–literature contro-versy'. There are still large numbers of people in English depart-ments who, for reasons of academic politics, feel obliged to parcel the world into two intractably opposed groups. This is not the proper place to make a fuss about that issue, since only by association does it affect the dispute between Mr Bateson and me. Modern

linguistics is only accidentally the 'successor' of the old philological medievalism. Linguistics lays fair claim to be an autonomous discipline in its central concern, the theory of *langue*; it provides a theoretical status for *parole*, but needs augmenting by other disciplines in the study of *parole*. In places where *parole* is studied (e.g. English departments) linguistics has obvious uses. But its value cannot be appreciated while people's words and votes are governed by oversimplified and historically irrelevant 'sets' towards imagined opponents. Reciprocal ignorance about literary criticism and linguistics is also, as I have several times argued, deeply inhibiting.

We can now attempt to rebuild the theory of style. I will argue that linguistic theory [7] provides a definition for a level of language which we may call 'style'. Since no workable theory has ever been constructed which uniquely isolates a category of language 'literature', there seems no good reason why the concept of style should be exclusively literary. (Whether or not a particular text is regarded by its readers as being literature is an important cultural fact, but an irrelevant fact from our point of view.) The linguistic theory which provides a definition of style by the same definition establishes the contribution, and the limitation of contribution, of grammar to the study of style. For the moment I will use the term 'style' in the sense which I believe Mr Bateson is attempting to propose: a formal, but non-grammatical, level of language at which interesting, if syntactically insignificant, patterns occur. It will already be obvious from Mr Bateson's discussion and mine that this use of 'style' is unconventional: too general, and inappropriate to some particulars. But the use of a mildly unsuitable known term is preferable to a neologism in a discussion such as the present. We can revise the terminology after we have established the concept.

The distinction between *langue* and *parole*, competence and performance, is well-motivated and essential. It reflects the gap between people's linguistic knowledge and what they do with it. Almost every sentence one encounters is a new sentence that one has never met before; a little reflection suggests that there is no reason why the number of such sentences should not be infinite: and yet, one understands these sentences. This comprehension cannot be explained by proposing that speakers have learned the meanings of an indefinitely large number of sentences which are then 'recognized' as they occur in speech. The explanation can only be that the fluent, mature, native speaker has acquired a finite device which recursively generates an infinite number of sentences. For example, the sentence *John likes apples and plums* is generated by a finite set of rules. The same number of rules plus one generates *John likes apples, pears, and plums*. Now the *same* rule that introduced *pears* can be *reapplied* infinitely many times to extend the list of fruits infinitely, and thus produce an infinite number of sentences of ever increasing length. The fact of *parole* is the infinite number of sentences; the fact of *langue* is the finite set of rules that generates them (i.e. that allows us to produce and understand an infinite number of sentences).

This finite mechanism *langue* can be represented in a grammar.[8] In this way a grammar represents a fluent speaker–hearer's linguistic competence, what he knows of his language which enables him to produce and interpret infinitely many sentences. A grammar seen as a finite body of rules is also descriptively useful: it will assign structural descriptions to the observed sentences of *parole* if they are grammatical; if they are ungrammatical ('deviant') a grammar will show this and will characterize the manner of deviation.[9] If a sentence is ambiguous a grammar will assign more than one structural description to it. If two sentences are paraphrases of one another, a grammar will acknowledge this fact, hopefully one day at a more valuable level than transformational equivalence. These are the capabilities and limitations of a grammar.

However, linguistic performance does not issue from the exercise of linguistic competence alone.[10] Other factors co-operate to determine the production and interpretation of real sentences. For example, the articulation and perception of speech depend on the use of an oral and auditory neurophysiological apparatus; successful communication depends on speakers' sensitivity to the type of communicative situation in which they are involved and the consequent selection of appropriate utterances; memory limitations, speech defects and other such accidental factors influence performance; non-grammatical formal conventions, e.g. metre, have their effect; the attitudes, beliefs, informedness, states of health and moods of performers are influential. For such reasons, texts (samples of performance) exhibit many features which are not causally linked to *langue* and which are therefore not describable by reference to a grammar. For example, the grammar does not explain why a particular sentence is about apples and plums and not about books, or tennis, or electricity; why a particular structure, or transformation, is evident; why one sequence of sentences or sentence-types occurs and not another; why a sentence, or a text, is in one tense or another or two tenses mixed; why speaker A speaks RP and B Cockney; and so on. Such characteristics (in *all* texts) do indeed transcend grammar; but they are not beyond applied linguistics—grammar is inescapably their base.

Categories of formal variation not dependent on linguistic competence include dialect, accent, voice set, paralanguage, register, and style.[11] I admit that the categorization is not well established—in particular, the boundaries between register and style have not yet been rigorously formulated—but the theoretical status of style within the *faculté du langage* is not, I believe, in doubt. For the sake of brevity I will illustrate this status by alluding to a simple example already discussed: the 'tripartite structures' in Bacon's essay 'Of Studies' (*ESL*, 18–22). These are obviously formal structures, since they exhibit a kind of 'syntactic' patterning. But their 'syntax' is not the syntax of the language; there is no rule which demands that all English sentences display arrangements of units in threes. This could be said to be a 'stylistic' rule, an extra rule applied to English units in English constructions generated by the grammar. The exponents of these stylistic structures may be described in terms of the grammar, but the grammar provides no term for the structures and no explanation for them. Their character, significance, value, and effect remain unexplained by the grammar, which is only to be expected because they neither stem from nor are recognized by the simple exercise of linguistic competence. They have an indispensable linguistic basis, however, and this makes grammatical description both valuable and necessary.[12]

Let us think of *langue* as an ability to produce sentences. This competence will *not* produce *parole* (utterances, texts) without the help of several other skills—a sound-producing apparatus, a sentence-selection process, a sentence-ordering skill, etc. One of these supplementary devices could be a rhetoric, as represented, for example, in one of the medieval or renaissance manuals. The style of a text produced by a grammar and a rhetoric together is described by the use of grammatical and rhetorical terms, and the rhetorical terms are explained and evaluated non-linguistically. Similar supplementary devices can be imagined which co-operate with the grammar to construct iambic pentameters, Milton's or Henry James's characteristic sentence structures, Spenserian stanzas or Euphuistic prose. And it is probable that such a model is appropriate to the production of local effects (e.g. metaphor, pun) as well as those (as above) which operate text-wide. Grammar is a human skill which is expressed in linguistic performance by the production and comprehension of an indefinite number of new sentences. The ancillary skills other than linguistic competence are expressed in performance by the selection, manipulation, and ordering of sentences in ways which are appropriate to the 'context of situation'[13] of an utterance. One set of non-grammatical skills works upon grammar to produce style.

I hope the general strategy of my reorientation is clear. The distinction between competence and performance provides the only fruitful way of understanding the special formal qualities (style among them) of texts. Wellek and Warren speak of 'the contrast of the language system of a literary work of art with the general usage of the time' (*Theory of Literature*, p. 177). The contrast attempted is evident from the mention in the next line of 'common speech, even unliterary speech': the false norm of non-literary language is being invoked to provide background for a spurious category 'literary language'. But in reality the sense in which there is a gap between the 'normal language' and any distinctive text is the same for *all* texts: there is the grammar (*langue*, competence) and what you do with the grammar (*parole*, performance, e.g. texts identified stylistically). In the light of this fundamental tenet of linguistic theory there is no formal category 'literature'. In my opinion no study of texts which recognizes the critical importance of 'style' can afford to define 'style' against any background other than that provided by a linguistic theory of this kind.[14]

Notes to Paper Five

1 Mrs Vendler (*Essays in Criticism*, xvi, 458) justly complained of the 'unholy fascination' of Dylan Thomas for linguists.
Discussion of poetry in terms of (un)grammaticalness is to be found in S. Saporta, 'The Application of Linguistics to the Study of Poetic Language' in T. A. Sebeok (ed.), *Style in Language* (New York, 1960), 82–93; S. R. Levin, 'Poetry and Grammaticalness' in H. G. Lunt (ed.), *Proceedings of the Ninth International Congress of Linguists* (The Hague, 1964), reprinted in S. B. Chatman and S. R. Levin, *Essays on the Language of Literature* (Boston, 1967), 224–30; J. P. Thorne, 'Stylistics and Generative Grammars', *Journal of Linguistics*, i (1965), 49–59.
2 See R. Quirk, *The Use of English* (London, 1962); M. A. K. Halliday, A. McIntosh and P. Strevens, *The Linguistic Sciences and Language Teaching* (London, 1964), Ch. 4.
3 Specifically, in his confusion of the medium of an art form with the medium in which one criticizes it.
4 I reserve judgment on this question. For typical arguments, see R. B. Lees, review of Chomsky, *Syntactic Structures*, *Language*, xxxiii (1957), 375 ff.; J. J. Katz, *The Philosophy of Language* (New York and London, 1966), 115 ff.
5 See Katz, 'Mentalism in Linguistics', *Language*, xl (1964), 124–37; Chomsky, *Current Issues in Linguistic Theory*, Janua Linguarum 38 (The Hague, 1964), especially 11 ff. An efficient presentation of 'taxonomic linguistics' is H. A. Gleason, Jr., *An Introduction to Descriptive Linguistics*, first edition (New York, 1955).
6 See Katz, 'Mentalism in Linguistics'.
7 The linguistic theory which informs the present discussion is most lucidly expressed in Chomsky, 'The Formal Nature of Language',

Appendix A in E. H. Lenneberg, *Biological Foundations of Language* (New York, 1967). For fuller treatments see Chomsky, *Aspects of the Theory of Syntax* (Cambridge, Mass., 1965); J. J. Katz and P. Postal, *An Integrated Theory of Linguistic Descriptions* (Cambridge, Mass., 1964); J. A. Fodor and J. J. Katz (eds.), *The Structure of Language* (Englewood Cliffs, N.J., 1964). The distinction between competence and performance is discussed at length by several of the contributors to J. Lyons and R. J. Wales (eds.), *Psycholinguistics Papers* (Edinburgh, 1966).

8 I use the term 'grammar' to include syntax, phonology and (part of) semantics, excluding phonetics and (probably) referential semantics.

9 See Chomsky, 'Some Methodological Remarks on Generative Grammar', *Word*, xvii (1961), 219–39: 233–9 reprinted in Fodor and Katz, op. cit., 384–9, under the title 'Degrees of Grammaticalness'; P. Ziff, 'On Understanding "Understanding Utterances"' in Fodor and Katz, 390–9; J. J. Katz, 'Semi-sentences' in Fodor and Katz, 400–16.

10 Unfortunately the theory of performance has been neglected in generative linguistics (since it is outside the bounds of linguistics in the narrow sense) and many statements about it in the works cited here are (I believe) unnecessarily negative.

11 On voice set and paralanguage see D. Crystal and R. Quirk, *Systems of Prosodic and Paralinguistic Features in English*, Janua Linguarum 39 (The Hague, 1964). On register see Halliday, McIntosh, and Strevens, op. cit., 87–98; G. N. Leech, *English in Advertising* (London, 1966), 67–73; but the usage of *style* by these authors is quite distinct from mine. Likewise, the hierarchization of styles implied in M. Joos, 'The Five Clocks', *International Journal of American Linguistics*, xxviii (1962) and Gleason, *Linguistics and English Grammar* (New York, 1965), Ch. 15, while related to that of Halliday *et al.* and Leech, has nothing to do with my usage, unless accidentally.

12 A compatible approach treating literary style in terms of characteristic selection of transformations (another aspect of my distinction between the grammar and the use of the grammar) is to be found in R. Ohmann, 'Generative Grammars and the Concept of Literary Style', *Word*, xx (1964), 423–39. See also his 'Literature as Sentences', *College English* (January 1966), reprinted in Chatman and Levin, op. cit., which updates the syntactic apparatus.

13 'Context of situation' is a term J. R. Firth developed after Malinowski; see Firth's *Papers in Linguistics* (London, 1957), 182–3, for an informal account of this notion.

14 The critical subdivision of this general concept 'style', and its status in the various kinds of literary texts, are a quite different subject-matter from that of the present paper: that I neglect it here does not mean that I underestimate its importance.

Six

Language and literature: reply by F. W. Bateson

Would I allow my sister to marry a linguist? It is a good question. And I suppose, if I am honest, I must admit that I would much prefer *not* to have a linguist in the family. But at least I would not forbid the banns—as Lincoln Barnett, for example, would certainly do. Here is a specimen passage from Barnett's informative if unprofessional *The Treasure of Our Tongue* (New York, 1964):

> To almost everyone who cherishes the English language for its grace and beauty, its combination of precision and flexibility, the social philosophy of the Structural Linguist seems past comprehension—epitomizing indeed the 'anti-intellectualism of the intellectual'. Among all the forces of cultural vandalism at work in the country, their influence has been, perhaps, the most insidious. The vulgarities of advertising and mudflows of jargon can be shoveled aside. But the impact of the Structural Linguists is like that of slow atomic fallout: through their influence on teachers' colleges and teachers, hence on the schools and the pupils within them they are incapacitating the coming generation. (pp. 285–6)

Mr Barnett is, of course, an American and the linguists who supply him with the monstrosities of prose style that he has collected in his book are also Americans. But one knows what he means, and the vandalism has, I am afraid, begun to infect some English linguists too.

Mr Fowler is not a vandal and I have no faults to find with his English. What I do find disturbing in his attempt to woo the literary critic and student is his inability to provide actual, concrete examples of the usefulness of the linguistic approach to a proper understanding and appreciation of particular poems, plays, or novels—or even particular parts or aspects of such works. Instead all that we get is theorizing—often of much interest simply as theory—and some skilful linguistic propaganda.

It will be remembered that the collection of *Essays on Style and Language* edited by Mr Fowler included a detailed linguistic analysis by J. McH. Sinclair of a poem by Larkin. Neither Mrs Vendler in her review nor I in the first instalment of this 'Argument' were able to derive any literary benefit from the exercise, and we said so with considerable emphasis. I had hoped that the second instalment might have given Mr Fowler the opportunity to explain to us what we had missed or where we had gone wrong. But I cannot detect a single reference either to Larkin's poem or to Sinclair's exposition of it. Is the essay perhaps, however linguistically sophisticated, *indefensible* critically? Mrs Vendler also commented on Mr Fowler's one descent into particularity—his description of the 'tripartite schemes' in Bacon's essay 'Of Studies'. The questions that she raised are clearly extremely pertinent for the study of Bacon's essay as literature:

> What is the effect here of threes in preference to twos or fours?
> Are there more threes elsewhere in Bacon? What do threes
> mean as an order for Bacon? Who else, like Bacon, has a liking
> for threes? Why?

Why, Mr Fowler? But, though he has a reference above to Bacon's 'tripartite structures', Mrs Vendler's actual questions are ignored. Presumably Mr Fowler does not know the answers to them. 'The grammar', as he now puts it, 'provides no term for the structures and no explanation for them'. In that case, however, if the patterns of threes in 'Of Studies' belong to 'style' and not to 'grammar', why need the literary student concern himself with grammar? And, as a matter of fact, much the most acute study of Bacon's style— Morris W. Croll's 'Attic Prose: Lipsius, Montaigne, Bacon' in the *Schelling Anniversary Papers* (1923), now reprinted in Croll's *Style, Rhetoric, and Rhythm* (ed. J. Max Patrick and others, 1966)— manages to make its points without any reference to grammar at all. It is not even clear to me that 'tripartite structures', as defined grammatically by Mr Fowler, are a significant feature of Bacon's style, and I suspect them to be mere figments of Mr Fowler's grammatical imagination. The *Essays* of 1597 were a part of the general 'Senecan' movement (though Croll demonstrates that Tacitus rather than Seneca was Bacon's principal model) in the later sixteenth century, and their distinguishing character as style is their aphoristic quality. Since the whole object of an aphorism is to pack as many related generalizations into as few words as possible, its structure naturally tends to be that of a *catalogue raisonné*. Mr Fowler's list of 'tripartite' grammatical elements in 'Of Studies' adds up to ten, two of which were added in Bacon's later revision of the *Essays*. Three others are the immediate logical consequence of preceding triads. The reason why this essay may give the impression of being dominated by series or patterns of three phrases or clauses is probably because the first sentence ('*Studies* serve for Delight, for Ornament, and for Ability') makes three related points—and not, as Mr Fowler seems to think, because Bacon tended to write in 'tripartite structures'. 'Of Discourse', on the other hand, begins with an antithesis (bipartite structure); 'Of Truth' limits itself to a single point. And even 'Of Studies' has two passages in which five points are made consecutively as well as nine two-point passages. To Mrs Vendler's 'Why' Mr Fowler should presumably have answered that Bacon, like Lipsius,[1] occasionally used a triad to add variety to the predominant antithesis. The conclusion would not have been earth-shaking—and a minimum of grammar is required to reach it. But in its small way it would have been a contribution to our understanding of Bacon's style.

The two stanzas from Chaucer's *Troilus and Criseyde* that I quoted and discussed in the first instalment of our 'Argument' (*E in C*, xvii (1967), 342 f.) were a direct challenge to the linguists, historical and descriptive, to apply their linguistic tools to literary interpretation. Mr Fowler avoids this passage altogether, and so far none of his colleagues has come to his rescue. Am I being unkind or unfair in ascribing their silence to a *necessary* incompetence? I mean by this simply that our two disciplines do not overlap. Under the condition that I have been assuming—viz. that the literary student is a sensible native speaker of the language whose literature he is studying—the linguistic assistance he will need is surely minimal. Occasionally, in the case of the long historical continuum that we think of as English literature (which gets spatially more extensive each year as well as temporally older), a glossary, dictionary or grammar will have to be consulted, but *linguistically* English literature remains essentially homogeneous. Once you have got used to Chaucer's spelling and pronouns, or the oddities of vocabulary employed by some Scotch, American or Australasian writers, there are really next to no language problems for an English reader that the context of the passage will not solve. Style, however, is different; its complexities and implications *are* almost infinite. Language, as we say, is 'picked up'; style, on the other hand, has to be learnt—and taught. It should not be forgotten that 'rhetoric' was the intellectual core of Greek and Roman education, and that the only *languages* the school-boy acquires by a conscious and deliberate process, then and now, are foreign languages. In an English-speaking country English is breathed in as part of the cultural atmosphere.

It is true that 'rhetoric' is a word that has now acquired unfavourable connotations. Unlike language, which whether spoken or written is either 'correct' or 'incorrect', style or rhetoric may be good or bad. The reason why this should be so is implicit, as Mr Fowler would no doubt agree, in the distinction that Saussure (whom Mr Fowler prefers to call 'de Saussure'—which seems like calling Montaigne 'de Montaigne') proposed between *langue* and *parole*. Language, the principal tool of man 'the tool-using animal', includes both aspects. Saussure's point of departure was *le circuit de la parole*, in which a man he calls 'A' communicates a concept to a man he calls 'B'. A and B belong to the same speech-community and so employ the same *langue*. But, as neither Saussure nor Mr Fowler seems fully to realize, *parole* (actual conversations between a real A and a real B) is always logically prior to *langue*. Some incentive to communicate—sexual, paternal or maternal, co-operation in the hunt, group-defence against a common enemy—is presupposed in the origins of language. Mr Fowler has recently published a useful Old English grammar. I need not tell him therefore why Old English —an inflected language with a complicated system of case-endings and genders, the adjectives 'agreeing' with the nouns, etc.—became obsolete and was superseded by the early form of modern English that philology has christened 'Middle English'. The root-cause was two extra-linguistic historical events—the settlement of large areas of northern and eastern England by Scandinavian invaders and the subsequent Norman Conquest. Because of these political events *le circuit de la parole* took place in a new human context and as a result a new or modified *langue* gradually came into general use to reflect and express it.

A similar process occurs whenever individual creative genius intervenes in the progress of literature. The new poet, dramatist, or novelist has inherited a particular *langue* and certain literary conventions, but extra-linguistic and extra-literary considerations continually impel him to modify them. He does not feel or think in quite the same way as his predecessors, and his external circumstances may also be very different from theirs. If he is to 'express' himself, if he is to balance or reconcile the opposite or discordant elements in his personality or his experiences, the *circuit de la parole* will necessarily be affected for him—exactly as when a primitive tribe turns from a pastoral to an agricultural mode of subsistence, or the influence of the Danelaw penetrated into new areas when conservative Anglo-Saxon pressures were superseded by the new Norman authoritarianism. In such circumstances *parole* will reconstruct *langue*, the older usage becoming bad ('fuddy-duddy') in comparison to the 'smart', fashionable, new usage.

Such changes will be registered by the linguist as changes of form or meaning. But to reduce them to mere revisions of the vocabulary or the grammar is to surrender to the behaviourist fallacy. The student of literature cannot be content with a description of the external mechanics or mere structure of *langue*. As he reads a work of literature he will have to almost identify himself with the author he is reading or with his various *dramatis personae*. Now the critical controls to be applied to prevent any misreading of this or that particular passage or work are *the inter-subjective phenomena of style*. Whatever Coleridge may or may not have meant by his 'homely definition', the study of literature written in one's native language reduces itself to a recognition that the words with which the reader is confronted are (or are not) *really*, in their context, approximately the best words in the best order. In the case of the author a style precedes the words. He knows more or less what he wants to say and how he proposes to say it *before* the final verbal formulation on paper. The reader, on the other hand, finds the process reversed, beginning with the specific individual words and working his way through them, as it were, to reach the style. And it is only via the style that he becomes capable of a proper literary response to what he is reading.

If I may judge by his comments on Bacon's 'Of Studies', Mr Fowler finds it difficult to pass from the linguistic to the stylistic phase, as I have described them. And as a consequence the full aesthetic response is apparently denied to him. Other linguists, of course, remain solidly stuck at the level of *langue*. Ultimately it is, I suggest, because of this verbal immobility, this failure to recognize that in literature language is for the reader a mere preliminary to style—as style itself is a preliminary to the literary response in its fullest sense—that the critic finds so little nourishment in modern linguistics in any of its forms. *Not here, O Apollo, are haunts meet for thee.*

Note to Paper Six

1 An example of a tripartite scheme in Latin will be found in the passage from Lipsius quoted in Croll (ed. J. Max Patrick), 31.

Seven

The structure of criticism and the languages of poetry

I

There are some statements by critics which, however vague and rudimentary, at least give the impression that, with a little more logical care, they could be derived directly from axioms in the theory of literature. These two assertions are of this kind; though woolly in expression, they are 'safe' and, I think, could be paraphrased to give incontrovertible truths:

> In considering the language of poetry it is prudent to begin with what is 'there' in the poem—'there' in the sense that it can be described and referred to as unarguably given by the words.
>
> (Winifred Nowottny, *The Language Poets Use*, p. 1)
>
> The novelist's medium is language: whatever he does, *qua* novelist, he does in and through language.
>
> (David Lodge, *Language of Fiction*, p. ix)

Others seem to proceed from the axiomatic by a much less direct route:

> There are four parts in this poetic composite [the lyric]: choice, character, thought, and diction. For choice is the activity, and thought and character are the causes of the activity, and diction is the means. The choice, or deliberative activity of choosing, is the principal part, for reasons analogous to those which make plot the principal part of tragedy. Next in importance comes character; next thought; and last, diction.
>
> (Elder Olson, 'An Outline of Poetic Theory', in R. S. Crane (ed.),
> *Critics and Criticism*, Chicago, 1963, p. 21.)

Can both kinds of statement be tolerated? I suppose this question would, conventionally, be answered affirmatively: after all, it is empirically evident that there are in existence many diverse critical 'metalanguages', the speakers of which operate happily and productively in their own literary fields—indeed the present volume [the volume from which this paper is reprinted; see Acknowledgments, above, xi] would seem to celebrate a multiplicity of critical schools, a healthy diversity of opinion and interest. Again, tolerance of different critical metalanguages seems to be justified on *a priori* grounds: the plea for pluralism, like pleas for religious or political toleration, is self-evidently reasonable and attractive. The range of literature—in this context I hardly dare to say the range of *kinds* of literature—is enormous, as is the range of readers, motives for reading, performances, audiences, markets for publications, teachers, and studying communities. In these circumstances diversity of method and interpretation is inevitable and, if the alternative is repressive and authoritarian bigotry, desirable. Freedom of interpretation, if responsible, can only be laudable; so also flexibility of method. This much admitted and approved, one begins to have doubts. In practice, twentieth-century pluralism has meant discord, intolerance, and mutual ignorance. One of the benefits of a true pluralism, one would think, would be healthy and productive interchange of views, informed agreement to differ, and certitude on what it is one is differing about. This is certainly not the case with contemporary criticism. It would be a grave mistake to regard the 'schools' as simply possessing alternative descriptive terminologies which could, in the last resort, be translated one into another. Critical discourse saturated with a distinctive and highly developed functional vocabulary is not merely in a situation of using certain special terms; it is conditioned by the terms it uses. As Olson and Crane make clear, a framework which is superficially a set of terms is more exactly a system of assumptions, attitudes, and expectations —to use a specialized vocabulary is to commit oneself to a specialized attitude. At the very least, learning a specific metalanguage may unfit one for understanding any other. (See, for example, Elder Olson's failure to understand Empson's language and method.[1]) It is a sad state of affairs if critic A cannot understand critic B, and the logical independence of A and B (the truth of A cannot disprove B) justifies neither A nor B, does not excuse their egocentricity, and certainly does not encourage our toleration of either. Since criticism, like literature, 'belongs to the public', the critic (as opposed to other, less reputable, sorts of commentators on literature) should earn his right of free speech by openness and clarity; willingness to understand and to be understood.

Ultimately, a pluralism of critical frameworks is a multiplicity of exclusive doctrines about the nature of literature. Most disputes reduce to this sort of question: whether poems are 'autonomous'; whether or not poetic language and ordinary discourse are to be distinguished; whether literature is language, or language just one of a number of 'elements' of literature. Judging by the writings of the critical theorists, there is a small range of central aesthetic questions about which passionate discord is inevitable, and about which there is not even the possibility of 'informed agreement to differ'. Often the friction between aesthetic theories is a consequence of failure to define stock terms—symbol, word, structure, image— or of dependence on terms of a necessarily highly abstract and there- fore potentially vague character—plot, tone, realism. The meta- languages employed in criticism of the arts and theorizing about the arts are notoriously slovenly, and they could easily be tidied up, to the benefit of harmony and constructive argument in general. But the incompatibility of competing poetics is not simply a mechanical result of the confusion of terms employed. It stems from the lack (despite appearances) of careful ontological discussion. We are offered *a posteriori* arguments proceeding from the critics' de- mands on literature rather than fundamental enquiries about what can be known about literature and stated formally. I would argue that we do not need a justificatory ontology, nor a speculative, quasi- logical ontology, but a scientific ontology; that is to say, an on- tology founded on a set of carefully controlled concepts derived from appropriate sciences and generating a wide range of descriptive terms available to critics with many different interests in the study of many different kinds of texts. An ontology so stable, so easily taken for granted, that it can be implicit in criticism, not demanding continual overt defence: an invisible theory which will tacitly in- form, not restrict the various compatible 'kinds' of criticism that can derive from it. This ontology should be of a kind which will serve *all* criticism; which should relieve critics of the necessity of redefining fundamental concepts for every new article and book. It should es- tablish concepts which are not redefinable in an *ad hoc* way.

(There are several predictable objections to this proposal for a single, unified, scientific theory of literature: for example, that it is unreasonable to expect critics to agree completely in their aesthetic presuppositions; that no science is absolute, but all are relativistic- ally dependent on their 'frameworks'; that science and art are by definition alien and must be kept apart.[2] No one who believes that these are disqualifying objections is going to be convinced by a di- gression here on pertinent issues in the philosophy of science.)

II

To return to the quotations with which this paper opened: it should now be clear that they are not harmless alternatives simply employing different kinds of descriptive terms. As I implied at the outset, they hold quite different positions relative to the ideal unperplexing theory of literature. The first two seek to present literature in terms of categories which are basic and which can be empirically justified: language, medium, words. The third operates with categories which claim to be fundamental but which are either not basic or are establishable empirically only with the greatest difficulty: thought, character, plot. These terms are secondary *at least*: they are not close to human behavioural reality and cannot be set up unless the primary terms have been defined. (The difficulties caused by a lack of primary terms—in this case not having an adequate semantic theory—are illustrated by Olson's vacuous note 8 in 'An Outline of Poetic Theory'.) This is not to say that statements containing non-primary terms cannot be tolerated in literary criticism—most critical and theoretical statements are such—but that these secondary statements make little sense unless they rest on a solid empirical base. Let it be understood that the 'scientific ontology' provides a base only; the secondary—and even further distanced than secondary—terms depend on it but are not replaced by it. No criticism can exist without secondary terms; these secondary terms have their conceptual content supplied by the primaries. My strictures against the secondaries—plot, realism, fiction, theme, structure, style, decorum, etc.—allege that they are too often employed in a conceptual vacuum (hence inefficient criticism) or confusingly used as if they were primaries (hence meaningless word-play posing as aesthetic theory).

It is of course no guarantee of theoretical or practical wholesomeness that a writer employs lots of words like *language, communication, concept, set, culture, semantic*, etc. The empirical bases of literary aesthetics have not yet been revealed so clearly that anyone can use primary terms with confidence. Let us consider again the quotations from Nowottny and Lodge (the first sentences of their books, as it happens). Both begin with a large assumption: that one can invoke a workable, commonsense, usage of the term 'language' without tortured definition. There is such a commonsense usage, I believe, and the general drift of both books suggests the authors intend it (as Empson does, but not, for example, Brooks, whose 'paradox is the language of poetry' uses 'language' metaphorically). However, to turn the commonsense term 'language' of practical criticism into the stable and overt term 'language' of axioms in critical theory needs

G

much effort, as anyone familiar with the turmoil of linguistics in this century might predict. Our two critics add qualifications. Nowottny asserts that there is an 'unarguable' quality in, or dimension of, language—an assertion that has to be squared with Empson's cornucopian polysemy and with the semantic arbitrariness of Humpty-Dumpty's sect. She implies—as does Wimsatt with his 'explicit meaning' (*Hateful Contraries*, pp. 221–2)—that all words have stable and statable meanings: this must be so, or we would not be able to communicate at all, but it is as well to realize the relativity of this fact. A workable theory of denotation and connotation, and some psycholinguistic studies of the facts of misunderstanding, would seem to be valuable projects in this connection. Lodge characterizes language as a 'medium', but does not make it clear whether he means the sculptor's marble or bronze or the communications engineer's telephone cables, air, bones, or whatever. In the indecisive 'in and through' he tries to suggest both definitions at once. Progressing further into Lodge and Nowottny, we find other important qualifications. Nowottny acknowledges that the structuring to be found in poems is not 'discontinuous with linguistic processes in ordinary life' (p. 82); this is a massive and essential concession to the empirical facts of linguistic usage. The language of poems is, however, 'more highly structured' than 'language outside poems' (p. 72). To judge by Lodge's methodological conclusions and by those sections of his criticism which deal with word-patterning, high structuring would appear to be for him important in novels too. But he does not regard structure—or 'verbal arrangements' as he calls it, quoting C. H. Rickwood—as merely independently beautiful or interesting. It also 'creates' other elements such as character and plot. Perhaps structure as structure is 'medium in which' whereas structure as creation is 'medium through which'.[3]

The general implications of Nowottny's and Lodge's remarks may be expressed in a series of propositions: that language is central to literature; that the description of the language of literature is central to criticism; that such description can be an objective process; that such description confers objectivity on literary criticism; that (to complete the circle) its linguistic character defines what kind of object a literary text is. There is a good deal of evidence (including the fact that much excellent criticism exists which seems to be founded on these ideas) that these propositions are true and essential. They also assume a general framework that is widely accepted today: the argument that a literary work is independent of its origins and its effects, an argument inaugurated by I. A. Richards and developed by Wimsatt and Beardsley. Richards' exposition is marred by basic contradictions concerning affectism, and Wimsatt and

Beardsley's articles are not without untidiness—chiefly flaws in the classification of genetic materials—but the general drift is clear enough. A poem is free of an author's intentions and his experiences, and of a reader's responses, because these are variable, irresponsible, undiscoverable, demonstrably erroneous, etc., while the poem remains stable. We cannot locate the poem in the author's state of mind at the moment of creation because this is inaccessible and may be changed by the act of writing—i.e. it may be an effect rather than a cause of the poem; we cannot allow the poem to reside in the individual reader's experience as he reads, because that would be tantamount to saying that there are as many poems as there are occasions of reading, whereas we know very well that there is only one poem. If a poem is not subjective in either of these two ways, it is objective: it is an object, with defining characteristics independent of the characteristics of poet and reader.

Having said that a poem is an object, it is essential (and extremely difficult) to specify what kind of an object it is. It is not a physical object, everybody agrees: it can be memorized and 'recited' silently; it can be printed in different typographies on different papers, and remain the same poem; some or all printed records of it may be destroyed, yet the poem can survive (contrast paintings). There are other related arguments; all conspire to make the point that a poem is not to be identified with any physical record, manifestation or performance of it. Nor is it a perceptual object, despite Beardsley (*Aesthetics*, Ch. 1), who regards all aesthetic objects (musical, graphic, dramatic, poetic, etc.) as perceptual objects. In fact, the usual gestures made towards the marbled page in *Tristram Shandy*, Herbert's 'Easter Wings', concrete poetry, etc., are gestures towards a poetically uncentral existence as perceptual objects. A particular printing of 'Easter Wings' is a physical object, an arrangement of letters; the reader or beholder *perceives* the object as a representation of a pair of wings. So poems are not basically perceptual objects (though they *may* exploit a perceptual dimension), whereas sculptures, for example, are essentially perceptual objects—forms perceived under the stimulus of physical artefacts.

A printed text is not a poem; a musical score is not a symphony. Is the likeness of music and poetry implied in this popular comparison illuminating? I would deny that it is. Certainly a score, like a text, implies both an underlying abstract formal structure and an acoustic realization. But whereas acoustic performance is vital to the symphony, it is quite accidental as far as the poem is concerned.[4] Undoubtedly Beethoven experienced the works he composed after he went deaf, and undoubtedly many musicians can experience pieces of music very adequately by reading scores. But this internal

music entails imagining acoustic performance, whereas silent reading, or recollecting, of poetry may not involve internal vocalization.
It seems inescapable that musical scores exist as directions for physical performance, whereas texts of poems, and oral performances of
poems too, exist as directions for the recovery of meanings. A literary object has semanticity, *pace* Cleanth Brooks; very little music
attempts to create this dimension, *pace* the post-Romantic com-
posers of what are called, significantly, tone-*poems*. (And classical
representational music, like Vivaldi's *The Four Seasons*, is stylized
away from the reality it pretends to imitate.)

This comparison with music fails to illuminate the nature of
poetry, because it attempts to establish music and poetry as variants
of the same thing, the same kind of aesthetic object, while semanticity differentiates them absolutely. However, one analogy (rather
than equation) of music and poetry does help, if we take it as an
analogy only.

Haydn's String Quartet in D Major, Op. 64 No. 5 'The Lark' opens
with a theme of great melodic simplicity stated in an impressively
detailed and complexly symmetrical arrangement:

We have eight bars of common time, a series divided into units of
2, 2, and 4. The two two-bar units at the beginning each divide into
1 plus 1. In bar 1 the second violin begins a simple and basically

falling tune which progresses by no more than one whole tone at a time; this is answered by a rising sequence in the same rhythm to be played by the 'cello. In bar 3 the tune of bar 1 is repeated slightly higher up throughout, but this time (in bar 4) the 'cello responds by a falling series. Bar 5 opens up the intervals between the elements in the second violin tune, but retains the basic shape, and, through bars 5–8, the falling sequence is repeated three times in a general melodic descent. Throughout the passage the viola matches the second violin note for note in a subtle counterpoint in which the viola traces a tune sometimes moving in the same direction as the violin tune, and sometimes (as in bar 5, where the viola rises as the second violin falls) contradicting it. It is all mathematically very tidy, simple yet involved, and very characteristic of Haydn's style. It is well known that eighteenth-century England yields poetic analogues of this style. The couplet as turned by Pope is a close parallel to the treatment of the eight- (and four-) bar theme by Mozart and Haydn. To avoid wasting space on gratuitous analysis I will quote a passage which has been discussed in these terms by Mrs Nowottny:

> Where-e'er you walk, cool gales shall fan the glade,
> Trees, where you sit, shall crowd into a shade,
> Where-e'er you tread, the blushing flow'rs shall rise,
> And all things flourish where you turn your eyes.[5]

Here the 'themes' and the counterpoint are a play of syntax and metre. As in the Haydn passage, the structure is one of units of almost algebraic abstractness: sentence-types and other structural components in regular and determinate relationships. It just happens that Haydn and Pope in these passages reveal their grammar with great clarity. These are no more than convenient examples; we are not for the moment concerned with the style itself. The grammar is an abstract system of materials out of which works are constructed. Of linguistic artefacts, such as poems, we may say that they are built with abstract, non-physical, formatives to which we give names like 'Sentence', 'Noun', etc. If we ignore the distracting level of physical performance, the answer to the question 'What kind of object?' is 'An abstract object'.

III

In order to state why any particular linguistic (or musical) object has the structure it does, one has to take into account two sorts of facts. A text is structured in a certain way because it is a distinct use of certain distinctive materials given in advance. We need to make a fundamental division between the musical or linguistic materials available (grammatical facts) and the use made of them (stylistic facts). To take the available materials first: Haydn had at his disposal a simple but very productive system of rules of pitch, harmony, and rhythm, the system stabilized largely by Bach and basic to most Western music ever since. The system is different from that, for example, on which Indian classical music is based, or the serial system of pitch conventions on which some twentieth-century music depends. The basic musical conventions known (and used) by Haydn could be seen as a kind of musical grammar, strictly analogous to the linguistic grammar possessed by Pope. This grammar distinguishes Haydn from Schoenberg as Pope's grammar distinguishes him from Racine. The rules of the linguistic system, like those of the musical, are abstract, finite in number but virtually infinitely productive, and conventional. This system of linguistic rules Ferdinand de Saussure called *langue* (*parole* being concrete use of the rules in a specific linguistic situation); Noam Chomsky, refurbishing this famous distinction, refers to the linguistic materials as *competence* (as opposed to *performance*). The status of this competence, this set of linguistic rules in which Pope is competent, must be determined very carefully. Sometimes grammar is thought of as a set of rules or patterns derived from texts by analysis. Such a view obliterates the distinction between the grammar of a language and the use that is made of it in constructing any particular text. A linguistic analysis of the language of a text (including literary texts) reveals less what is uniquely possessed by that text than what properties it has by virtue of being a use of a certain grammar: the grammar is external to the text and prior to it. This grammar, and therefore the texts founded on it, is the public property of all speakers of the language. I am a native speaker of English. Like Pope, W. K. Wimsatt, Winifred Nowottny, Queen Elizabeth I and II, and many hundreds of millions of others, I acquired linguistic competence in English in my infancy. Apart from certain superficial differences caused by historical, geographical, social, and personal factors, my command of English is much the same as Pope's. I could converse with Pope with no greater linguistic difficulty than conversing with an Irishman or Cornishman. The grammars of natural languages being what they are, any sentence of English that Pope might write is my property just as much as his: though I may never have uttered the sentence 'cool gales shall fan the glade', I know its meaning all the same, and know its meaning in advance of reading it in Pope.

To understand this assertion, it is necessary to grasp the principle of the *creativity* of natural languages. Apart from quotations and trivial standardized utterances like 'Good morning', 'Dear Sir', speakers are constantly producing (and understanding) new sentences. Although for obvious reasons this can never be proved as an empirical fact, it seems that the number of sentences possible in any language is infinite. Repetition is the exception rather than the rule. It would be a mistake to believe that each individual acquires, as he matures linguistically, a vast store of completely formed sentences from which he selects, from moment to moment, appropriate off-the-peg utterances. Contemporary linguistics suggests rather that each speaker of a language learns a finite system of rules (*langue*, competence) which enables him to produce an infinite number of sentences, i.e. the infinite set of grammatical sentences which constitutes the English, or whatever, language. (It is not possible to defend this hypothesis here, but many of my readers will see the point if I say that we propose a finite grammar with recursive properties, e.g. a grammar containing some rules which can be applied over and over again to form sentences of theoretically infinite length.) Pope uses this creative grammar to produce something which is unique, but not untypically unique or untypically creative, and not cut off from all other uses of English. A poem of his is not a quite self-contained assemblage of sentences, and not to be regarded as his personal property to the exclusion of his readers. We must adopt this position if we do not want to reject such analytic truths as 'speakers of English speak the same language' and 'readers of English can read Pope'.

This theory of linguistic competence has two immediate and fundamental implications for literary theory of the kind we are considering. First, it gives clear support for those who, like Empson and Nowottny, have claimed that the language of literature is not different in essence from language at large. Since nobody has ever managed to devise any workable criteria for distinguishing 'poetic language' from 'ordinary language', it seems foolish to retain a spurious terminological distinction which effectively denies commonsense. From the point of view of the present theory, those texts commonly regarded as literary are not to be differentiated from those regarded as non-literary, at least not by the invocation of any absolute criterion at the level of linguistic competence, the level of the available materials. Nor is any absolute distinction forthcoming in the study of linguistic performance, consideration of the use made of the materials. This is not to say that descriptive statements of variability among literary texts at the level of performance are impossible: such description is central to criticism. The second implication for criticism of contemporary linguistic theory is that it makes nonsense of the cruder assertions of the 'autonomy' of single works of literature. The extreme of the New Critical aesthetic, developed by argument and by the pressure of metaphors such as 'icon', 'urn', and 'monument', maintains that each poem is a self-sufficient symbolic object, by the act of poetic creation severed from its roots in language, culture, and personality, with the power to teach the reader its own unique context and language. Hence no appeal is desirable or possible to anything except 'what is "there"' in the poem. It is of course sound advice that the evidence of the page should be given priority over evidence off the page; some kinds of non-textual evidence are not evidence at all, or inadmissible, or misleading. But accepting this advice does not entail believing that poems are utterly free, linguistically, culturally, or psychologically. Certainly, authors can control and restrict the meanings of words by manipulating collocations; and to some extent poems, especially long poems, can enforce a new variety of the language. (Milton's syntax is a case in point.) But ultimately, in the experience of readers, poems are unequivocally in a language which exists independently outside the poems, and this fact guarantees 'reference out', connection with the outside world. Poems do not create out of nothing their own meaning and logic; the language they use imports from outside concepts and organizations of concepts as firm and demanding as the grain in the sculptor's medium. It is only a superficial paradox that 'what is "there"' in a poem, i.e. its language, ensures that the poem is linked essentially to the outside world.

IV

Criticism not being linguistics, critical statements are not statements about grammar (materials available) as such. However, it seems to me that they cannot but be improved by knowledge of what grammar is. In so far as critical statements make reference to language, they make reference to particular *uses* of the grammar, i.e. they are concerned with linguistic performance. Of course reference to language may be only implicit and indirect, but it is nevertheless unavoidable: criticism cannot do without a sense of the functioning of language. I am aware that that is a provocative assertion, even with the concession that criticism is not concerned with grammar as such. It can be justified only if we are equipped with a sufficiently rich theory of linguistic performance. Now I must make it clear that the construction of a theory of linguistic performance is a task that a linguist *qua* linguist cannot carry out alone. Chomsky has very little interest in linguistic performance, rightly defining the role of the strict linguist in terms of competence. We must look to the anthropologist for help, and we ought also to be able to consult critics who are well informed about language, but in practice find little assistance in the critical literature. The anthropologist rather than the linguist is the key figure because the 'unit' of linguistic performance is not the sentence but the language situation defined culturally, or communicative event, which gives sentences a function and a characteristic shape. I am now rephrasing the distinction between competence and performance, grammar and use of grammar, in the following terms. About any sentence, we can make two quite different kinds of statement. We can say 'This sentence is generated by a grammar of English' and then proceed to identify its structure; say whether it is grammatical, or, if deviant, in what way it is deviant; if it is ambiguous, state its alternative meanings; if it is a paraphrase of some other sentence, point this fact out. All this is simple observation and description, dependent merely on accepting the sentence as being in existence and bearing a definable relationship to the grammar of English. On the other hand, we could seek to answer the questions 'Why this sentence? Why have all the other possible sentences been rejected?' It is obvious that grammar in itself, the individual's ability to produce English, or French, or Russian, sentences, gives no reason at all for the production of one sentence rather than another—a speaking machine programmed just with a grammar of English could produce English sentences only in an utterly unmotivated fashion. But sentences do not occur randomly: there are always good reasons why in normal linguistic performance a certain sentence should be produced rather than some other. These reasons have to do with topic, style, social etiquette, tradition, rhetorical design, and so on: factors external to language but central to the structural organization of the culture which employs the language. As a general rule, we may say that the formal linguistic characteristics of every text or discourse are determined by the role it plays in the network of communicative conventions which defines a culture. 'Every particular *use* of English is to some extent reflected in and determines the *form* of the language that is used for that particular purpose', as Randolph Quirk puts it (*The Use of English* (London, 1962), 19). So a 'sufficiently rich' theory of linguistic performance demands not merely a cataloguing of the types of sentences that occur in texts but also a powerfully explanatory model of the culture (or relevant parts of it) which makes texts the way they are. Texts must be seen as possessing certain internal formal characteristics as a consequence of performing a certain role within a conventional type of communication situation.

It is not difficult to demonstrate that there is correlation between the uses to which language is put and the form it assumes. The sentences used for advertising are immediately recognizable as different from those used for reporting Parliamentary business; the style of the instruction book for a car is distinct from that of romantic stories in women's magazines; the conventions for lecturing are different from those adapted to light conversation; and so on. These usages are easily explicable by reference to the external circumstances of linguistic performance. There is a growing body of studies by anthropologists and linguists (see many of the papers in Hymes, *Language in Culture and Society* and Gumperz and Hymes, *The Ethnography of Communication*) of patterns of discourse in culturally institutionalized speech situations. The more we think about these patternings, the clearer it becomes that *all* linguistic performance makes reference to recognized cultural conventions of a very regular and restrictive kind. The overall structure of performance in a language seems to be isomorphic with the network of communicative relations which maps a culture: one could draw a diagram of the structure of a community by making a classification of its modes and styles of linguistic performance.

Learning to be a mature participant in a community means primarily learning flexibility in an enormous range of 'registers' of language, acquiring the skill appropriately to perform linguistically according to the situation one is in, the role one is playing, the function of one's speech, one's audience or interlocutor, etc. One has to learn the way to perform linguistically as a father, son, colleague, neighbour, customer, husband, lover, and so on. There are also corresponding passive roles: it is vital to recognize significant differences in the character of linguistic performance as it is to produce them. A mature member of the English-speaking community might be said to have attained 'sociolinguistic competence' as well as 'grammatical competence' in English. An habitual and successful reader of literature broadens and refines his sociolinguistic competence—his sensitivity to and skill in the patterned variability of English. Learning to read late Henry James is not an activity different in kind from learning to recognize and understand some equally circumscribed variety outside literature, for example the language of scientific articles. We have now provided another angle from which the common opposition of literature and non-literature, or literary language and non-literary language, appears less than sensible. The communicative activities of a society are not duolithic, split gigantically into two masses; they are split again and again and again with great delicacy and complexity into perhaps thousands of functional adaptations: commercials, sonnets, workshop manuals, recipes, odes, metaphysical lyrics, obituaries, specifications, political speeches, textbooks, academic articles, sermons, newscasts, short stories, labels and notices, dirty jokes, classical plays, Mozartian libretti, meteorological reports, epics, sports commentaries. . . .

I have brought the argument to this point for theoretical and cautionary, rather than practical and methodological, ends. The practical benefits of accepting this model of intra-language variety are simple and perhaps trivial. Much of the spadework in literary studies has always consisted of constructing taxonomies of styles and genres. The above theory—suggesting external causation of verbal distinctiveness by distinct cultural situations—allows for varieties of language in literature to be sifted by a categorization of situational types, thus making stylistic categories intrinsically more interesting by imparting cultural content to them. Methods for this kind of classification are readily available. One thinks of, for example, J. R. Firth's (ultimately Malinowski's) notion of 'context of situation', designed as a schematic representation of the influencing circumstances in which language functions, and useful for the classification of situations, functions and forms. Nils-Erik Enkvist has proposed a literary adaptation of this device (Spencer and Gregory, *Linguistics and Style*, 30–1). The methods of anthropologists, especially their treatment of ritual situations and oral folk-literature, would also assist in the development of procedures. The simplicity and cultural responsibility of this approach to stylistics and generic study recommend it highly. The theoretical gains are higher still, however. This proposed model of linguistic performance in society removes some of the most obsessive oppositions in modern poetics: language *v.* society, text *v.* context, internal *v.* external, autonomous *v.* dependent, linguistics *v.* sociology; language *v.* literature, ordinary language *v.* poetic language; static *v.* creative, convention *v.* innovation, habit *v.* invention, conformity *v.* licence, regularity *v.* deviation. All language is language, all language is creative, all language interpenetrates with culture.

V

The above is a fragmentation model, an analytic model, adapted to stylistics. The thesis is: every bit of linguistic performance has its associated bit of culture. There is also a synthetic paraphrase of the theory: language is culture. (That is exaggerated, but not grotesquely: language is the most potent systemic base of a culture.) Someone who attempts to come to terms with a society but knows *nothing* of its language is a profound alien indeed. His alienation embraces three degrees of severity: he cannot talk to others; he does not know the appropriate sociolinguistic rules, as above; he is perceptually paralysed. The last of these three handicaps—or its positive converse—is of the greatest interest to the critic: language is essentially, and not only in literature, a fiction-making device—a capability consequent upon its having a semantic dimension. I invoke here a commonplace belief, that language conditions perception. The belief has been prominently asserted in many quarters. There is Wittgenstein's dictum that the limits of one's language are the limits of one's world; Benjamin Lee Whorf's theory (developed from Sapir) of linguistic relativity, that speakers of languages with different semantic organizations have different world-views; the principle in the psychology of learning that concept-formation depends on language. Undeniably we are here moving into a field that is rife with confusion, absurdity, and metaphysical speculation. Whorf committed himself to an extreme and untestable doctrine; others—chiefly those who have debated the priority of language and thought—have descended to a chicken-and-egg dilemma. Nevertheless, it seems clear that man is a fiction-making animal, and that language assists the making and stabilization of fictions. Man has always been a great cataloguer and segmenter, a designer of calendars, numerical systems, units of measurement, and so on. Adam's first task was to name all the beasts and fowls, bestowing order and relationship on their collective presence. That myth is a myth of creation and security as well as of ownership: what is amorphous, contingent, and undifferentiated is made into something manageable by imposing a conceptual structure on it. We understand our universe by naming its parts—or so we like to think. Of course what we really do is partition our universe fictionally by an imposed grid of language: the parts are created by the separateness of the linguistic symbols. Edmund Leach postulates that

the physical and social environment of a young child is perceived as a continuum. It does not contain any intrinsically separate 'things'. The child, in due course, is taught to impose upon his environment a kind of discriminating grid which serves to distinguish the world as composed of a large number of separate things, each labelled with a name. This world is a representation of our language categories, not vice versa. ('Animal Categories and Verbal Abuse', in E. H. Lenneberg (ed.), *New Directions in the Study of Language*, Cambridge, Mass., 1964, p. 34.)

A culture is one set of people's particular organization of the chaos of physical universals. The organization is made largely (not wholly) through language, and in this sense language is culture. Whatever 'reality' is, we do not think directly in terms of it, but in terms supplied by language. I segment the continuously gradated series of light frequencies into a set of colours structured by my colour vocabulary; manufacturers of paints, fabrics, etc., attempt to increase the size of my set of colours by extending my colour vocabulary. Or, to adopt Leach's example, I distinguish trees and bushes —there is no absolute distinction in nature—because I possess the terms 'tree' and 'bush'. The fictional concepts symbolized by 'tree' and 'bush' are items in a structured network of concepts, the semantics of my language. The semantics of my language comprise a matrix of logical oppositions and relations by which I chop up the flux of the world. Syntax allows me to juggle with concepts, and thus to demand that my audience attempts to follow my conceptualization as I speak. Every sentence is a fiction. And so the interrelationship of syntax and semantics in poems becomes peculiarly interesting. The semantics of a poem do not constitute a bald, extractable 'content' divorced from the mechanical forms of syntax and phonology: they are a fragment of a society's linguistic conceptualization of its experiences, actively arranged by the syntax to induce novel fictional perceptions in a reader.

Fictions are language-reinforced conceptualizations. Where the need for order is overwhelmingly powerful, myths and sensory percepts are created. Frank Kermode's *The Sense of an Ending* (1967) is a stimulating discussion of the fictional ordering of time. The bulk of the argument concerns apocalypses as examples of man's imposition on continuous temporality (*chronos*) of the significant but unempirical moment (*kairos*), bestowing crisis on mere flow. Put into language, artificially structured time becomes plot. As the paradigm of plot he alludes to the primitive fiction of 'what the clock says': *tick-tock*. It is a fact, presumably biologically-determined, that, presented with a sequence of equispaced acoustic stimuli, people perceive them not as equally spaced out but as grouped into pairs with longer alternate intervals. This perception transcribed linguistically—*tick-tock*, with the *tock* indicating elongation of the second, fourth, etc., interval—becomes an emblem of fictionality, a micronovel.

We are to view language, then, as the way fictional orderings of experience are created. Such a view is more promising for criticism than that which considers language as having two rather mechanical possibilities: making patterns ('medium in which') or acting as a transparent channel for the passage of ideas ('medium through which'). We avoid any hint of the form/content dualism which, though denied, has bedevilled New Critical practice. With this development of the theory of language in mind, let us return to Pope. When I introduced the quotation from the *Pastorals* (using it because it displays its grammar very clearly), I suggested that the abstract materials of the grammar were organized into structural patterns which could be characterized as partaking of a certain style. Later, methods of integrating such stylistic conventions of linguistic performance in a cultural framework were touched on. Now it becomes apparent that such an exposition would fall short of the potential of a criticism founded on an organic model of the reciprocity of language and culture. I shall refer briefly to Pope's *Essay on*

Man to suggest what might be done. This 'general Map of Man' is a reasoned assertion of man's place and function in relation to the rest of created nature. It is thus fair game for the historian of ideas, and also happens to be excellent quarry for materials on Augustan syntax, metre, and imagery. A way of combining these two concerns is offered by Pope's own justification for writing these principles of philosophy in verse rather than prose: 'I found I could express them more *shortly* this way than in prose itself; and nothing is more certain, than that much of the *force* as well as *grace* of arguments or instructions, depends on their *conciseness*.' We must ask, then, how the poetic style enforces the argument. The basic premise is that nature is ordered on the 'great chain' principle (i, 34, 245, etc.): Man is a 'system' in a vertically ordered set of interdependent systems gradated 'justly' from inconceivably high to lowliest low. But though the poem is eloquent on the dependency of chains, it is silent on their linearity, extension, continuity. It presents no catalogue of systems, no survey, no explanation of each, one after the other. Rather it insists on the 'middle state' of man (ii, 3), and in a rather odd way. Simple paraphrase might affirm that Pope sets man comfortably midway between angels and beasts, telling the reader that we may have grounds to be contented with the convenience and justice of our position. But the language is not contented: it rages with oppositions and paradoxes so severe that man can at one point be addressed as 'Vile worm' (i, 258), a slur superficially quite at odds with the philosophy as a whole. Man is not in the middle as, say, the digit 5 is in the middle of a series of 9, stable and symmetrical; he is in the middle as a piece of iron between two magnets is—being pulled and wanting to move two ways. His position is defined by negations and oppositions: not angel, not brute; reasonable, but passionate; physical, yet weak; wise, yet blind; neither one thing nor the other, and at the same time all things. The language is dense with syntactic and metrical opposition and antithesis, imagery in terms of absolutes (light and dark, etc.), opposed processes (rise and fall), oxymoron, paradox. The habitual discords of Pope's grammar and metre, the internal and external tensions of the couplet and its parts, contribute in a major way to inducing our conception of man through this poem: man occupies a state of just the same tension and contradiction as the poetic style itself. The language creates the fragile order of the great chain of being: an ordered and firmly conventional form so full of basic conflict that it is continually on the point of losing its fictional equilibrium (but never does).

Consider another kind of example. At the end of Ch. 9 of *Washington Square*, Morris demands a private interview with Catherine; she asks him to come to the house and he exclaims, 'I can't enter your house again. . . . Your father has insulted me.' Nevertheless, he acquiesces, and Ch. 10 opens:

> Catherine received the young man the next day on the ground she had chosen—amidst the chaste upholstery of a New York drawing-room furnished in the fashion of fifty years ago. Morris had swallowed his pride, and made the effort necessary to cross the threshold of her too derisive parent—an act of magnanimity which could not fail to render him doubly interesting.
>
> 'We must settle something—we must take a line,' he declared, passing his hand through his hair and giving a glance at the long, narrow mirror which adorned the space between the two windows, and which had at its base a little gilded bracket covered by a thin slab of white marble, supporting in its turn a backgammon-board folded together in the shape of two volumes—two shining folios inscribed, in greenish-gilt letters, *History of England*.

Morris's 'line' is then suspended for two pages, and it is this last sentence that 'causes' the suspension. He entered confident: confidence derived from his self-bestowed judgment of magnanimity— he had set aside his honour to enter the house for Catherine's sake. But the chosen ground of Catherine asserts itself: a casual (vain?) glance at himself in the mirror leads his eyes through a train of objects epitomizing the inescapable material presence of the Sloper household and its master. As the sentence drags out, and the objects it presents become more extraordinary (I think there is no specific symbolism in them), the dissipation of his will is dramatized before us. The perception is so powerful that it destroys his 'line'; it is Catherine who makes the decision, two pages later when the suspended action begins again.

A rather more complicated example of the structure of a sentence presenting to the reader the fictional ordering of an environment comes in Ch. 16 of *Mansfield Park*, at the end of an account of the history and contents of the East room, just before Fanny enters it to 'try its influence on an agitated, doubting spirit':

> The room was most dear to her, and she would not have changed its furniture for the handsomest in the house, though what had been originally plain, had suffered all the ill usage of children—and its greatest elegancies and ornaments were a faded footstool of Julia's work, too ill done for the drawing-room, three transparencies, made in a rage for transparencies, for the three lower panes of one window, where Tintern Abbey

held its station between a cave in Italy and a moonlight lake
in Cumberland; a collection of family profiles thought unworthy
of being anywhere else, over the mantle-piece, and by their
side and pinned against the wall, a small sketch of a ship sent
four years ago from the Mediterranean by William, with H.M.S.
Antwerp at the bottom, in letters as tall as the mainmast.

The complexity here is all in the ambivalence of the narrator's inter-
vention: the sentence ostensibly gathers a set of physical objects,
about to be seen and reflected on by Fanny, but in actuality juxta-
poses all kinds of judgments. Far from being a nest of comforts, it
is a concrete précis of all Fanny's conflicting affiliations, from the
cruelty of Mrs Norris to the love and security of her thoughts of
William. She thinks to go to a room with objective characteristics
from which she can learn; in fact she goes to a room in which her
own and the novel's moral dilemmas are jostled together by the
language of 'description'.

A language is a structured repository of concepts, and every use
of language is a particular ordering in a (partly language-dependent)
circumscribed cultural situation. This ought to be a tacit principle
for criticism, because it is an inevitable fact of all writing. The
reader, whose linguistic conceptualization of experience answers
closely to that of a poet who uses the same language, has his perceptions guided by the poet's performance in language. Imagist
theory (which I can do no more than mention here) was an attempt
to exalt this fact to a normative rhetoric. Pound championed
Fenollosa because he presented written Chinese as a 'language close
to *things*': an active, concrete language in which nouns were derived
from verbs and there were no copulas, a language which did not
place a barrier between reader and events and objects represented,
but enacted them directly.[6] This is, I understand, a questionable
view of Chinese, and is certainly an unhappy model of English. (Note
also that it implies a literal belief in the existence of 'things' prior
to language.) Nevertheless, it provided a poetic to be strained for.
In fact, English pretty consistently resists the Imagists' efforts to
make it construct (i.e. induce perception of) concrete symbolic
objects. The extension of language in space and time makes it very
difficult to assemble complex concepts at one point of time. For
example, T. E. Hulme's 'Autumn' is not a moment of unified perception but a procession of cold, night, walking, moon, farmer, not
stopping, nodding, stars, faces, and children:

> A touch of cold in the Autumn night—
> I walked abroad.
> And saw the ruddy moon lean over a hedge

Like a red-faced farmer.
I did not stop to speak, but nodded,
And round about were the wistful stars
With white faces like town children.

The linear organization of syntax disperses the image and creates an expectation of narrative rather than an instantaneous perception.

VI

In a paper of this scale the theory has had to be hurried and the analysis fragmentary. Many major issues have had to be neglected altogether: one that I particularly regret having to ignore is the question of how 'fictional worlds' are created by long-range semantic organization in novels. I hope that the examples at the end have made it clear that I have not been arguing for a practical criticism founded on the techniques of linguistics, but for a unified criticism based on a theory of language and a theory of the mutual interpenetration of language, conceptualization, and cultural organization. Whereas R. S. Crane, in *The Languages of Criticism and the Structure of Poetry*, suggests that criticism is disparate and literature unified, I would claim that the only criticism capable of treating, at a public and non-idiosyncratic level, the diversity of literature, is a profoundly unified criticism. Literature is diverse linguistically: poems and novels are linguistic universes in which the fictional orderings of experience can be traced in diverse manipulations of language. A subject of such difficulty and complexity demands a very stable empirical theory from which meaningful descriptive terms can be derived; I do not think the anarchy which the Chicago Critics' offer of pluralism entails can satisfy so high a demand.

Notes to Paper Seven

1 'William Empson, Contemporary Criticism, and Poetic Diction', in R. S. Crane, *Critics and Criticism*.
2 Cf. my comments on the issue of 'art *versus* science' in *Essays in Criticism*, xvii (1967), 327–8 and xviii (1968), 168–9. (This volume, pp. 47–8 and 68–9.)
3 Creation by structure is much more interestingly discussed in Lodge's article 'Towards a Poetics of Fiction: An Approach through Language', *Novel*, i (1968), 158–69.
4 In 'Suprasegmentals and the Performance of Poetry', *Quarterly Journal of Speech*, xlviii (1962), 366–72, Samuel R. Levin offers an ingenious, and I think rather convincing, case against the oral performance of poetry.
H

5 Pope, *Pastorals* ii, 73–6; see *The Language Poets Use*, 11–12.
6 See Ernest Fenollosa, *The Chinese Written Character as a Medium for Poetry*, San Francisco [n.d.]. The work was discovered by Ezra Pound among Fenollosa's papers after his death in 1908, and hailed by him as 'a study of the fundamentals of all aesthetics'.

Eight

Criticism and the language of literature: some traditions and trends in Great Britain

Ignoring the traps of ontological speculation, we can nevertheless assert that a work of literature is usefully considered as a verbal structure, whatever else it may be. This verbal structure may be described. But we assume that description and criticism pursue different goals, since they do not imply one another reciprocally: description, as an activity, is most efficient without critical direction; yet criticism, according to most theoretical and practical efforts in this century, entails the activity of description. 'Efficiency' is no doubt an impertinent ideal for criticism, although 'objectivity' is probably a desirable attribute—hence the willingness of the twentieth century to accept the label 'descriptive criticism' as a shorthand indication of what it is doing.

Most of this survey will be devoted to the growth, the rationale, and the techniques of descriptive criticism in England. This emphasis is not intended to imply dismissal of non-critical descriptive studies such as stylistics, metrics, and formal classification of genres. We reject only undirected description of a kind which might result from the logical extension of the New Critical belief that a poem is an autonomous verbal object all of whose characteristics can be discovered by a structural analysis which excludes appeal to externals. This pseudo-procedure would run counter to the most obvious facts about the way we read and come to understand pieces of literature. We start off a reading with information and hypotheses, and the growing perception of literary form depends on progressive accretions and rejections of facts, hunches, and working metaphors. And as we begin a reading active and informed in this way, we begin also with a purpose, a tentative direction. There can be no unmotivated literary study. The value of stylistics is different from that of literary criticism because of a distinction of ends (and of course the goals of stylistics are very much more readily definable than those of criticism). Stylistics attempts taxonomic generalizations about the recurrent local formal characteristics of individual texts, authors' complete works, cross-author corpora of various sizes.[1] It yields demonstrations for statements like 'X's style is different from Y's in such-and-such ways.' It also seeks to validate labels like 'high', 'middle', 'low', 'Baroque', 'Senecan', 'florid', 'staccato', etc. If these are more than convenient recognition tags, they pretend to attach significance to generalizations about linguistic structure. So, for example, an author's psychology is investigated, his rhetorical purpose is suggested, traditions and schools and periods emerge. Sometimes stylistics directed these ways extends towards the edges of literary criticism. However, since stylistic characterizations can perfectly easily be found for language outside literature, it would seem that stylistics must always abandon its defining techniques if it is to get nearer to criticism than the fringes.

'Strict stylistics' as we have just described it has never been much practised by English literary scholars. Carlyle, Ruskin, and Newman expressed a Victorian preoccupation with style but failed to provide an adequate motive for stylistics; the French, on the other hand, had Flaubert as a model and as an impetus towards study. We may make a similar contrast between the English amateur theorists, Walter Raleigh, Middleton Murry, and Leo Spitzer, who promised a methodology and a new discipline. The domination by the Continent of Europe in post-Spitzerian 'New Stylistics' may be gauged from the select bibliography in Wellek and Warren;[2] and Hatzfeld's guide[3] confirms the impression of European bulk against English sparseness. In England, the work of Stephen Ullmann is outstanding and untypical, probably outside our brief, and certainly too wide-ranging to present in this short survey.[4] Equally untypical but simpler is a book by R. A. Sayce, *Style in French Prose* (Oxford, 1953), an 'attempt to produce a literary or aesthetic grammar of the French language': an attempt alien to the Anglo-Saxon literary mind. Seven chapters are devoted to the parts of speech; a section of one only to metaphor; and the three chapters which appear to state conclusions are called 'Period style', 'Individual Style' and 'Good and bad style'. Apart from a few other excursions into Romance scholarship such as this, and some scattered works in stylo-statistics,[5] the English have left style alone or attempted to make it subservient to some higher critical purpose.

While arguing the inevitability and necessity of evaluation, Sayce remarks: 'The critic's first and most important task must be to discover, as far as he is able, the objective characteristics of the work under consideration' (p. 126). The recommendation is not without ambiguity; does not point directly to any simple course of critical action. Nevertheless, it is the central truism of modern critical theory, and its genesis and development are readily understandable. Historically, it is a reaction against two linked failings among critics at the turn of the century: the conviction that it was adequate and desirable merely to communicate evocatively one's—perhaps quite private—response to an art stimulus; and the lack of a significant and shared critical vocabulary, except at the trivial levels of philology and scholarly annotation. In 1923 T. S. Eliot complained against this quirky irresponsibility and inarticulateness:

> we perceive that criticism, far from being a simple and orderly field of beneficent activity, from which impostors can be readily ejected, is no better than a Sunday park of contending and contentious orators, who have not even arrived at the articulation of their differences. Here, one would suppose, was a place for quiet co-operative labour. The critic, one would suppose, if he is to justify his existence, should endeavour to discipline his personal prejudices and cranks . . . and compose his differences with as many of his fellows as possible, in the common pursuit of true judgment.[6]

Eliot implies an ideal of the harmonious critical academe. Although one may be sceptical of the desirability of all strife ceasing, one can appreciate his real and valuable objection: an objection to oratory, not mere contention—the art of criticism had become not an art of description or analysis but an art of persuasion, an art *founded* on oratory. He complains against exhortations to approval or disapproval, invitations to delight or disgust. He hopes for a criticism founded on a sense of and respect for the literary object and a certain maintained detachment. At the best, oratorical criticism can have the kind of curious successes typified by the impressionism of Bradley on the colours in *Macbeth* or the prose poem of Pater before the 'Mona Lisa'. However splendid, these attempts at re-creation are essentially the presenting of another version of what the critic claims as his imaginative experience of the work: trying to catch the pitch and intensity of the experience without investigation of its cause. The comparative lack of interest in the object, the excessive subjectivism, made for a difficulty of communication that resulted in Eliot's contentious orators.

The impressionism against which Eliot and others have protested thus has two facets. One is emotional self-indulgence by the critic, at its most blatant producing Desmond MacCarthy's censure of Leslie Stephen: that he was 'deficient in the power of transmitting the emotions he had derived himself from literature; he seldom, if ever, attempted to record a thrill.'[7] If the critic does no more than record his thrills, his 'criticism' is just pages from his emotional autobiography: an essentially disreputable and uninteresting use of the public work of art. The second side to impressionism is the refusal to analyse, to say *why* in terms of one's perception of the verbal organization of texts one makes the statements and judgments one does. This has been a more persistent failing, and we may illustrate it from a critic whose writings have continued long after Eliot's stricture; a reminder that the need for descriptive criticism remains with us. F. R. Leavis makes gestures towards analysis, but is really only pleading for a feeling of value and character which the reader of his criticism is forced to reconstruct without Dr Leavis's explicit help. Introducing three quotations from Yeats, he suggests:

> This (but for the last two lines, which suggest Tom Moore) Morris himself might have written:
>
> . . .
>
> And Tennyson is behind this (though it could hardly be mistaken for Tennyson):
>
> . . .
>
> And this, with its characteristic burden, modulates into Keats and out again:
>
> . . .

Again, speaking of the influence of Milton on the nineteenth century, he hints at and then avoids analysis:

> Language was used in a generally Miltonic way even in un-Miltonic verse. To justify the phrase, 'a generally Miltonic way,' a difficult and varying analysis would be necessary; but I have in mind Milton's habit of exploiting language as a kind of musical medium outside himself, as it were. There is no pressure in his verse of any complex and varying current of feeling and sensation; the words have little substance or muscular quality; Milton is using only a small part of the resources of the English language.[8]

Though Leavis is often regarded as a pioneer of close verbal analysis, he is actually anti-analytic: a contentious orator preserving a mode of criticism which Eliot's pronouncement and the efforts of his English and American contemporaries and successors sought to displace.

Leavis's critical aims have taken him away from descriptive criticism. But his early years at Cambridge placed him in the midst of events which lay claim to constituting the origins of modern criticism. Immediately after the First World War the teaching and examining of English literature in the University of Cambridge were reformed and expanded. In 1919 I. A. Richards, a philosopher turned literary theorist, began teaching at Cambridge. He had two aims; as Tillyard puts it:

> first to supplant the easy-going and vaguely laudatory criticism that was still largely the vogue by something more rigorous, and secondly to apply the science of psychology to the processes of making and enjoying literature.[9]

It has long been assumed by critics on both sides of the Atlantic not only that the first of these aims was attained (the second, as J. C. Ransom pointed out, never provided a consistent or helpful theory of literature) but moreover that the early writings of Richards— *Principles of Literary Criticism* (1924) and *Practical Criticism* (1929) —were specifically and directly productive of what came to be known in England as 'Practical Criticism' and in America as the 'New Criticism'. With certain reservations, W. K. Wimsatt has voiced this conviction as recently as 1965:

> With all its up-to-date paraphernalia of verbal analysis, Richardsian aesthetics was readily available or at least convertible for the purposes of cognitive literary talk, and for that reason Richards became a venerable name in the schools and among analysts and grammarians, persons who recognised their business to be not the fanning nor the feeding and watering of emotions but the explication of the sources of emotion in the uses of language.[10]

It is true that Richards, in *Practical Criticism* at least, directs attention towards individual poems, to the details of isolated texts, and tries to provide a guide for analysis; but we would argue that the ends to which the detailed scrutiny is addressed, as well as the terms and assumptions it employs, suggest a distinctly non-cognitive and non-verbally directed quality. This quality we detect in both Richardsian analysis and, to some extent, the tradition that looks back to it.[11]

In *Principles* the fundamental effort is towards a redefinition, in terms of the 'new psychology', of the traditional Romantic apologies for poetry. The motive is very clearly a belief in the need for a scientific basis for enquiry; it leads to a concentration on the modes of production and the modes of reception of a poem—these being, in Richards' view, psychological processes describable in scientific terms—with a consequent minimization of attention to the poem as a verbal structure. There are two corollaries to this approach which are, in a sense, both reasons and results. First, there is a reluctance to consider a poem as having an intrinsic verbal interest. Second, there is a suspicion, at that time understandable, of theories proposing for art a secondary and indirect relation to experience, with a consequent desire to assimilate art into a general theory of psychological experience. Both of these attitudes may be thought of as part of a traditional English distrust for non-utilitarian explanations of artistic value. Thus we grant Richards' influence on descriptive criticism, with a most important qualification. It is true that the sophistication of his development of Romantic, particularly Coleridgean, theories of the systematization and harmonizing of emotional impulses in poetry has been the inspiration of much valuable new critical terminology—paradox, ambiguity, irony, and their kin. But on the other hand, the consequences of his marked indifference to the poetic object, and therefore to the organization of language which constitutes or underlies that object, have been evident in the erratic development of stylistically orientated criticism in England. In fact, much English 'Practical Criticism' since Richards has displayed fundamentally affective and emotional tendencies—except where it has been explicitly and uncompromisingly moralistic—for which the terms of descriptive criticism function as a screen of pseudo-objectivity.

To turn in more detail to Richards' argument, we note the insistence with which he asserts the fallacy of the objectivity of the work of art; he mounts a frontal assault on the object-directed terms commonly employed for aesthetic description:

> we continually talk as though things possess qualities, when
> what we ought to say is that they cause effects in us of one
> kind or another, the fallacy of 'projecting' the effect and mak-
> ing it a quality of its cause . . .   (*Principles*, 21)

> Before [the critic's] insight can greatly benefit, however, a very
> clear demarcation between the object, with its features, and
> his experience, which is the effect of contemplating it, is neces-
> sary.   (*Principles*, 23)

No doubt such a demarcation between the object-cause and state-effect is necessary and natural (though the exotic perceivers who people Benjamin Lee Whorf's pages might quarrel with this); but the use to which Richards puts it is quite insupportable—and quite at variance with the beliefs of the critical progeny he so strangely fathered:

> All remarks as to the ways and means by which experiences
> arise or are brought about are technical, but critical remarks
> are about the values of experiences and the reasons for re-
> garding them as valuable, or not valuable.   (*Principles*, 23)

And it naturally follows that critical remarks are merely a branch
of psychological remarks, and that interest in the 'technical' features
of a poem is attention to valueless superficialities:

> We pay attention to externals when we do not know what else
> to do with a poem.   (*Principles*, 24)

That triumphant 'externals' would be much less misleadingly persuasive today if the bias which led to it were more clearly apprehended.

Richards goes on to define poetry as a means of communication
among other means. The artist's disavowal of communicative intent
is irrelevant—the very act of 'getting it right', of 'fully embodying
the precise experience', is the perfecting of art's communicative
function. Richards sees the poem as a vehicle, a medium, which the
poet uses, perfects, to exactly transmit a 'real' emotional experience
which he has had, or has: and the means of transmission are quite
subordinate in interest to the experience communicated. This notion
of poetry as transmitted experience is directly related to the identification of criticism with the making of value-judgments noted
above. The critic is interested in works of art, Richards asserts, because 'They record the most important judgements we possess as to
the values of experience' (*Principles*, 32).

The effort to tackle systematically this concept of value leads to
a remarkable extension of Coleridge's remarks on Imagination in
which poetry becomes simply one of many factors, if an important
one, operating towards the well-being of man, assisting in his continual struggle to attain maximum satisfaction through a coherent
systematization of impulses:

> We pass as a rule from a chaotic to a better organised state by
> ways which we know nothing about. Typically through the
> influence of other minds. Literature and the arts are the chief
> means by which these influences are diffused.   (*Principles*, 57)

The fineness of these sentiments conceals an assumption that some
kinds of art must be more effective in this function than others and
provides the impetus for a covert shift to the equation of moral
value and literary excellence. If

> The most valuable states of mind then are those which involve
> the widest and most comprehensive co-ordination of activities
> and the least curtailment, conflict, starvation and restriction.
>   (*Principles*, 59)

then, apparently logically but provocatively,

> To set up as a critic is to set up as a judge of values . . . For
> the arts are inevitably and quite apart from any intentions of
> the artist an appraisal of existence.   (*Principles*, 60-1)

That this kind of argument, minimizing the role of the poet as
verbal artist, undermines any ideal of objective scrutiny of the linguistic details of poetry is obvious. In *Principles* it leads to a disabling indifference to the uniqueness of a verbal structure. Pointing
out that critics undergo different 'experiences' when reading a poem,
Richards argues that

> Provided the ends, in which the value of the poem lies, are
> attained, differences in the means need not prevent critics
> from agreement or from mutual service.   (*Principles*, 115)

But how can the ends of a poem be split off from its own organization? If this organization—this 'means'—is not perceived and understood, how can a poem be apprehended?

The position in *Practical Criticism* is not so extreme—merely the
fact that a corpus of poems is offered as material suggests an adjustment of attitude. But Richards' concern is far more centrally with
the psychological and emotional inhibitions exhibited by his 'proto-
cols' than with the details of the thirteen poems. He is impressed by
the widespread incompetence in the reading of poetry displayed by
his subjects and is thus prompted to put forward some claims for the
possibility, even the desirability, of the intellectual analysis of
poetry. In Ch. 3 of Part III he discusses some of the problems of the
relationship of the critical account to the poem. But while the cor-
rective offered to aspiring critics—'exercise in analysis and cultiva-
tion of the habit of regarding poetry as capable of explanation' (216)
—is close enough to the assumption of descriptive criticism, the
comments on the 'means available' to critical articulation seem to
offer little hope of practical objectivity; he claims that critics have
an efficient apparatus for talking about the Sense of poems, but

> For handling feeling we have nothing at all comparable. We
> have to rely upon introspection, a few clumsy descriptive
> names for emotions, some scores of aesthetic adjectives and the
> indirect resources of poetry, resources at the disposal of a few
> men only, and for them only in exceptional hours.
>   (*Practical Criticism*, 217)

Apart from being bedevilled by his habit of simplistic distinctions—
two uses of language, four kinds of meaning—Richards is showing
the same bias as we found in *Principles*: the critic he has in mind is

attending not to the poem but to the feeling the poem produces in him. Because of his distinction between Sense and Feeling he can assume an instantaneous apprehension of the poem—the 'plain sense' is easily understood—so that the critical process is reduced to the articulation of something presumed already comprehended and felt; hence the 'critical' difficulty, it is alleged, lies in the poverty of the language relevant to emotion. A more sophisticated theory of language in poetry would have recognized that typical resistance to understanding which poems offer, a resistance which demands that criticism should be a process of exploration and discovery of the characteristics of poetic form ('means') rather than a process of articulating morally valuable states of feeling in readers.

Richards is, through these two early books, the father of modern critical theory in two powerful ways: first, his desire to professionalize literary criticism—although his appeal to an eclectic contemporary psychology brought little benefit and a great deal of confusion—has been a valuable example against irresponsible forms of amateurism; second, his revival and expansion of Coleridgean theory raised critical theory to a level of serious abstractness that has been fruitfully maintained: even though his speculations on the nature of poetry have proved misleading, he showed theorists how high they must set their aim. Gains in method, however, have been less impressive. His neo-Romantic, new-psychological, insistence on the complexity of art led, in the next generation of critics and literary theorists, to the battery of familiar concepts: Empson's 'ambiguity', Brooks' 'paradox', Blackmur's 'gesture' and everyone's 'irony', 'tension' and 'dramatic structure'. But because Richards located the complexity in the reader's responses rather than in the linguistic structure of texts, some adjustment was necessary before the concepts could become descriptively useful. The terms had to be more concrete than vaguely deferential to the sense of complexity, of polyvalent language, of a more than usual activity of language; and they had to be given meaning by a sensitive insight into the way language works, for Richards' dogmatic linguistic categories could not impart meaning to a descriptive terminology. It is precisely a keen sense of the formal complexity of poetry, an awareness of its central significance for criticism, and a realistic view of the critical importance of a flexible theory of language, that so effectively distinguish William Empson from his tutor Richards. We would argue that Empson's controversial *Seven Types of Ambiguity* (1930) is the major, and continuing, stimulus to descriptive criticism in England. John Crowe Ransom (though giving Empson a subordinate place to Richards) regarded the book as 'the most imaginative account of readings ever printed, and Empson the closest and most resourceful reader that poetry has yet publicly had'.[12] The sheer abundance of his readings makes Empson a more powerful and influential model for practical criticism than Richards; but more significantly, his aesthetic assumptions and his view of the nature of language give a better base than those of his teacher.

His response to Richards' problem of the relationship of apprehension and articulation, or reading and criticism, is to transfer the sense of difficulty, of complexity, from the mind to the poem itself. More subtly, he collapses the distinction between reading and criticism:

> Indeed, what often happens when a piece of writing is felt to offer hidden riches is that one phrase after another lights up and appears as the heart of it; one part after another catches fire, so that you walk about with the thing for several days. To go through the experience in question [i.e. apprehension] is then slower, not quicker, than the less inspiriting process of reading an analysis of it; and the fact that we can sometimes grasp a complex meaning quickly as a whole does not prove that a radically different mode of thought (an intrusion of the lower depths) is there to be feared.   (*Seven Types*, xi)[13]

This identifies criticism as a kind of articulate reading rather than a rationalization of felt emotion; it also lays a basis for the justification of analytic criticism in suggesting that the process of reading may consist of simultaneous apprehension *and* exploration. The distinction is not that of Richards—between reading a poem and criticizing it—but between reading or criticizing a poem and reading someone else's criticism of it. The argument for the rational analysis of poetry gets another, more clinching if more irreverent, formulation somewhat later:

> Critics, as 'barking dogs,' on this view, are of two sorts: those who merely relieve themselves against the flower of beauty, and those, less continent, who afterwards scratch it up. I myself, I must confess, aspire to the second of these classes; unexplained beauty arouses an irritation in me, a sense that this would be a good place to scratch; the reasons that make a line of verse likely to give pleasure, I believe, are like the reasons for anything else; one can reason about them. . . .
> (*Seven Types*, 9)

The problem of value in poetry, and the problems of the evaluative critic, that so taxed Richards, are neatly and effectively sidestepped by Empson. In reply to a reviewer who complains that a critic 'has as his first business the passing of a judgment of value',

Empson voices a position which is fundamental to the effective practice of descriptive criticism:

> You think the poem is worth the trouble before you choose to
> go into it carefully, and you know more about what it is worth
> when you have done so. . . . No doubt the study would be
> done badly if there were wrong judgments behind it, but that
> is another thing. (*Seven Types*, xiii)

The term 'ambiguity' is often in Empson a convenience, a gesture at complex linguistic functioning, 'any verbal nuance, however slight, which gives room for alternative reactions to the same piece of language' (p. 1), and the methods for discussing it are correspondingly eclectic. But it does also refer to a characteristic of poetry that is more organic and more elusive of definition than mere complexity. In affirming his conviction that ambiguity is necessarily present in all great poetry, Empson suggests that there is, in poetry, 'a feeling of generalisation from a case which has been presented definitely' (p. xv), a reference, that is, both outwards to inclusiveness, to other poems, to experience, and also inwards to precision and accuracy. The poem itself becomes a nexus for a mass of relationships and yet retains a specific form. It is this sense of multiplicity that underlies most New Critical theory and this very paradox of an infinitude of reference and an exactness of form that exercises Winifred Nowottny in *The Language Poets Use*, a book heavily indebted to Empson, which we will discuss below.

The First Type of Ambiguity, and indeed the whole idea, is based upon a concept of metaphor as an engagement of a number of possibilities none of which is ever wholly subservient to the other(s): there is, then, no possibility of a clear distinction between tenor and vehicle. However, it is possible to push the idea back from metaphor to language itself. The potential ambiguity of all language, all words, is, in 'normal' communication, controlled by all we know about the context into which it enters and by deliberate techniques of qualification, exclusion, and definition. But poetry, freed from any given context, exploits richly the complex potential references and relationships of language. This notion of poetry as an exploitation of the characteristics inherent in language seems to us fundamental to the development of an adequately flexible verbal criticism. It avoids, for example, the prescriptivism, what has been called the 'critical monism', of Cleanth Brooks' concept of paradox as 'the language of poetry', with its implications of a language, or structure of language, peculiar to poetry, to all poems, and its tendency to seek its justification in a discovery of paradox at the heart of human experience itself. Paradox, after all, is not an inherent characteristic of language; ambiguity or polysemy is, must be, because language works semantically by *arbitrary* symbolism. It is not surprising that Empson's writings are full of insights on the nature of language, without restriction to the 'language' (that 'language' is a metaphor) of poetry: as he says in a later book (*The Structure of Complex Words* [1951], 1), he is a writer 'on the borderland of linguistics and literary criticism'. The central insight is that the language of poetry is language. Since language has an objective public existence, its characteristics can be, as he claims, 'reasoned about'.

As for the method proposed, it is basically, as are all effective criticisms of verbal functioning, a matter of paraphrase. Not indeed paraphrase of the kind that Brooks identifies as heresy, but a mass of multiplying local paraphrases, a profusion of minor allegories that attempt to map out the layers of meaning in the poem. It is perhaps hardly a 'method' at all—but then it seems likely that the idea of a truly 'critical' as distinct from a 'descriptive' method is fallacious. As Empson points out,

> the words of the poet will, as a rule, be more justly words,
> what they represent will be more effectively a unit in the mind,
> than the more numerous words with which I shall imitate their
> meaning so as to show how it is conveyed.   (*Seven Types*, 6)

The last part of that sentence might serve as a rough indication of the processes of descriptive criticism. Empson's contribution has largely been his insistence on the astonishing co-presence in poems, in the words, the sentences, the syntax, the metrical structures of poems, of meanings, from the near equivalence of two shades to the stark opposition of contraries. And this insistence has been made clear in scores of analyses probably unequalled in brilliance, if also, at times, unequalled in ingenuity, which proceed for the most part as fragmented, linear imitations of the many-dimensional poetic object.

Scrutinizing language, Empson discovers the heart of poetic structure in the potentiality for richness of semantic organization natural in the polysemy of all words. With a few tentative probes into wider aspects of language, his aesthetic is largely lexical and semantic, for his linguistic background is occupied by Ogden and Richards and Gustav Stern. For Donald Davie, twenty-five years later, the linguistic world of poetry is a syntactic world, and thus syntax is the focus of descriptive criticism. In *Articulate Energy: An Enquiry into the Syntax of English Poetry* (1955) his purpose is to demonstrate the power of syntax in setting the character and quality of poems, and to provide criticism with a descriptive meta-language and categories adequate to the display of the workings of syntax. His confidence in the domination of style by syntax is evident in his final generalization:

> If the foregoing pages have tended to any one conclusion it is this: the break with the past is at bottom a change of attitude towards poetic syntax. It is from that point of view, in respect of syntax, that modern poetry, so diverse in all other ways, is seen as one. And we can define it thus: *What is common to all modern poetry is the assertion or the assumption (most often the latter) that syntax in poetry is wholly different from syntax as understood by logicians and grammarians.* When the poet retains syntactical forms acceptable to the grammarian, this is merely a convention which he chooses to observe. (p. 148)

Whether we believe this is just a trite generalization depends on the faith imparted by Professor Davie's analyses, which are often spectacular but sometimes opaque. His five categories of poetic syntax ('objective', 'dramatic', 'subjective', 'like music', 'like mathematics') of course produce the disappointment natural to that kind of categorization: one should not be asked to believe that there are *n* and only *n* types of syntax, ambiguity or whatever. Empson's categories are thrown off with a marvellous disbelieving panache—if there had been eight and not the magical seven we might have had to worry—but there are really as few or as many types as you want: the universe is not being mapped out into parceis. Davie is somewhat more careful and therefore perhaps rather less convincing. The five-fold classification emerges from Davie's critique of three exciting but limited theories of poetic syntax: those of T. E. Hulme, Susanne Langer, and Ernest Fenollosa (Chs. 1, 2 and 4; the objections are summarized on pp. 65–6). Some of the analyses—for example the readings of Sackville in Ch. 3—convey the impression that Davie is beginning to uncover the roots of Empson's flower of beauty, but this is not carried off consistently, and the attempt may be inhibited by the introduction of the supposedly exhaustive five types. An overall problem is that his 'syntax', and its relation to thought and logic, are not explicitly defined; perhaps they could not be: but the fact remains that Empson's 'ambiguity' is much more readily understood than Davie's 'syntax'. Nevertheless, *Articulate Energy* is fully within the tradition of verbal descriptive criticism: it views poetry as existing linguistically and describable by use and extension of the concepts natural to the description of language.[14]

Davie is within the broad tradition of descriptive criticism, but outside the narrow channel of the New Criticism. The next book we review, Winifred Nowottny's *The Language Poets Use* (1962), reveals

the whole force of that Anglo-American tradition behind it, the
theoretical and procedural influence of the writings of Richards,
Empson, Brooks, Ransom, and the rest. Between *Seven Types of
Ambiguity* and *The Language Poets Use*, what had begun as a small
body of writings by English critics was welcomed and absorbed into
an international critical doctrine. We cannot chart the history of the
New Criticism here and must emphasize that the national limitation
of the present survey in a sense distorts that history. It must be
remembered that English critics of the sixties are no longer in a
specifically British tradition.[15]

Mrs Nowottny takes for granted the linguistic basis of literary
form and the necessity to found literary criticism on verbal analysis.
Her first sentence is a declaration which could be a motto for all of
descriptive criticism:

> In considering the language of poetry it is prudent to begin
> with what is 'there' in the poem—'there' in the sense that it
> can be described and referred to as unarguably given by the
> words.   (*The Language Poets Use*, 1)

The heritage of aesthetic theory—belief in the value of structural
and semantic complexity—is overt on the next page:

> a verbal structure is literary if it presents its topic at more
> than one level of presentation at the same time—or, alterna-
> tively, if one and the same utterance has more than one
> function in the structure of meaning in which it occurs.

Mrs Nowottny is, however, less specifically committed to ambiguity
than she is to the more inclusive notion of complex, unified structure; indeed, in Ch. 8, 'Ambiguity', she dissociates herself from the
extremes of Empsonianism. Her thesis is that 'meaning and value
in poems are the product of a whole array of elements of language,
all having a potential of eloquence which comes to realization when,
and only when, one element is set in discernible relation with another' (p. 18). If this is so, there is no aprioristic reason why any
single element of poetic language should, if isolated, be uniquely
significant; that is, there is no need to set up one feature, say 'paradox', as the defining characteristic of poetic structure. An extremely
valuable consequence of this thesis is that, wherever one begins an
analysis of a poem, one is going to be led off into other corners, detect
new relations between elements, interpret details in the light of
unique confrontations of linguistic levels. So, if the critic is explicating syntax, he must expect to make unpredictable discoveries about
metre or meaning. Such a progress—not method—seems intuitively
to be true to the activity of coming to understand a poem, again

underscoring the lack of distinction between 'criticism' and 'reading'. The implication is of unsystematicness, as the author confesses; but, equally, dispensing with method allows the use of fragments of method drawn from all kinds of sources, and Mrs Nowottny is fruitfully eclectic. Her analyses are often brilliant (but sometimes not as persuasive as the 'unarguably' in her opening sentence implies) and range widely through period and style.

Like Empson, Mrs Nowottny relies on an informal and only partly articulated theory of language. She stresses the continuity of language inside and outside poems—she is not really dependent on the aesthetic differentiation that she provides in answer to Northrop Frye. The willingness to accept poetry as language immediately adds new dimensions of value to her proposition 'what is "there" in the poem', since it then becomes possible to go beyond the view of poetic language as primarily exemplifying old or new rhetorical categories. The language found in poems thus has a force and structure derived from its opening up of the potentialities of speech, and it is in turn opened up to a range of techniques and insights excluded by the limited rhetorical methodology of the classic American New Critics. Mrs Nowottny's 'complexity' of poetic language, because it is really the latent complexity of all language, does not force her to head straight for Donne and the structure of complex urns. On this theory, simple poems may be complex.

David Lodge's book *Language of Fiction* (1966) emerges from substantially the same critical and linguistic background as Nowottny's. The Anglo-American tradition of descriptive criticism is active in his thinking: it lends him methods and a motive for his book. His account of the corpus of significant twentieth-century critical theory 'extending from T. S. Eliot and I. A. Richards, to, say, W. K. Wimsatt' (p. 3) checks with the history we propose; and in his Preface (pp. x–xi) he acknowledges his indebtedness to a wholly predictable set of authors. The tradition of verbal analysis makes the book possible and at the same time problematical. It is not through the lack of interest of critics that twentieth-century novel criticism is a story of under-achievement; simply, New Critical methods are not obviously applicable to the verbal structure of works of prose fiction without disabling neglect of an enormous aesthetic dilemma, which Lodge recognizes: how can criticism 'carry its study of the language of extended prose works beyond the limits of stylistic description'? (p. x). This question was raised by Ian Watt in his important article 'The First Paragraph of *The Ambassadors:* An Explication', *Essays in Criticism*, x (1960), 250–74. Watt gives an excellent brief summary of the triumphs and inherent drawbacks of the methods of Practical Criticism, *explication de texte*, European stylistics and historical

I

stylistics, and concludes with the opinion that he must undertake his analysis 'virtually helpless'. The problem of extending the practice of descriptive criticism to novels is really a special version of a general aesthetic difficulty which descriptive criticism forces on our attention: does language 'constitute' or merely 'underlie' the formal structure of works of literature? This is the very question we announced that we would dodge in our opening sentence, and we believe it is not disastrously ignored when poems are the object of criticism. Novels transform it into a direct challenge and a stumbling-block. The sheer length of novels has two consequences: first, there cannot be coextensiveness of linguistic units with the novel considered as a spatio-temporal object—a sonnet can be co-terminous with a single sentence, but a novel can never be linguistically determined in any such way. Second, there is the problem of 'perception', as it is called, although it is more accurately a problem of the limitation of immediate memory: we can at least convince ourselves that a short lyric poem can be perceived 'as a unit', but there is obviously no such possibility with a thing that takes many hours to read. For the verbal analyst, these two problems express themselves as difficulties of selection: since one cannot analyse a complete novel, how does one decide what parts to discuss? Watt and Lodge are both very conscious of this particular difficulty. Another is that the medium of prose has no inbuilt (metrical) advertisement of its principles of formal control: heroic couplets or blank verse make the descriptive critic's initial technical tasks much easier—he has a direct entry into formal organization. Finally, the status of style in novels is ambivalent and various: is Henry James's style 'style', or is it rather a means of creating abstractions which transcend style? We cannot discuss these dilemmas fully here, although we concur with Lodge's judgment of their centrality. Lodge skirts around the question by a seventy-page survey of versions of the problems, divisions of the problems, methods, and attempted solutions. There is probably no better presentation of the material relevant to instituting a discussion of the practice of novel-criticism.

It is clear that Lodge does not solve the dilemma, and does not pretend to: *Language of Fiction* is preliminary and tentative. Probably no critic who has the New Critical monkey so firmly on his back—and we are inclined to think that New Critical method *is* a burden if lifted bodily and transported to the analysis of the novel—can sort out this difficulty. Lodge, like most of us, seeks solutions in method, and at that level the yield is predictably meagre:

> the alternative principles . . . are (1) to isolate, deliberately or at random, one or more passages, and to submit them to close

and exhaustive analysis, or (2) to trace significant threads
through the language of an entire novel. One might label these
approaches 'textural' and 'structural' respectively. (p. 78)

Lodge's analyses (seven chapters ranging from Jane Austen to Kings-
ley Amis) vary considerably in technique and success. They do not
derive simply from his two methods: their achievement depends on
the critic's variable aims and sensitivity. As models of the application of various kinds of verbal analysis to the language of novels they
make useful demonstration-pieces. For this reason, and because of
the welcome self-consciousness about the business of descriptive
criticism, we have found the book very valuable as a text in courses
in critical theory.

   In 1962, R. F., reviewing *The Language Poets Use*, observed that
Mrs Nowottny 'just fails to embrace' descriptive linguistics as an
aid to analysis.[16] If this was a suggestion, it was intended to be less
pushing than Harold Whitehall's extravagant 'as no science can go
beyond mathematics, no criticism can go beyond its linguistics.'[17] It
seems natural that a discipline devoted to the exact study of language would have something to offer to a brand of criticism orientated to the description of the language of literature. Although it
would be ridiculous to claim a dependence on formal linguistics as
inevitable as that implied by Whitehall, many linguists in America
and Great Britain have argued for close co-operation between linguists and critics.[18] In America, the initial exploration of the use
of linguistic methods in literary studies was marked by the 1956
Kenyon Review symposium on metre[19] and by the conference in 1958
which led to Sebeok's *Style in Language*.[20] Progress by the pioneers
was impeded by over-commitment to the Trager-Smith statement
of the phonology of English and by the instability and cumbersome-
ness of early versions of the theory and procedures of generative
grammar. The theoretical and methodological backgrounds to
British work in 'linguistic criticism' have been quite different, except
for a small number of publications. Discussions of metre by Thompson,[21] Hawkes,[22] and Fowler[23] have been continuous with the work
of Chatman and others in America. An article by J. P. Thorne represents the only excursion so far by a British linguist into the area
of 'Stylistics and Generative Grammars'.[24]

   Apart from these few writings which make contact with American
linguistics and American linguistic stylistics, the greater part of
work in this field in Britain has started from a basis in neo-Firthian
linguistics. In the late fifties M. A. K. Halliday, then at Edinburgh
University, was attempting to make explicit the kind of grammar
implied in Firth's fragmentary and often cryptic writings.[25] Halli-

day's most influential article is 'Categories of the Theory of Grammar', published in 1961.[26] This theory offers a precise and explicit version of the immediate constituent, or labelled bracketing, technique of analysis. Though this theory is of course subject to the Chomskyan criticism of the 'limitations of phrase-structure grammar', it nevertheless provides a minutely discriminating terminology for textual analysis. John Spencer and Michael Gregory offer an enthusiastic argument for this mode of analysis in literary studies,[27] and examples of analysis are provided by Halliday,[28] Sinclair,[29] and Fowler,[30] and by others in unpublished works.

Though the terms of Hallidayan scale-and-category grammar are mechanically useful in explicating the syntactic structure of texts, attention has been drawn to the inherent inadequacy of 'mere description' by this or analogous methods.[31] We cannot welcome the belief in easy and automatic transition from syntactic analysis to critical description implied in Halliday's

> The linguistic study of literature is textual description, and it is no different from any other textual description; it is not a new branch or a new level or a new kind of linguistics but the application of existing theories and methods.[32]

It is certainly not true that linguistic analysis—any more than the discovery of Shakespeare's laundry bills—automatically achieves anything of interest to literary criticism. As much is admitted by Halliday's own dependence on the notion of 'cohesion', structural patterning across the boundaries of sentences:[33] here the technical terminology of descriptive linguistics is supplemented by a concept which is not derived from the grammar of English but which is necessary to make structural sense of supra-grammatical patterning; and, of course, the addition of this term does not take one into criticism, but only advances slightly in that direction. Despite Halliday's assurances, 'cohesion' is not a grammatical concept. In Chomskyan terms, it is a construct devised to account for certain regularities in linguistic performance which cannot be explained by a grammar seen as a theory of competence. Thus to claim that linguistic analysis opens straight into literary criticism is to miss two disqualifications: that description is different from criticism; and that the assignment of structural descriptions to sentences is distinct from the exposition of the patterned form (style, etc.), of texts. Clarification of these issues is the theme of a recent dispute in *Essays in Criticism*.[34] The more moderate claim for linguistics which we would make is that the analytic concepts of grammar are, like other methods available to the cognitive critic, aids to the exploration of the linguistic structure of texts and to the articulation of one's perception of linguistic structure within a critical statement; and that the theory of language provided by a sophisticated linguistics could be an invaluable guide to a critic who regards literature as an enriching of language in the way we have suggested.[35]

Two specific neo-Firthian concepts, *lexis* and *register*, seem to promise well for the study of the language of literature. Lexis is claimed by Halliday to be an independent level of linguistic form, the level of patterning of lexical items as distinct from the syntactic patterning in which they exist.[36] Rules for lexical patterning are statable as *collocations*, co-occurrence probabilities within a particular (but not syntactically definable) short span of utterance. So *white* collocates with *snow* independently of their possible occurrence together in an adjective-noun syntactic construction, while *feline* has perhaps a zero probability of collocating with *book* even though they could, syntactically, be put in an adjective-noun construction. The uses of a properly formulated lexis in the study of the deviant principles of word-combination in certain kinds of poetry, and in general the implications of the concept in the study of metaphor, are obvious. Register is a generalization which relates the typical formal characteristics of discourses and texts to their functions in certain 'contexts of situation'.[37] Briefly and somewhat crudely, the proposal is that every piece of language has (at least) two dimensions of structure: first there is the syntactic structure of sentences, determined simply by the fact of communication in a specific language with a certain grammar; additionally there is patterning not required by the grammar and determined by factors external to the language— the topic of discourse, the function of the discourse, and the situation in which it functions, etc. Since the linguistically external pressures on language are not random or arbitrary, but are structured and repeated according to the organization of the speech-community (which includes the patterning of its corpus of literature), then non-grammatical structure in texts tends to be significant, characterizing and recognizable. Categories of contextually significant textual ordering are registers; so we can speak of the registers of advertising, journalism, legal documents, scientific report, and so on. The importance of the notion of register is that it opens the way for a description of the total set of (overlapping and sub-dividable) categories of textual variation in a speech-community answering to the cultural patterns which identify that community. Such a theory of variation in linguistic performance would both include and provide a model for an account of formal literary variation. It seems likely that a blend of Chomsky's 'performance' and Firth's 'context of situation' may produce just such a theory. D. Crystal and D. Davy are preparing a book presenting the main varieties of spoken and written English in the light of a general 'theory of variety'.[38] Such a theory, and with it the precise definition of the concept 'register', would assist greatly our understanding of the processes and causes of formal variation in literature.[39]

Besides discussions such as those surveyed above, which deal with generalities and specifics in the theory of the application of (mainly neo-Firthian) linguistics to literature, there is a considerable body of writings by British linguists which succeed well either through a sensitive eclecticism or through building useful bridges between linguistic competence and literary performance. Two collections, a volume of the *Review of English Literature* devoted to 'New Attitudes to Style'[40] and Fowler's *Essays on Style and Language*, include papers on a range of literatures and periods. In these two collections or elsewhere, the writings of Angus McIntosh,[41] Randolph Quirk,[42] and Geoffrey Leech[43] are especially interesting.

We have ended with a review of recent British attempts to apply the methods of linguistics to the style and structure of literary texts chiefly because our survey has been chronological and these attempts have been recent. However, we might suggest that the linguists' position at the conclusion of this article represents, in a sense, something more than an accident of time. The story of verbal analysis in England starts with a proposal to professionalize literary criticism by importing part of the discipline of psychology. Contemporary linguistic discussions in the context of literary criticism suggest the continued need for professionalization, made more respectable now by criticism's sharpening focus on language as the basis of literature. The only objective existence that can be proposed for literature is a linguistic existence: the public language of a culture, shaped in conventional and inventively unconventional ways to make literary texts. This shaping is not to be discovered by subjecting texts to the complete apparatus of any brand of descriptive linguistics, because the analysis which is technical linguistic analysis stems from a discipline which is linguistics and not literary criticism (whether linguistics 'is' a science is quite irrelevant to this issue). Descriptive criticism, as we said at the outset, is not linguistic description. But the critic will make informal use of bits of method from analytic disciplines such as linguistics, because he must always believe in the objectivity of language and its availability to be 'reasoned about': this is the only way a critic can possibly locate literature as a patterned, valuable product of a literary community.

Notes to Paper Eight

1 A useful brief survey of some orientations in stylistics is provided by S. Ullmann, 'Style and Personality', *Review of English Literature*, vi (April 1965), 21–31.

2 *Theory of Literature*, third edition (Harmondsworth, 1963), 343–6.

3 *A Critical Bibliography of the New Stylistics Applied to the Romance Literatures, 1900–1952* (Chapel Hill, 1953).

4 *Style in the French Novel* (Cambridge, 1957); *The Image in the French Novel* (Cambridge, 1960); *Language and Style* (Oxford, 1964).

5 See Rebecca Posner, 'The Use and Abuse of Stylistic Statistics', *Archivum Linguisticum*, xv (1963), 111–39.

6 'The Function of Criticism', *Selected Essays*, third edition (London, 1951), 25.

7 Quoted by Q. D. Leavis, 'Leslie Stephen: Cambridge Critic', *Scrutiny*, vii, No. 4 (March 1939), 405.

8 *New Bearings in English Poetry* [reprinted, Harmondsworth, 1963 (first published 1932)], 33 and 71.

9 E. M. W. Tillyard, *The Muse Unchained* (London, 1958), 89.

10 W. K. Wimsatt, 'Horses of Wrath: Recent Critical Lessons', in *Hateful Contraries: Studies in Literature and Criticism* (Lexington, Ky., 1965), 7.

11 The specific tradition that claims descent from Richards is 'Practical Criticism', a form of close analysis prominent in English education in the University of Cambridge and elsewhere. See C. B. Cox and A. E. Dyson, *Modern Poetry: Studies in Practical Criticism* (London, 1963). For a critique of this practice, see Helen Gardner, 'The Academic Study of English Literature', *Critical Quarterly*, i (1959).

12 John Crowe Ransom, *The New Criticism* (Norfolk, Connecticut, 1941), 102.

13 Page references in roman numerals refer to the 1947 preface to the second edition of *Seven Types*.

14 Francis Berry, *Poets' Grammar: Person, Time and Mood in Poetry* (London, 1958), is only superficially and metaphorically about grammar.

15 One regrettable consequence of this simplification is that it obscures the fact that *within* 'the Anglo-American New Criticism' there are important differences. The most obvious is that between the self-conscious critical movement associated with the Southern group—Fugitive Poets and at times editors of influential magazines —of John Crowe Ransom, Allen Tate, Cleanth Brooks, and Robert Penn Warren, and those British and American critics whose writings are in the same general spirit but do not form part of that self-announced new critical group. To some extent parallel to that necessary distinction are differences in the degree of commitment to the belief in the autonomy of each text and its

amenability to total explication without external reference: at one
extreme (perhaps most clearly represented by Brooks) this facet of
the 'strict New Criticism' can be very inhibiting.

16 *Critical Quarterly*, iv (1962), 288.
17 Review of Trager and Smith, *Outline of English Structure*, in
    Kenyon Review, xiii (1951), 713.
18 For a selection of views and of analyses from both sides of the
    Atlantic, see S. B. Chatman and S. R. Levin, *Essays on the
    Language of Literature* (Boston, 1967).
19 *Kenyon Review*, xviii (1956), 411–77.
20 T. A. Sebeok (ed.), *Style in Language* (New York, 1960). See also
    A. A. Hill, 'An Analysis of *The Windhover*: An Experiment in
    Structural Method', *PMLA*, lxx (1955), 968–78.
21 J. Thompson, *The Founding of English Metre* (London, 1961).
22 T. Hawkes, 'The Problems of Prosody', *Review of English
    Literature*, ii (April 1962), 32–49; cf. E. L. Epstein and T.
    Hawkes, *Linguistics and English Prosody*, *Studies in Linguistics*,
    Occasional Paper 7 (Buffalo, 1959).
23 R. Fowler, ' "Prose Rhythm" and Metre', Ch. 5 of Fowler (ed.),
    Essays on Style and Language (London, 1966); 'Structural Metrics',
    Linguistics, xxvii (November 1966), 49–64 (reprinted in Chatman
    and Levin, op. cit. and Paper 9 of this volume); 'What is
    Metrical Analysis?' (this volume, Paper 10) is basically genera-
    tive. For a different methodology, see D. Abercrombie, 'A
    Phonetician's View of Verse Structure', *Linguistics*, vi (June
    1964), 5–13.
24 *Journal of Linguistics*, i (1965), 49–59.
25 See J. R. Firth, *Papers in Linguistics: 1934–51* (London, 1957);
    R. H. Robins, 'John Rupert Firth', *Language*, xxxvii (1961),
    194 ff.; G. Bursill-Hall, 'Levels Analysis: J. R. Firth's Theories of
    Linguistic Analysis', *Journal of the Canadian Linguistic Association*,
    ii (1960–1), 124–35, 164–91; Fowler, 'A Note on Some Uses of
    the Term "Meaning" in Descriptive Linguistics', *Word*, xxi (1965),
    411–20.
26 *Word*, xvii, 241–92.
27 'An Approach to the Study of Style', in Spencer (ed.), *Linguistics
    and Style* (London, 1964). The volume also includes a valuable
    chapter 'On Defining Style', by Nils-Erik Enkvist.
28 'Descriptive Linguistics in Literary Studies', *English Studies Today*,
    Third Series, ed. G. I. Duthie (Edinburgh, 1964), 25–39; reprinted in
    A. McIntosh and Halliday, *Patterns of Language: Papers in
    General, Descriptive and Applied Linguistics* (London, 1966), 56–69.
29 'Taking a Poem to Pieces', Ch. 4 of Fowler, *Essays on Style and
    Language*.
30 'Linguistics and the Analysis of Poetry', *Critical Survey*, iii (1967),
    78–89; 'Some Stylistic Features of the *Sermo Lupi*', *JEGP*, lxv
    (1966), 1–18 (this volume, Papers 14 and 13,
    respectively).

31 Fowler, 'Linguistics, Stylistics; Criticism?' *Lingua*, xvi (1966), 153–66 (this volume, Paper 2).

32 'Descriptive Linguistics in Literary Studies', 64. Cf. Halliday's 'The Linguistic Study of Literary Texts', *Proceedings of the Ninth International Congress of Linguists*, ed. H. G. Lunt (The Hague, 1964), revised version in Chatman and Levin, op. cit. (NB p. 217) for a similar sentiment; also Halliday, McIntosh, and P. Strevens, *The Linguistic Sciences and Language Teaching* (London, 1964), 5.

33 See Halliday in Chatman and Levin, 218–19.

34 Helen Hennessey Vendler, review of *Essays on Style and Language*, *Essays in Criticism*, xvi (1966), 457–63; editorial postscript by F. W. Bateson, ibid., 464–5; reply by Fowler, *Essays in Criticism*, xvii (1967), 322–35; rejoinder by Bateson, 335–47; further comments by Bateson and Fowler forthcoming in *Essays in Criticism*, xviii (April 1968) (this volume, Papers 3–6).

35 Cf. Fowler, 'Linguistic Theory and the Study of Literature', Ch. 1 of *Essays on Style and Language*.

36 See Halliday, 'Categories of the Theory of Grammar'; 'Lexis as a Linguistic Level', in C. E. Bazell, *et al.* (eds.), *In Memory of J. R. Firth* (London, 1966), 148–62; Sinclair, 'Beginning the Study of Lexis', ibid., 410–30; McIntosh, 'Patterns and Ranges', *Language*, xxxvii (1961), 325–37, reprinted in McIntosh and Halliday, op. cit., 182–99.

37 The term 'context of situation' is Malinowski's, adapted and popularized by Firth. A somewhat unrigorous (though rigour is hardly achievable yet) account of register is given by Halliday, McIntosh, and Strevens, *The Linguistic Sciences and Language Teaching* (London, 1964), 87–94. See also G. N. Leech, *English in Advertising* (London, 1966), Chs. 7–10.

38 *Investigating English Style* (London, 1969).

39 Cf. Leech on 'institutional delicacy' in *Essays on Style and Language*, 138 ff.

40 vi (April 1955).

41 'Saying' in 'New Attitudes to Style', 9–20; ' "As You Like It": a Grammatical Clue to Character', *REL*, iv (April 1963), 68–81, reprinted in *Patterns of Language*, 70–82; 'A Four-Letter Word in *Lady Chatterley's Lover*', *Patterns of Language*, 151–64.

42 *Charles Dickens and Appropriate Language* (Durham, 1959); 'Some Observations on the Language of Dickens', *REL*, ii (July 1961), 19–28; *The Use of English* (London, 1962), especially Ch. 14.

43 ' "This Bread I Break"—Language and Interpretation', in 'New Attitudes to Style', 66–75; 'Linguistics and the Figures of Rhetoric', in *Essays on Style and Language*, Ch. 8; *A Linguistic Guide to English Poetry* (London, 1969).

Nine

Structural metrics [1]

Over the past fifteen years we have witnessed a good deal of activity in one compartment of applied linguistics, the application of 'supra-segmental' phonemics to the analysis of English metre. Starting with a suggestion by Harold Whitehall in 1951 that this was a possible use of Trager-Smith phonology,[2] it has culminated (perhaps) in a full-scale discussion by another of the pioneers, Seymour Chatman. The publication of this book provides an occasion for an appraisal of the assumptions and achievements of the approach.

Structural metrics could be said to be concerned with the reconciliation (through phonemics) of two extremes of analysis. On the one hand is the old belief in two fixed degrees of stress alternating with perfect regularity and uniformly disposed in time. At the other extreme are the instrumental revelations that each of the syllables in a line is realized differently by various complexes of intensity, pitch, and length; that there is no identity of weight among the stresses; that there is no clear binary distinction between 'stress' and 'unstress'; and that there is no equality of time-interval.

Both of these extremes are rejected by modern linguists: the first, 'graphic' analysis, derived from classical, quantitative metrics, because it does not fit the facts of English, even if one substitutes 'stress' for 'length'; the second, because acoustic display gives too much information and is thus meaningless unless a phonemic or other categorizing selection is made.[3] And yet both these modes of analysis do convey sorts of reality: the first is a reflection of a demonstrable perception by readers of verse, even though rationalized unrealistically; the second, the physical reality of actual performance. Neither, by itself, tells us much about the structure of a line; but both are genuine dimensions for study. The aim of reconciliation, often unexpessed, is to discover a means of fusing these dimensions, of bringing the notion of 'abstract' or 'perceived' metre into line with the facts of language.

Structural metrics has always operated with a multi-dimensional or complexly stratified model of verse structure in mind. Whitehall views English metre as a product of two dimensions:

the traditional 'ideal' metrical patterns of much English verse —patterns based on the two-level contrast of stressed versus unstressed syllables—have been 'orchestrated' since Marlowe by a poetic adaptation of the actual four-level contrast of speech. [4]

'Orchestration' appears to be the modification of the 'ideal' metre by natural suprasegmental phonology to give a 'real' and phonemically valid metre: the two-stress metrical system is actualized by four degrees of stress, and the artificial isochronism of feet is modified by superimposition of an isochronism of phrase-stresses. Whitehall's analyses look just like analyses of any sort of English, with no concessions in notation to metre: that 'ideal' has been submerged:

The curfew / tolls the knell / of parting day /

But Hawkes, giving a later exposition of Trager-Smith metrics, makes explicit note of the ideal metre and so hints at its survival (in what is presumably a non-phonological state):

The hol| y time | is qui | et as | a Nun | [5]

His strategy is to sophisticate the idea of the foot. Under the influence of the natural stresses of speech, the metrical matrix ∪ ⁻ will be capable of actual (i.e. phonemic) realization as ∪ ∕, ∪ ∧, ∪ ∖, etc. [6]

Those linguists who have retained the idea that the metre still somehow 'exists', despite the phonemic actuality of four stresses, have toyed with such notions as 'tension', 'counterpoint', 'interplay' between what a verse-line is and what it is thought to be. Chatman speaks of 'a tension between TWO systems: the abstract metrical pattern, as historical product of the English verse tradition, and the ordinary stress-pitch-juncture system of spoken English, determined as it is by requirements of meaning and emphasis' (1956, p. 422). He goes on to describe the results of tension as '"promotions" or "suppressions" of the stress levels of normal non-verse speech under the pressures of the abstract metrical pattern' (p. 424). His analyses here and in the article of 1960 [7] show metre and suprasegmental phonology, with a full display of stress, pitch, and juncture.

Warren and Wellek posit three dimensions: SPECIFIC PERFORMANCE which is 'irrelevant to an analysis of the prosodic situation, which consists precisely in the tension, the "counterpoint", between the METRICAL PATTERN and the PROSE RHYTHM'. [8] This interplay between metrical pattern and prose rhythm, with a product describable in terms of English suprasegmental phonology and yet different from English non-verse, is a theory of metre which I find attractive. And yet it is a theory full of snags and dangerous assumptions, not least of which is the feeling that metre is easily and relevantly described according to the practices of linguistics. As Wimsatt and Beardsley point out, 'you cannot write a grammar of the meter's interaction with the sense'.[9] The linguist can talk only about the CAUSES of tension (prose rhythm and metre) and recognize them both; the PRODUCT of the tension (performance reduced to phonemic form), as shown by Whitehall, or the upper lines of Chatman's and Hawkes' analyses, has the status of a symptom only.

Since I am going to conduct my essay on *A Theory of Meter* by means of annotated summary and quotation, I pass over Ch. I, which is itself a presummary. In so far as this is also a statement of intentions and presumed achievements, I shall refer to it piecemeal in the course of my account.

The approach of Ch. II, 'The nature of rhythm', is basically psychological, for it presents rhythm (and hence metre) as a product of a natural human perceptual tendency. There is 'primary' or 'cardiac' rhythm, 'the simple repetition of single events between equal time intervals' (p. 22). Although this may exist, it is unlikely to be perceived. We perceive 'secondary' rhythm: events will appear to be grouped, perhaps into pairs, and we will believe that there is an alternation of relative prominences:

> When a series of sounds precisely equal in loudness, pitch, and
> length, and occurring at precisely equal intervals is presented
> to a subject, the chances are that he will not hear the series
> as the cardiac rhythm it really is, but as grouped rhythm, that
> is, he will overestimate every other interval, thus creating a
> purely subjective distinction between external and internal
> intervals. He may also begin to perceive a regular difference
> in prominence (either loudness or pitch or length) among alter-
> nating events. (p. 25)

Chatman concludes that

> meter is basically *linguistically determined 'secondary rhythm'*—
> linguistic events grouped regularly in time, such that each
> group has unity in its internal composition and in its external
> relations. A 'foot' can be defined as one of these groups of
> events. (p. 29)

This chapter establishes clearly that metre is in the ear of the beholder, in his ability to group and equate sequentially random and physically disparate sound-stimuli. Obviously, there is here a great advance over such unexplained locutions as 'abstract metre' or 'ideal metre', which were hardly sufficient to encourage the non-linguist to believe that linguists were positively interested in anything but sheer sound. Much antagonism has sprung from a belief that physical and phonemic investigations must destroy the notion of metrical pattern. Chatman himself, while paying homage to the idea, has consistently denied its linguistic existence. I would like to think of the phonetic variation revealed by the spectrograph as corroboration of the psychological or abstract 'existence' of metre. An analogy is the principle of the phoneme. Phonemes are abstractions that, for the sake of communication, we agree to believe in. Phonetics reveals that no sound is ever repeated, but there is not phonetic anarchy: physical 'cues' exist: plosion, voice, etc. Similarly, metre is our own simplification and categorization of phonetic variety on the basis of cues: lexical stress, syllable-count, etc.[10]

Chatman examines these cues in Ch. III, 'Phonological backgrounds to metrical analysis', which is a treatment of suprasegmental matters arranged in an order to be of use in metrical analysis, and (with the Appendix, 'The stress systems of Pike and Trager-Smith' [pp. 225–9]) a survey of phonemicizing approaches to these matters.

As Chatman is concerned with isosyllabic or syllable-counting verse (p. 113), he first discusses the nature of the syllable, which is 'the event' in metre, 'the essential rhythmic integer' (p. 30). Theories of chest-pulse and sonority are surveyed, but Chatman favours the phonological definition as formulated by O'Connor and Trim:[11] a syllable is a segmental sequence (C)V(C), the exponents of the pattern being selected according to the order- and clustering-rules of the language. He concludes:

> Although there are differences of opinion about the constitution of the syllable, the problem does not seem serious from the point of view of metrics. Metrics is concerned mostly with the number of syllables-as-events; syllables are easily recognized, and the problem of identifying their boundaries rarely matters. . . . The only important question for metrics is 'How many syllables are there?' (p. 39)

All we need to know is how many syllables a line has—this is the first of the 'configurational' features which start the 'metrical set', the pattern-in-our-minds superimposed on the phonological pattern.

Among syllables, some are more prominent than others. When metre occurs, there appears to be a regular relation between prominent syllables: a metrically prominent syllable, recurring at regular intervals and of the same 'weight', is an ictus—Chatman keeps the old term. Prominence, he says, cannot be attributed to one phonetic or phonemic feature alone; a syllable may be felt to be prominent, and so signal ictus, because of characteristics of pitch, stress, vowel-quality, or length, or all four. His particular (and deserving) butt here is the view that it is 'loudness' (stress defined as a correlate of articulatory energy or amplitude) which is the only or chief producer of prominence. This was the belief of traditional metrists after the quantitative model had been buried, and is reflected today in the practices of those who rely exclusively on the Trager-Smith stress-levels. Instrumental analysis reported later in the book reveals that prominence is a matter of high redundancy, achieved by a selection from the four 'suprasegmental' features, with the human ear incapable of isolating any ONE feature as significant (p. 49).

Chatman no longer espouses the Trager-Smith formulation of suprasegmental phonology, and it seems that any notion of 'degrees' of prominence must be foreign to him.[12] He confesses elsewhere[13] to using 'a binary phonemic model' (a cryptic phrase) in his recent work. 'Stress' and 'non-stress' correspond simply with ictus and non-ictus. But I suspect that much is to be gained by preserving a multi-level view of prominence in order to keep what might be called 'allophones' of ictus—different degrees actualizing metrical points as a result of the so-called 'tension' between metre as a mental categorization and the variety of cues which signal the categories.

The last section (pp. 52–76) of the phonological chapter is devoted to the linguistic qualities which produce prominence. He follows Bolinger's restatement of a familiar distinction:

> Stress is a fundamental property of full vowel monosyllabic words, and of one syllable in polysyllabic words, which in any environment, accented or not, can serve to distinguish them from what are otherwise homonyms. The actualization of stress is not uniform; its phonetic cues will vary according to the phonological context in which the word finds itself. Nevertheless, it is real; speakers will not ordinarily differ in their sense of where it occurs, and can always make it more prominent on demand. Accent, on the other hand, is the prominence which one syllable in an uttered phrase receives when it is the center of the pitch contour; it is not fixed to the word but to the phrase. (p. 58)[14]

A third concept is introduced, 'pitch obtrusion' (p. 62), which is the use of accents involving relatively large pitch-contrasts for 'emphasis' and similar functions.

He has outlined those indispensable features of all utterance which produce prominence. All words have (through lexical stress) the potential at fixed points. When words are put together, some syllables will have this potential realized through accent and/or pitch obtrusion. All stretches of utterance have this composite stress-pattern, which I would like to call PROSE RHYTHM.[15] Manipulation of word-order, and rigorous control of number of syllables, together with the presence of other configurational features such as rhyme, can encourage a reader to transform the prose rhythm into a metre of binary, alternating contrasts of prominence. For Chatman, the transformation appears to be complete, for the prose rhythm succumbs to the 'on-off' contrast of metre. I would prefer to think that the variousness of prominence of prose rhythm survives, in some degree, WITHIN the binary categorization. To use the analogy of the phoneme again: we agree that we use substantially the same phonemes as the speakers of other dialects of our language, but we recognize the allophonic variety which sets them off from us; so every iambic foot is ◡‾, but we remain conscious of—and derive pleasure from—the variety of its realization.

Ch. IV, 'Objective analyses of metrical properties: a survey', has two parts: one on mechanical analysis of actual performance, and the second on 'The structuralist approach to meter': respectively, phonetics and phonemics. Kymograph, oscilloscope, and spectrograph are described, and some research surveyed. Chatman has said before, of the limitations of acoustic metrics, that 'one cannot get more structure out of a machine than one puts in' (1956, p. 422).[16] Now the phonemic value of suprasegmental distinctions is denied (1965, p. 69), and it is somewhat of a puzzle what use is to be made of acoustic data now he has removed that 'structure'.

In the disappointingly brief second section of this chapter, he comments (pp. 95–6) on some statements by Roman Jakobson. Jakobson makes what I take to be a three-level differentiation which depends on type-token relationships. VERSE DESIGN is the abstract metre; VERSE INSTANCE is a line written in that metre, and it has 'invariant features' determined by the design; DELIVERY INSTANCE is an actual performance of that line. Chatman re-words this position, which I among others[17] accept:

> Three ideas now seem clearly established: 1) it is the linguistically relevant, not the unanalyzed speech sounds which signal metrical features; 2) meter itself is a system, parallel to and actualized by, but not to be confused with, the linguistic system; and 3) there is an essential difference between performance (recitation, realization) and abstract meter. (p. 96)

The author makes a further—and less clear—use of Jakobson's proposition, which can be quoted as a way of getting into Chs. V and VI:

> It is but one logical step from this position to recognize the verse instance as a sum or common denominator of all meaningful delivery instances, a hypothesis which underlies much of my own theory of meter. The sum or common denominator is part of the poem itself, the 'enduring object' in contradistinction to the many performances of it, which are merely 'events'. (p. 96)

The difficulty is to understand what procedures he has in mind. 'Metrical analysis' is the discovery of the verse instance, and here it is said to be deducible from delivery instance, performance. In fact, in Ch. VI it is deduced from PERCEPTION OF performance—the testimony of himself and the '21 professors of English literature' (p. 159). The acoustic analysis (surely, in the true sense analysis of performance?) is used only as secondary evidence. Chatman's words in *Style in Language* (p. 208) show that he is conscious of the essential irrelevance of performance *qua* physical event, and in fact proceed more logically from the position of Jakobson:

> I am not attempting to analyze English meter on the basis of performances; to the contrary (and it is apparently a point I cannot repeat often enough) the phonemic notation of a reading is *not* a metrical analysis. It is simply a way of accounting for the differences in readings, all of which may satisfy the same metrical pattern.

But they by no means resolve the difficulties stumbled over in the present book: difficulties not clarified by the procedurally imprecise 'sum or common denominator'.

In Ch. V, 'The components of English meter', the first component considered is the syllable. The author has already argued (p. 39) that syllable-count is not problematical, despite the indeterminacy of syllable-boundaries; he now minimizes the difficulties of elision, reducing it to rule and category. 'The poet may select his words in part by considering the number of syllables they contain, and ordinarily he can be sure that this feature will be conveyed to his reader' (p. 112). And 'since syllable-count is the most relatively constant feature of meter . . . we may give it priority of application in the analysis of isosyllabic verse' (p. 113).

The grouping of syllables is into lines and feet. The line is numerically determined, and the foot also: for analytic convenience, at least, it is 'the smallest *submultiple* of the normal line' (p. 117). The foot Chatman presumes to be 'a pure metrical convention with no relation to English or to the sense of the poem' (p. 14). Like all other components of metre, it is a concept; but less based on a percept, one supposes, than the others (for the distinction, see p. 105). I would agree that the foot has only a tenuous relation to linguistic reality (ictus is 'cued' by prominence, and is an additional foot-defining quality, although the concept is chiefly numerical); but once it has been proposed as an analytic or descriptive category, further use of it can be made. Although boundaries between feet have no linguistic basis, to say that a foot-boundary falls within a word is to say something significant.

We come now to the treatment of ictus, a discussion for which most of the earlier linguistic theory has been a preparation. The author again gives attention to the linguistic conditions—lexical stress and phrase-accent—which determine the siting of ictus and hence the metrical pattern. He believes (p. 126) that it is the lexical stress of polysyllabic words which is most useful in creating the metre. When this has been established, it can be carried on in the absence of an explicitly metre-fixing prose rhythm:

> If ictus is not totally discoverable in the linguistic structure itself it must partly be the product of some extralinguistic phenomenon, like the metrical 'set' (in the psychological sense), the running disposition of ictus and non-ictus established by preceding sequences, particularly where these were linguistically unequivocal. (p. 121)

After a disposition to iambs has been created, it will be sufficient for the poet to distribute points open to the imposition of ictus. Certain types of syllable are especially receptive:

> Syllables with full vowels are likely to be more prominent than those with reduced vowels in length, loudness, and pitch-obtrusion, but the prominence is not significant. (p. 125)

Chatman distinguishes

> four different sorts of syllables, or more accurately, syllabic *weights*: **a**) full-vowel monosyllabic words, **b**) stressed syllables of polysyllabic words, **c**) unstressed full-vowel syllables of polysyllabic words, and **d**) unstressed reduced (degraded) syllables of polysyllabic words.

Then, under the heading 'Foot-types',[18] he lists the various combinations of types of syllable ($\bar{\text{a}} + \breve{\text{b}}$, $\breve{\text{a}} + \bar{\text{b}}$, etc.) with illustrations of each. His purpose here is to distinguish between 'metre-fixing' and

K

'metre-fixed' types. A metre-fixing foot can be exemplified by $\overset{\smile}{\mathbf{d}}$ + $\overset{\_\smile\_}{\mathbf{b}}$ | aloft | where the stress-pattern is invariable: such a foot will be of first importance in establishing metrical set.

The classification is not offered for its own sake; the author has, in the Introduction, disclaimed an interest in the classification of feet:

> I take the position that the metrist's function is not to find out
> how many kinds of feet there are, but rather to insure that
> there aren't any more kinds than necessary. (p. 14)

But he gives the game away by admitting that his distinctions are based on 'syllable-weight' (pp. 15 and 123) and this confirms one's suspicion that, with the substitution of other parameters, the classification could have some very positive value. Of course, the provision of as minutely (and immensely) discriminated a categorization as possible is not a viable or useful project.[19] But one must account somehow for differences of 'feel' between lines. And the most useful hypothesis that structural metrics can lead us to adopt is that this variety arises from the realization of ictus and non-ictus by syllables of varying weight or prominence.

Chatman's picture of English metre includes level feet, reversal, ambiguity, and stress-shift. Some passages, he says, make best sense if equally-stressed feet are allowed into the metrical pattern, despite the impossibility of equal stress in linguistic reality. (And despite Wimsatt and Beardsley [p. 594]; in this matter Chatman is more traditional than his conservative opponents.) Reversal can obviously be caused by dominating lexical and/or accentual pressure, and often by pitch obtrusion. He is more cautious about ambiguous feet. His footnote on p. 149 reveals him as still tender from the exchange with Arnold Stein on 'hovering' feet.[20] An ambiguous foot is one 'which can be scanned with either the normal disposition of ictus and non-ictus or a reversal'. Several examples are to be found in his analysis of Shakespeare's Sonnet 18. Where semantic criteria justify either of two (or more) readings, and formal features select neither unequivocally, he marks both:

$$\overset{\_\ \overset{\smile}{\_}}{\underset{\smile\ \ \_}{\text{Shall I}}} \mid$$

Stress-shift is the opposite of reversal. Here metrical demands override lexical stress:

The rich proud cost | of $\overset{\smile\ \_}{\text{out}}$ | worn buried age

(Sonnet 64)

After a brief skirmish with Substitutions, Chatman ends his survey of the components of English metre with a dismissal of caesura and enjambment as 'pure performance features' (p. 156; cf. Chatman, 1960, pp. 165–70). I cannot allow this judgment to pass unchallenged. His unwillingness to consider metrical stretches more than two syllables long (here and p. 10) is culpable enough, and I shall return to this later. I have written elsewhere on caesura and enjambment,[21] and will at this time say only that semantically and grammatically signalled terminal junctures, both within and between lines, are an essential part of verse-structure. They cannot be ignored without violence to language and meaning. Of course, they may be realized in a variety of ways, as Chatman says; but this does not make them optional, nor alter the fact that they can have a profound effect on the shape of line and line-sequence.

The climax of *A Theory of Meter* is the treatment of Shakespeare's 18th Sonnet. Chatman took eleven commercially available performances of the poem (chiefly by professional actors) and subjected them to spectrographic analysis. He then (presumably; the exact procedure is not well described) applied the linguistically unrevolutionary techniques of syllable-count and foot-division, and marked ictus where it was clearly suggested by stress and accent. His own perceptions were then checked against those of an academic panel in an attempt to find scansions which would eliminate all indeterminacy except in cases of genuinely ambiguous feet. At each stage, the panel's assignments of ictus were compared with the acoustic evidence, demonstrating only (as far as I can see) the acknowledged uselessness of physical data, and the more positive fact that stress, accent, and metrical set can and do compensate for lack of phonetic signal. It is important to realize that performance *qua* physical data forms no part of the analysis itself: just as Chatman has claimed (e.g. p. 142).

It turns out that the apparently dubious relation between 'scansion' and 'metrical analysis' is a quite simple one. A scansion is an informed assignment of foot-division, ictus and non-ictus to one performance; a metrical analysis is a CONFLATION [22] of semantically and linguistically justified scansions of several performances, showing agreements and REASONABLE difference of opinion. This is what the analysis looks like:

1. Shall I | compare | thee to | a sum | mer's day?

2. Thou art | more love | ly and | more tem | perate:

3. Rough winds | do shake | the dar | ling buds | of May,

4. And sum | mer's lease | hath all | too short | a date: (p. 182)

His experience with the Sonnet allows him to state his hypotheses as conclusions:

1. Lexical stress unambiguously marks ictus, regardless of the phonetic actuality, unless overridden by accent.

2. Pitch change is most effective in marking ictus if lexical stress is not a definitive criterion. It functions most powerfully if it is accentual, but pitch obtrusions which are allophonic may also signal ictus in a clear-cut fashion. Length is less effective, although it does operate where pitch is not sufficiently obtruded. Loudness seems least effective; it occasionally operates in the absence of other cues, but most of the time it has little impact. Indeed, it often actually conflicts with concurrent features without upsetting the perception of ictus.

3. Foot-reversal may be effected where lexical stress is not definitive, but ictus then requires a comparatively greater degree of prominence than it does in the normal foot. The metrical set operates so strongly that a pitch change usually needs to be accentual to reverse the foot.

4. Vowel reduction generally shows that reducible monosyllabic words are unstressed and hence non-ictic. In very rare cases, accentual features may promote a syllable containing a reduced vowel to ictus.

5. The difference between the pyrrhic foot and spondee is largely one of the relative length of the syllables. The clearest instances of spondee occur where both syllables are accented in the same way, preferably with an intervening terminal. (pp. 182–3)

Such a set of statements calls for a judgment, and I think this must be 'excellent as far as it goes'. He has tested a good many basic assumptions in experimentally valid ways; he has established some useful techniques. Above all, he is enlightening on the linguistic cues to ictus: lexical stress, accent, fullness of syllable, syllable-count, and the various other minor signals.[23] He convinces one of the psychological reality of 'metrical set'. But if the book teaches us only to produce ictic analyses by committee, its ultimate message is too limited. It does not take structural linguistics to allow us to carry out that sort of operation (but Mr Chatman has used linguistics brilliantly to show us by what mechanisms we do it so confidently).

What structural metrics is well fitted to do is explain the differences
between, say,

> Pinn'd, beaten, cold, pinch'd, threaten'd and abus'd

and

> Immutable, immortal, infinite . . .

A generalization to

$$\cup - \mid \cup - \mid \cup - \mid \cup - \mid \cup - \mid$$

is not adequate, and if Chatman had pursued the implications of his
earlier theory (1956, pp. 422–5), he could have shown how both are
iambic pentameters and yet both quite individual.

I accept his account of how metrical stress and its arrangements
are perceived. The perception of the verse line as a sequence of groups
of ictus and non-ictus comes about through the stimulation, by the
disposition of certain linguistic features, of an innate human tendency to hear secondary rhythm. Once the metre has been established, the stimulation need not be so explicit. An established metre
does not, of course, turn the prose rhythm into a system of two-level
prominence contrast: an approximation to this state may occur in
some excessively 'metred' performances

> (The boy | stood on | the bur | ning deck
> Whence all | but he | had fled . . .

> Cf. Chatman, p. 105)

but ordinarily a metrical line retains multi-level prominence characteristics. To account for differences between iambic pentameters,
one must record not only the position of ictus, but this full surviving
suprasegmental pattern. One must recognize ictus and simultaneously the varying prominences which realize it: I differ from Chatman in believing that these are metrically significant.

If we substitute composite prominence for stress, we may find the
germ of the idea in the earliest writings on Trager-Smith metrics:

> The two extreme stresses, primary or weak, are poetically
> fixed, the first being necessarily always a poetic strong, the
> second always a poetic weak. The two middle stresses, secon-
> dary or tertiary, may be poetic strongs, or poetic weaks. The
> principle of poetic stress is that a syllable is strong if it is
> stronger than those which surround it; so that as indicated
> above, a tertiary stress followed by a weak may count as a

poetic strong, while if followed by a secondary or primary
stress, it may count as a poetic weak. Those English poets
who are generally admired as metrists make use of these differences to produce variety . . . [24]

There is no need to believe that a line- or foot-analysis in these terms
is phonemic, however. All we need is a means of symbolizing finer-
than-binary prominence. I propose that the Trager-Smith notation
(╱, ∧, ╲, ∪) be adapted to this task on the assumption that four degrees will provide enough contrasts. As has been said many times,[25]
once we 'dephonemicize' the system, there may be more than four;
but four relative degrees may be enough. And the degrees are of
prominence, not stress. Interpreted in this way, the phonemic
notations of the pioneers make a good deal of sense.

The notion of 'tension' also makes sense if we can accept the simultaneous existence of metre as a concept and of the physical reality of
multi-level prominence. But the term is undoubtedly misleading, as
is 'counterpoint'.[26] I have argued elsewhere for 'syncopation'.[27]
Syncopation is an effect produced when, holding the metrical set in
our minds, we read a line which is not composed entirely of 'metre-
fixing' syllabic patterns. Obviously such an effect is not open to adequate linguistic notation; but the factors which produce it are, and
the 'prosodic product', which is composed neither of ictic contrast
nor of lexical and accentual prominence patterns, could be said to
be a reflex of it.

An understanding of the operation of syncopation depends on the
analysis of prose rhythm IN CONTINUITY. Chatman merely picks out
a lexical stress from a polysyllabic word and uses it as a cue to ictus
within one foot: if the rest of the word falls in another foot, that is
quite another matter. So we have

$$\breve{a} + \bar{b} \mid \text{Sw}\bar{e}\breve{e}t \text{ } \bar{im} \mid$$

in one foot, with the rest of the word making up a different foot under a different rule:

$$\breve{d} + \bar{d} \mid \breve{a}g\bar{e}s \mid$$

The formula **a** + **b** + **d** + **d**, broken up into two parts, conceals the
continuity of prose rhythm in 'images': under the influence of metrical set, ìmágês, perhaps. Similarly, Whitehall and Hill's principle
that ictus and non-ictus are variously realized as ╱ ∧ ╲ and ∧ ╲ ∪ is not
fully expressed in a translation of ∪ — into ∪ ╱, ∪ ∧, etc.: the continuity
of prose rhythm is essential. Although the foot is an abstraction, it
need not be thought to have internal structure only: it has boundaries and external relations.

So syncopation is an accentual effect produced by the fit or non-fit of GROUPS of metrical stresses and GROUPS of prose prominences. I will demonstrate the results of this interplay in several pentameter lines.

Her eyes, her haire, her cheeke, her gate, her voice.

Chatman would comment that phrase-accent coincides entirely with ictus: this is a perfect 'metre-fixing' line. I would add that foot- and phrase-boundaries coincide, and that the junctural separation and grammatical identity of the phrases lead easily to a prosodic interpretation close to simple two-way contrast.

In the next example, the boundary between the fourth and fifth feet does not coincide with a terminal juncture:

I burne, I burne, I burne, then loud | he cryde

and hence we must make a different 'bridge' between *loud* and *he* from that between *burne* and *I* and *burne* and *then*. I suggest that *he* is slightly more prominent than *I* or *then* ($\setminus$ instead of $\cup$ perhaps) but it is still non-ictic. In

So long as men can breathe or eyes can see

non-ictus is relatively close to ictus throughout, except that a minor 'caesura' is marked by an extra contrast between *breathe* and *or*.

Rocks, caves, lakes, fens, bogs, dens, and shades of death

has syntactic boundaries within the foot, strong phrase-accents coinciding with non-ictus. Here non-ictus is signalled by the highest level of prominence available for the function, $\wedge$.

Immut | able, | immor | tal, in | finite |

requires foot-boundaries within words; but the words must be retained as wholes by allowing only one $\diagup$ on each (therefore two ictuses are realized as $\wedge$) and 'promoting' certain non-ictic syllables to $\setminus$ so that they will not be detached from the words they belong to.

The most common form of syncopation is found where a two-syllabled word maintains its prominence-pattern across a foot-boundary. Lexical stress is perfectly adjusted to the position of ictus, but the 'light' second syllable of the word, often necessarily in the next foot, cannot be reduced to $\cup$, or it will detach from the word.

When yel | low leaves,

Bare ru | in'd choirs

the twi | light of

In iambic metre, no word with initial stress can be realized as /◡; but words with stress on their second syllable can utilize the contrast between the lowest and highest degrees of prominence:

in me | behold

against | the cold

The prose rhythms of English are in fact the phonology of its grammar, and are quite open to analysis, whether by the Trager-Smith or any other sophisticated method. They need not be deduced from performance. Metrical analysis should see how they are fitted to metre by the manipulation of lexical stress, accent and full vowels, as Chatman has demonstrated. But they cannot be TOTALLY manipulated, or, if they were, English verse would be a very dull thing, with no grammatical units longer than two syllables, and only two degrees of prominence; no syncopation. I believe that metrical analysis should go further than the documentation of ictus, to consider the patterns formed by its implementation throughout the line. Metrical analysis based on grammatical signals of prose rhythm might then be grammetric[28] prediction rather than phonological description, but it would at least attempt to show how verse in such an inflexible matrix can remain interesting.

Notes to Paper Nine

1 A review-article prompted by Seymour Chatman, *A Theory of Meter* (= *Janua Linguarum*, Series Minor, 36) (The Hague, 1965).

2 Harold Whitehall, 'From Linguistics to Criticism', *Kenyon Review*, xiii (1951), 710–14.

3 S. Chatman, 'Robert Frost's "Mowing"': an Inquiry into Prosodic Structure', *Kenyon Review*, xviii (1956), 421, 422 (hereafter referred to as Chatman, 1956); A. Warren and R. Wellek, *Theory of Literature*, 3rd ed. (Harmondsworth, 1963), 166, 168.

4 *Kenyon Review*, xviii (1956), 418.

5 T. Hawkes, 'The Problems of Prosody', *A Review of English Literature*, iii (April 1962), 45.

6 Ibid., 39.

7 'Comparing Metrical Styles', in T. A. Sebeok, *Style in Language* (New York, 1960), 149–72 (hereafter referred to as Chatman, 1960).

8 *Theory of Literature*, 169.

9 W. K. Wimsatt, Jr., and Monroe C. Beardsley, 'The Concept of Meter: an Exercise in Abstraction', *PMLA*, lxxiv (1959), 596.

10 This is not to say, of course, that metrical units are part of the phoneme-system of a language; they are 'produced' by the same mental process, the equation and classification of different physical phenomena.

11 J. D. O'Connor and J. L. M. Trim, 'Vowel, Consonant, and Syllable—A Phonological Definition', *Word*, ix (1953).

12 Intermediate degrees are challenged, pp. 68–71, in terms which recall some of the critics' attacks on the Trager-Smith system (e.g. Wimsatt and Beardsley, 593): 'If *disestablish* is said to have, say, four levels of stress (dîsĕstáblìsh), what is to prevent us from saying that *antidisestablishmentarianism* has eight?' (p. 71). On p. 68 he comes out into the open: 'stress in the limited view we have adopted operates in an "on-off" fashion; either it is there, or it is not . . .' Ictus, indeed, is an 'on-off' concept; but the 'ons' and 'offs' can, paradoxically, be distinguished, even if the differences are not phonemically significant.

13 Sebeok, 207.

14 See Dwight Bolinger, 'A Theory of Pitch Accent in English', *Word*, xiv (1958), 112. For the older account, see Daniel Jones, *An Outline of English Phonetics*, 9th ed. (Cambridge, 1960), 248–73.

15 Warren and Wellek's phrase. See my ' "Prose Rhythm" and Metre' in *Essays on Style and Language* (London, 1966), 82–99.

16 Quoted with approval by Wimsatt and Beardsley, 586.

17 Jakobson, in Sebeok, 365–6; R. S. Wells, in Sebeok, 197–200; Wimsatt and Beardsley, 596–7.

18 The phrase has a more traditional meaning, pp. 118–19.

19 Epstein and Hawkes (*Linguistics and English Prosody*, Buffalo, 1959) are noticed by Chatman (1965, p. 99) as having attempted classifications.

20 'Mr Stein on Donne', *Kenyon Review*, xviii (1956), 443–51, a note which provides important background for the part of *A Theory of Meter* currently under examination.

21 ' "Prose Rhythm" and Metre', 85–92.

22 Chatman's confusing expressions of this relationship are found on pp. 14 'token/type'; 96 'sum or common denominator'; 105 'process of summing'; 121 'consensus or common denominator'; 167 'consensus'.

23 By abandoning multi-level prominence, he has missed one useful principle, the tendency of adjacent syllables to have different weights. For example, *(tem) perate* is rendered |pĕrăte|, 'pyrrhic

as far as *perception* goes, but . . . metrical set suggests the
possibility of iambus' (p. 181). But if the lexical stress is written
out for the whole word, we see that the final syllable will in any
case tend to be heavier than the second, granted that primary
stress goes on *tem-* (surely the trochaic reading |mōre tĕm|,
offered as one possibility, goes too much against lexical stress?).
And he seems to be talking about TENSION, here, not AMBIGUITY.

24 H. Whitehall and A. A. Hill, 'A Report on the Language-literature
Seminar' [of the Linguistic Institute at Indiana, 1953], H. B.
Allen, *Readings in Applied English Linguistics* (New York, 1958),
395. R. S. Wells has the same idea in Sebeok, 199.

25 E.g. Wimsatt and Beardsley, 596–7.

26 Wimsatt and Beardsley suggest 'interplay' as an alternative: John
Hollander, Sebeok, 202, adeptly reveals the inappropriateness of
the melodic analogy implied in 'counterpoint'.

27 ' "Prose Rhythm" and Metre', 95.

28 For the term, see P. J. Wexler, 'On the Grammetrics of the
Classical Alexandrine', *Cahiers de Lexicologie*, iv (1964), 61–72, and
the same author's 'Distich and Sentence in Corneille and Racine'
in Fowler, *Essays on Style and Language*, 100–17.

Ten

What is metrical analysis?

The verse situation is extremely complex; moreover, it is not one, but several situations: for example, reading a poem aloud; listening to a poem being read aloud; reading a poem silently.[1] If we ask questions about it (such as the one which gives this article its title) we must realize that there are several very different questions which can be asked. A criticism of existing metrical theory is that most writers on the subject have thought that one question and one answer (various to each) are all they need consider. Most solutions to 'the problem of metrics' are unsatisfactory because of this limitation and simplification. This is not the whole reason why metrics has such a low value in literary studies, but it is a good part of it.

The first motive of the new linguistic metrics,[2] the desire to approach verse with the aid of a knowledge of the workings of living language (where 'stress' is astonishingly more subtle than the 'stress-or-not-stress' of traditional metrics), was a reaction against the linguistic unreality of the Saintsbury school. It was good to be reminded that verse is language as well as stylized pattern. But the orthodoxy demanded by the Trager–Smith metrists, the formalization of the line always in terms of the complete suprasegmental array, took away the simple pattern, or at least our means for understanding this pattern, this 'abstract metre'. By isolating one function of metrical analysis, other functions were ignored. Not unnaturally, Trager–Smith metrics has lost its excitement.[3] It is difficult today to understand what the 1956 *Kenyon Review* pioneers intended: what question they were asking, and what their answer was, in the total set of answers that are proper to questions in metrics.

Some of the questions which must be distinguished in a theory of metre are these: When we refer a poem to a verse tradition, what kind of generalization are we invoking and what, in the poem, is the nature of the evidence which allows the attribution? When a practised reader of poetry reads a poem silently or listens to an oral reading, what is the nature of his experience? What features of the language of a line tell us how to scan it? What is there in the arrangements of different words which causes one line to differ texturally from another, although they are 'metrically' the same? How do we describe consistent textural difference of one poet/poem from another within the same verse design? In what depth of detail does the language of a line dictate its oral reading? How does a poem establish for oral interpreters a permissible range of styles of delivery?

This article suggests a range of related answers to the questions posed in its title, setting up levels for analysis with reference to both a scheme for understanding verse situations and a consideration of practical purposes in describing verse. The specific motive is dissatisfaction with two positions. The phonemic analysis of oral performances must be disqualified because it does not proceed from best evidence, the language as more or less neutrally represented in a written text: this approach, in its simplest and most straightforwardly descriptive form, is only a little closer to metrical reality than pure phonetic methods such as those of E. W. Scripture.[4] The dangers of ignoring primitive ictic pattern, of being misled by irrelevant or at least disputable performance features, and of not taking into account the perceptual factor, are obvious. On the other hand, Chatman's current reduction of metrical analysis to a statement of ictic patterning, though a deliberate restriction and understandable within his own terms of reference, give less information about metre than is often necessary. We need to specify line-structure in detail in order to distinguish poems and poets within the same metrical scheme. Individual poets achieve distinctive 'textures' through their manipulation of language within a chosen metre, and such texture is not captured by an analysis which reveals only which syllables are metrically stressed. A poem full of multisyllabic words (for example) is quite different from one which largely utilizes monosyllables and disyllables, different in ways which go beyond the selection of diction. There is, I would claim, a metrical difference, because there is an inevitable phonological difference; moreover, this part of metrics (if established) is of particular critical interest since here metrical form is more closely intimate with other 'poetic' details of the language than are the framing patterns of ictus and non-ictus.

The most useful exposition of metrical levels comes from Roman Jakobson:[5]

> Far from being an abstract, theoretical scheme, meter—or in more explicit terms, *verse design*—underlies the structure of any single line—or, in logical terminology, any single *verse*

instance. Design and instance are correlative concepts. The verse design determines the invariant features of the verse instances and sets up the limits of variations . . .

The verse design is embodied in verse instances. Usually the free variation of these instances is denoted by the somewhat equivocal label 'rhythm'. A variation of *verse instances* within a given poem must be strictly distinguished from the variable *delivery instances.* The intention 'to describe the verse line as it is actually performed' is of lesser use for the synchronic and historical analysis of poetry than it is for the study of its recitation in the present and the past . . .

How the given verse-instance is implemented in the given delivery instance depends on the *delivery design* of the reciter; he may cling to a scanning style or tend toward prose-like prosody or freely oscillate between these two poles. We must be on guard against simplistic binarism which reduces two couples into one single opposition either by suppressing the cardinal distinction between verse design and verse instance (as well as between delivery design and delivery instance) or by an erroneous identification of delivery instance and delivery design with the verse instance and verse design.

These are distinct and necessary components of metre from its inception by a poet to its realization by a reader. Briefly, the *verse design* of a poem is its place in the formally defined set of kinds which make up a poetic literature; *verse instance* is a particular segment of a poem seen as different from comparable segments within the same verse design; *delivery design* is a chosen style of recitation; *delivery instance* is a recitation. To these we add *verse type,* in which a poem is identified by reference to the phonological features used in its metre (e.g. stress as opposed to length); *metrical set,* the psychological reflex of verse design, the disposition of a reader, variable according to his experience and to the metrical regularity of the poem in question, to impose a certain reading on it.

These levels of manifestation of metre are chiefly (but not wholly) derived from a level which must be presumed to exist independently of them: 'the language of the poem'. Verse is language with additional formal constraints; it is nevertheless language and embodies not only the formal restrictions of metre, but also characteristics which are necessary to the syntax and vocabulary of the occurring sentences whether or not the sentences are contrived to make a poem. Moreover, these are features which do not always co-operate with the metre-fixing qualities. One could regard the language as doing more than is strictly necessary to realize the verse design, manifesting verse design more or less complexly, neutrally, or efficiently. It is relevant to enquire what part of the linguistic structure of the text is 'active' in this way: a vague concept such as 'the language of the line' is inadequate. The language of a text, as it figures in a linguistic description, has three components: syntactic, semantic, and phonological.[6] The syntactic component enumerates sentences each of which has a *deep structure* and a *surface structure.*[7] The deep structure does not concern us, since it is not directly related to the overt form of a text—it is the point at which the lexical formatives (with their semantic features) and categorial relations are introduced, and many transformational and phonological operations intervene before a deep structure 'becomes' a well-formed sentence. Surface structure in the syntactic component contains the following information:

(*a*) identification of lexical formatives according to their phonological composition;

(*b*) specification of junctures, i.e. directions on how the formatives are to be concatenated;

(*c*) segmentation into grammatical phrases (e.g. *grammatical phrases* but not *on how the*);

(*d*) functional characterization of the types of phrases involved – noun, verb, etc.

(Chomsky: 'the surface structure of a sentence is a properly labelled bracketing of a classificatory matrix of formatives and junctures'.)[8] Given this information, the phonological component assigns a *phonetic contour* to a surface structure: if we have this information we know what the sentence sounds like.[9] We need no information about deep structure: for example, although we need to know the nature of the juxtaposition *grammatical phrases* in surface structure, we do not need to know that this construction presupposes a deep structure which would be represented as *the phrases are grammatical*; nor do we need to know anything about the 'meaning' of *grammatical* or *phrase* or *-s*.

A verse design may be fulfilled by a certain phonetic contour, a configuration of stresses, pitch tunes, sound qualities, linearly patterned and dependent on surface structure. If the surface structure of a poem can be determined, the metre can be stated, without reference to an 'oral rendition' or a 'written text' but relying on the linguistic form which underlies both of these *representations* of a poem.

Verse type[10]

The first division necessary to metrics is that between verse and non-verse. Verse is measured language. It has defining regularities of patterning additional to those demanded by linguistic structure as a matter of course. In theory, any feature of a language which can be regulated against a time-scale is available for metrical use. Repetition of a syntactic structure, as in some kinds of free verse (e.g. Old Testament Hebrew), will suffice in theory. In practice it is inadequate unless the syntactic repetition also entails constancy of phonetic reiteration. Metre is an oral/aural phenomenon, and its language is measured by control of features capable of perceptible phonetic realization. Linguistic features available for metrical use are those which are phonologically distinctive in a language: that is, those sound-distinctions which are structurally regular. So 'stress' (syllabic prominence achieved by one or more of several phonetic qualities), being phonologically active in English, is metrically relevant for English verse, but not for French or Japanese; 'tone' (where 'the pitch levels or the rising and falling pitches are properties of the words as lexical items')[11] can be the metrical basis for Chinese or Vietnamese but not English.

The range of phonological qualities found in natural languages (independent of historical links and boundaries between them) sets the possible range of verse types. A particular type is identified by the phonological features used in metrical organization. The categories are 'tonal', 'stress-timed', 'syllable-timed', 'quantitative' and so on. Issues in metrics which are typological in nature are, for example, the difference between Chaucer's and Langland's verse, and, much the same question, Hopkins' distinction between Running or Standard Rhythm and Sprung Rhythm.[12] Of course, the supplanting of the stress-based metre of Old English by isosyllabic verse-forms can be explained by appeal to externals of history (French cultural influence) but the primary differentiation is of type.

We may illustrate the character of a typological statement by considering Old English poetry.[13] 'Stress' is an important component of Germanic phonology. By whatever phonetic means a syllable is made more prominent than its neighbours, the prominence is available for syntactic or semantic use: parts of an utterance may be picked out for emphasis; some pairs of words are distinguished only by differential prominence of syllables; polysyllabic words consistently take stress on one syllable rather than another; finally, the 'stressed' syllables of an utterance tend to occur relatively evenly spaced in time—English is naturally 'isochronous'. This regularity means that it is naturally rhythmical. It was made metrical[14] in Old English by control of the linguistic fact by which it was rhythmical. Stresses were grouped to make a metrical unit—the four-stress line with its component half-lines—by strict alliteration (most often AAAB, but patterned variation was allowed, as in *The Battle of Maldon*) and by the consistent concurrence of phrase- or clause-boundaries with the ends of half-lines. There was one other ingredient in this recipe for a verse type: limitation on the number of unprominent syllables between stresses. In a sample of 100 lines from *Beowulf* (710–809) the average number of 'unstressed' syllables between the first and second stresses was found to be 1·49. Hopkins (ed. cit., pp. 9–10) speaks of 'one, two, or three slack syllables' between the stresses in sprung rhythm. Although count of syllables is not fundamental to this verse type (which may be called 'isoaccentual' or 'stress-timed'), it is not difficult to see why relative consistency, and limitation of number, are important in the treatment of slack syllables. Even though they may be validated by theme or mood, Old English hypermetrical lines[15] lack the momentum and insistence of the short lines of *Beowulf*; and in Middle English *Piers Plowman* is surely, for this reason, justly accused of metrical inertia: it is not unlike prose.[16]

Verse design

Statements next in generality to those of metrical type are descriptions of verse design. A verse design is a generalization which accounts for broad similarities and differences of metrical structure among poems and poets. It may be described and formalized by the literary historian, used to identify and label verse traditions. A study of the verse designs of a period may or may not be helped by noticing contemporaneous theory or prescription: in fact, it is immaterial whether a particular verse design had a label during the period of its currency: the design 'iambic pentameter' is no less real simply because this name was not applied until it had been flourishing for several centuries. Nor need words like 'design' or 'selection' (natural to a historical classification) imply clear consciousness or perfect analysis by the poet.

'Iambic pentameter' is a verse design; so are 'blank verse', 'heroic couplet', and 'sonnet'. The first, however, is a superordinate of the others: descriptions of verse designs are variable in generality—up to a certain level, where the ground is covered by verse type, and down to a lower limit, where verse instance takes over. Verse design distinguishes, within the same type, octosyllabic from decasyllabic metres; rhymed from unrhymed verse; iambic from spondaic; couplets from four-line stanzas, etc. Shakespeare's blank verse, that of *Paradise Lost*, and that of *The Prelude* may be classed together; but a broader category can accommodate these and *The Rape of the Lock* and *The Deserted Village* too. Subdivision of the iambic class ('pentameter' is one subdivision) can be as delicate as one wants (down to a certain limit), taking into account historical factors and questions of genre. (Below the lower limit of verse design, the line between it and verse instance, some of the descriptive metrical statements most important to criticism are made: for example, distinguishing between the metrical texture of *Hyperion* and *Paradise Lost*; *The Rape of the Lock* and *The Deserted Village*; Shakespeare's early and late blank verse.)

Verse design is a generalization of verse instances. In view of the fact that verse instances are based on linguistic entities (sentences capable of full phonetic realization), Jakobson's denial that verse design is an 'abstract, theoretical scheme' is apposite—with the qualification that design is often relatively far removed from the particularities of utterance. However, verse instances are not arrived at by downward extension of classes of verse design. Verse design is set for a poem as a whole, and does not vary from line to line. So, *at the level of verse design*, a poem in iambic pentameters has every line a 'regular' iambic pentameter. 'Variation' or 'irregularity' is noted at the level of verse instance. We can have an *instance* | – ∪| | ∪ – / ∪ – / ∪ – / ∪ – / which is at the same time the *design* | ∪ – / ∪ – / ∪ – / ∪ – / ∪ – /. This may seem odd and uneconomical. It would be easy to state possibilities for reversed feet as subclasses in the design rules for the pentameter. So | – ∪ / ∪ – / ∪ – / ∪ – / ∪ – | could be listed as a permitted alternative to | ∪ – / ∪ – / ∪ –/ ∪ – / ∪ – /; another rule would exclude | ∪ – / ∪ – / ∪ – / ∪ – / – ∪|. Similarly with the rules for feminine endings: | ∪ – / ∪ – / ∪ – / ∪ – / ∪ – (∪) | could be offered as an alternative selection to | ∪ – / ∪ – / ∪ – / ∪ – / ∪ – /. Optionally, the design rules could be two-part, first giving possibilities for the foot and then showing where the selections could be used within the line. In either case, each line would consist of a selection at the level of design. I find this aesthetically and psychologically unsubtle. In a sense, every line in a poem 'written in iambic pentameters' *is* | ∪ – / ∪ – / ∪ – / ∪ – / ∪ – /, even if it demands to be scanned with a different sequence of ictus and non-ictus. The verse design in its perceptual reflex 'metrical set' is | ∪ – / ∪ – / ∪ – / ∪ – / ∪ – /, and this serves as a frame for variant actualizations (instances). We see instance through the grid of metrical set, and where the grid will not fit there can be a point of high rhetorical marking:

> But oh! if e'er thy *Gnome* could spoil a Grace,
> Or raise a Pimple on a beauteous Face,
> Like Citron-Waters Matrons' Cheeks inflame,
> Or change Complexions at a losing Game;
> If e'er with airy Horns I planted Heads,
> Or rumpled Petticoats, or tumbled Beds,
> Or caus'd Suspicion when no Soul was rude,
> Or discompos'd the Head-dress of a Prude,
> Or e'er to costive Lapdog gave Disease,
> Which not the Tears of brightest Eyes could ease:
>
> ‾   ‿
> Hear me, and touch *Belinda* with Chagrin,
> That single Act gives half the World the Spleen.
>
> (*Rape of the Lock*, iv, 67—78)

This is not to imply that all deviant realizations of verse design are heavily charged rhetorically—this is not the case even with the basically regular and profoundly rhetorical Pope. But however the 'effect' of a reversal or substitution is described, it is most satisfyingly seen as an effect of the opposition of instance and design-based set, not as neutral selection of an alternative design.

A second dimension of line-variation best treated at the level of instance may be illustrated by comparing two lines from *Tamburlaine*:

1. One thought, one grace, one wonder at the least

is different from

2. My discipline of arms and chivalry

although both are, ictically, perfect and identical examples of the design $\smile - / \smile - / \smile - / \smile - / \smile - /$. Yet they are very different in feel: randomly and informally, one could notice the interrupting major junctures after *thought* and *grace* in 1, which cannot be inserted at the corresponding points in 2; the very different prominence of the tenth syllable in each line, a direct result of the different grammatical status of the syllables in question; the word-boundary between the third and fourth feet in 2 contrasted with the overlapping word *wonder* at the corresponding point in 1. The overall difference in texture may be tested by selecting a reading appropriate to 1 and attempting (ludicrously) to transfer it to 2. It is clear that the phonetic contours required by the syntax of these lines are absolutely non-interchangeable.

It would be unsatisfactory to regard these two lines as metrically distinct lines selected ready-made from a vast inventory of distinct design pentameters. Setting aside the implausibility of this as a model of poetic composition, it has an over-mechanical suggestion of the process of reading poetry: if each line is a different design, the two-level model which seeks to explain 'tension' is lost and the principle of underlying sameness through the constancy of verse design is removed. Another criticism concerns the size of such an inventory. If the Trager–Smith system is used, the number of such designs within the iambic pentameter class is enormous. The work of Epstein and Hawkes (see note 2) is the most notorious example of this confusion of instance and design. They compute 6,236 kinds of iambic feet, 2,376 trochees. The figures soar even higher when the combinatorial possibilities in lines are considered. Just such vast numbers of lines *may be* encountered: but the numbers are so formidable that we are better off viewing each instance as unique, a distinctive product of the marriage of metrical set and syntactic structure. Chatman (who comments on Epstein and Hawkes, *Theory*, pp. 98–9) asserts (p. 14): 'I take the position that the metrist's function is not to find out how many kinds of feet there are, but rather to insure that there aren't any more kinds than necessary.' At the level of design, this is fundamental: design, whether of foot or line, must be regarded as simple and constant.

If verse design is not often present at the poem's surface, how can we know what it is? Recognition is probably much more informal, more based on hunch and trial and error, than any systematic discovery technique a linguist might propose:

> If I see an English poem printed on a page with lines of a certain length, on a page of a certain size, in a certain type face; if I happen to notice pairs of end rhymes here and there, then even without bothering to count syllables I will make a guess. I will say that these are probably pentameter lines, probably heroic couplets, even though I don't know when they were written, even though I am only glancing at the page (not *reading*, or *counting*). When a sophisticated reader reads iambic pentameter verse, his expectations are going to get more flexible the more of a total stock of iambic pentameter lines he has experienced.[17]

The rough-and-ready contribution of the practised reader of poetry is probably a quick and reliable short-cut to experiencing a verse design in a new poem. But even if we imagine a situation where the reader does not readily detect the metre on the basis of his past experience, and the language itself has to do all the work, the process is not difficult to understand. A line of poetry—an *efficient* line of poetry—incorporates definite signals, open to anyone who knows the language, which establish it as a particular verse instance or at least as one of a small range of possible alternative instances. The signals —lexical stress in polysyllabic words, phrase accent, rhyme, etc.— are, largely thanks to Chatman's book, now well understood. Instance can be established, and design is an 'average' of instances: the most prominent ictic patterning in the poem is the design of that poem, and we read all lines with it in mind. It is sometimes claimed that poets make the openings of poems dense with 'regular' lines to fix metrical set early. The truth of this claim is doubtful, and in fact it does not matter where the design-fixing lines are sited: understanding is a tentative and cumulative process, and a second reading refines one's perception of the first. The numerical basis of this 'average' is, it must be admitted, difficult to imagine, if indeed it exists. We would not want to say that a poem with 51 per cent of lines beginning $- \cup$ has the verse design $/ - \cup / \cup - / \cup - / \cup - / \cup - /$, for the 'experienced reader' could compensate for this marginal preponderance.

For describing verse designs in their historical or generic relations, only a curtailed and abstract apparatus is required. Because of the indirectness of connection between verse design and language, this is not a technical linguistic vocabulary. The terms are such as 'iamb', 'couplet', 'tetrameter'. The description for iambic pentameters will include: decasyllabicity, achieved by a single rule for the segmental construction of syllables—syllables 10 and 20, 30 and 40, 50 and 60 . . . n–10 and n must rhyme;[18] lexical stress and phrase accent must mark around five ictuses (sometimes less but rarely more) in a considerable majority of lines—this determines rhythm or, as Chatman terms it, 'primary rhythm . . . simple periodic return of a given stimulus'; the sequence of ictus and non-ictus is $\cup -$: this defines secondary rhythm (sequence of *grouped* stimuli) for that design. Whether one calls this sub-unit a 'foot' is optional. Sometimes, as in describing verse which contains many substitutions (e.g. trisyllabic for disyllabic), the foot is indispensable. But it is only an analytic convention and has little to do with language—it is 'purely "notional"'.[19]

Metrical set[20]

Hollander speaks of 'the experienced reader', reminding us of a fact too often ignored by metrical theorists: that metre is located in the responses of a reader as well as in the linguistic features of a poem. The reader makes an active (which is not to say conscious) contribution, compensating readily for the linguistic inefficiency so necessary if a poem is to be attractively various in its verse instances. For some readers, knowledge of a poem's author or period of composition is all that is required to induce perception of design. For most, 'metre-fixing' lines act not so much to enforce a verse design as to confirm a hypothesis: 'let us see whether this poem makes sense read as iambic pentameters.' Although one must assume some linguistic presence for a metre-fixing design, it may be that its power is rather to prevent misreading than to dictate a reading absolutely.

Metrical set may be informally defined as 'a reader's disposition, through past experience and through design-signals in the poem, to impose a familiar reading on any metre which does not absolutely forbid it'. We have two uses to make of the notion: as an explanation of how readers of poetry discover designs in relatively irregular poems, and as a factor in the determination of instances. The metaphor of a 'grid' was intended to suggest a frame through which we see poetry, a frame simpler in structure than language most often is. More accurately for the theory of verse instance, and psychologically more credible, metrical set exists as a sequence of expectations that the phonetic contour of a line will fulfil the prescription of verse design in several respects: number of events (e.g. syllables) capable of bearing metrical marking (e.g. prominence in any of its aspects— stress, pitch, length, etc.); lawfulness of the linear sequence of ictus and non-ictus (e.g. $/ \cup - / \cup - / \cup - / \cup - / \cup - /$); binicity[21] of the design's marking-parameter (long *v.* short syllabic, high *v.* low pitch, etc.). These must be understood to be categories of verse design,[22] not of metrical set: metrical set must not be spuriously reified. It is a behavioural disposition on the part of (silent) readers and of listeners, acquired by experience of and generalization from a formally homogeneous body of poetry. It is not random or idiosyncratic. For a given design, metrical set is relatively stable for the individual reader at one stage of his literary education, and is culturally shared, with significant variation only in readers with very little experience of poetry, just as the native language and the texts of the literature are shared. Metrical set in this sense gives meaning to such locutions as 'abstract metre' and 'ideal metre' which have been so troublesome in the past.[23]

Verse instance

Verse instance is one of the products of the meeting of determinate sound and determinate meaning.[24] John Crowe Ransom, focusing on the composition end of the poetic process, presents the character of an individual line as the result of the poet's compromise between the demands of his chosen metrical form and those of his intended meaning. Ransom's 'indeterminate sound' is (or at least includes) verse instance. From the point of view of the poet, 'determinate sound' is verse design. However, we are more interested here in the reader's experience of the finished line, and we may express the situation this way: verse instance is the quality of a line which will emerge for a reader who has an adequate metrical set as he interprets adequately the syntax of the line.

Truth to behavioural reality does not ensure descriptive convenience, and it is apparent that there is a grave descriptive difficulty here. For a useful descriptive metrics, we must assume that the character of a line is inherent in the poem (as Jakobson, Sebeok p. 366, says of 'tension'): yet my account suggests that verse instance is a matter of individual (and thus idiosyncratic) reader experience. This inference is not wholly accurate: verse instance is indeed vulnerable to the personal contribution of the reader, but the criterion of adequate interpretation is built into the definition. Both of the variables producing verse instance must be adequately achieved to generate instances which really derive from the poem. An adequate metrical set is one which embodies expectations of phonetic fulfilment appropriate to the verse design: for example, that each upcoming syllable will be ictic or not, in a certain sequence and within a certain numerical limit. Verse design, unlike metrical set, contains analytic categories, and these may be invoked in the study of instances: for descriptive convenience, though not in the construction of a valid model of reader participation in verse. The concept of an adequate interpretation of the language of a line is realizable, but it will not do to ignore the complications. Difference of opinion on the determinate meaning of poetry is a major fact of the critic's professional life. But metrics does not require the discovery of one true and uncontested meaning: what is required is one or more meaning(s) which the interpreter can justify by an articulate and conscientious account of the line's semantic and syntactic composition. In this way a metrist can say that a verse instance is, if not one single thing, at least one or other of a set of understandable and discussible alternatives.[25] A second caution to the automatic acceptance of the concept of 'the language of the line' is that, although its grammar or possible grammars may be readily describable, it is not grammar *per se* that we are concerned with, but the phonetic implications of the surface structure as providing confirmation or denial of metrical set. Linguists no longer believe that a particular syntax is specified in detail by a unique suprasegmental realization. That the loss of this certainty of phonological prediction does not prejudice the whole enterprise will, it is hoped, be demonstrated; but we must be aware of the limitation.

Though metrical set can be handled through the categories of verse design (as long as we realize the artificial conflation of levels involved in doing this), and, given certain cautions, an adequate linguistic interpretation may be assumed, verse instance is neither metrical set nor the language of the line, but a product of the two. The ontology of verse instance remains uncertain, and means of direct description cannot be devised. As Wimsatt and Beardsley say, 'you cannot write a grammar of the meter's interaction with the sense'.[26] However, a product of two variables can be treated in terms of those variables. In what follows, metrical set is understood as adequate and constant for a stated verse design; therefore, where verse instance varies it does so under the influence of varying linguistic form. Subject to the qualification that we have not yet decided on the exact correlation between syntax and phonology, we will say that verse instance varies consistently with syntactic variation and that a description of the surface structure of a line serves as the description of a verse instance. (But the line as syntax is not the same as the line as verse instance.)

J. R. Firth maintained that all texts (presumably including verse) have 'implication of utterance'.[27] This seems a necessary and sensible assertion: it is a fact that oral readers of written texts can agree fairly closely on a phonetic contour. Chomsky, Halle, and Lukoff notice 'that native speakers can assign stress patterns to new utterances in a fairly consistent and uniform manner'.[28] However, the assumptions underlying these statements have been denied frequently, and enter into one of the fiercest debates in recent linguistics, the dispute over the relation of syntax and phonology. One denial comes from Robert P. Stockwell:

> If we assume, with Chomsky, that the crucial undertaking of linguistic analysis is to discover and describe the rules of sentence formation, we must assume a variety of 'elements' or 'formatives' on which rules operate to generate sentences. Among these formatives we must include intonation patterns, unless we believe they are all morphophonemically predictable by rules constructed in terms of the nonintonational sequence of formatives. This latter assumption is certainly a possible one, but no one has, to my knowledge, succeeded in constructing even a remotely approximate set of rules which will succeed on this assumption. There is, furthermore, a good deal of evidence . . . that intonation patterns are the absolutely minimal differentiators of numerous utterance tokens.[29]

The contention here is that stress-pitch-juncture patterns are units in the grammar, on a par with, say, structural order and word-class and as active as these non-phonological features in determining meaning. A distinctive intonation pattern, it is said, may be the only means of distinguishing two linguistically different but 'syntactically identical' utterances:

ímports: impórts
íncrease: incréase

I'm going home no~w~: I'm going home now

You know what to d^o [question]: You know what to do

líght hóusekeeper: líghthouse-keeper

I do not deny that disambiguating phonologies can be created—or at least one can persuade an interlocutor that he hears them—when adequate verbal and non-verbal context is not provided. However, we can almost invariably understand an utterance given proper context; in so far as this is verbal context, we are saying that interpretation comes from syntax without the mediation of phonology. Suprasegmentals do not uniquely specify syntactic structures in a systematic way, are not reliably diagnostic for syntax except in some very broad distinctions, and are manifestly not indispensable (written language exists). A patterned phonetic contour is an obligatory concomitant of speech; the patterns are regular and predictable, and certain broad regularities are *derived from* syntactic organization; conscious reference may be made to intonation contours in rare cases where context is inadequate. There is some scope for manipulating such variables as syllabic prominence for special emphasis or attitudinal annotation, but the phonetic contour comprises, on the whole, 'the tunes one has to play' rather than the 'tricks one can play on the tunes'. The distinction is so worded by Lee S. Hultzén, who gives due weight to the automatic, unchosen character of intonation:

> In every utterance, a man has to do certain things intonation-wise because he speaks a particular language or dialect with a particular accent and is the man he is, in the mood he happens to be in at the moment. The communication in this part of the tune, if the hearer can interpret, is that and nothing more . . . Whatever is specific in the interpretation [of the text rather than the tune as above] may be got more from the text in its material and linguistic context than from the refined shape of the intonation.[30]

Speaking a particular language involves, for example, giving prominence to prescribed syllables of English polysyllabic words; shaping intonation patterns to a certain predictable 'fit' with a clause. Such rules as these are part of Chomsky's 'systematic phonemics', the input end of the phonological component of a grammar.[31] The output end ('systematic phonetics') is a 'phonetic contour' which is 'largely an automatic reflection of the syntactic structure' (Chomsky, *Topics*, p. 88, cf. p. 83). That the phonetic contour of a text is systematic does not mean that its organization is the source of our intuitions of structure. We understand written texts in the absence of a phonetic contour, and spoken utterances with incorrect contours (in listening to an unskilful yet fluent foreign speaker). 'Since in any event, the phonetic contour is largely an automatic reflection of the syntactic structure, it follows that any one who understands an utterance and thus, in particular, has determined its surface structure should be able to predict the phonetic contour by rules that constitute part of his linguistic competence.' This states elaborately the obvious fact that people can read aloud, but the elaboration gives the phonetic contour its correct status and so justifies the descriptive strategy necessary here: without bothering about the 'phonemic' (old-style) character of our predictions, we can propose a distinctive phonetic contour (and so, by juxtaposition with metrical set, a distinctive verse instance) if we can describe the overt syntax of a line. Furthermore, since that part of the phonetic contour which concerns only the shared rules of utterance for the language (excluding style, paralanguage and voice set) varies automatically and consistently with syntax and choice of lexical items, we can identify verse instances by reference to the non-phonological make-up of a line, without a refined phonetic apparatus. The following rules are all that are needed for discovering the distribution of ictus and non-ictus in an English poem:

I. In all English words of more than one syllable, one particular syllable is more prominent[32] than the other(s): *repáir, bánkrupt, dáughter*. Where there are three or more syllables, there are regular gradations from the most to the least prominent syllable, with 'relatively prominent' and 'relatively unprominent' syllables alternating in a patterned way:

2 4 1 5 3	3 1 4 2	2 4 1 5 3	2 3 1 4
opportunity	eradicate	mathematical	approbation

The pattern is learnt with the word; lexical selection automatically selects the pattern.

II. In all grammatical English sentences certain words are more prominent than others: *It was an interesting expérience for the péople who atténded*. Pitch-change is most effective in signalling the syllables which are prominent in this pattern. In some sub-sentence sequences, relative prominence is firmly prescribed: e.g. *to the cóuntry, not very búsy, didn't sée them, he will cóme*. For the effect of changing these patterns, see rule III. Some other sequences enjoy greater latitude: *a big dog* may be *a big dóg* or *a bíg dóg* (but *a bíg dog* brings rule III into play). It seems natural to say that under rule II it is the 'most important' words which are sentence-prominent, defining 'importance' in terms of word-class (see Jones, p. 262). However, no one has yet succeeded in writing out all the details of rule II in a systematic way.

III. The 'normal' pitch-stress contours of rule II can be optionally overriden where a word is picked out for special emphasis (e.g. *he spends áll his time reading*); to contrast a word with some other in the immediate context (*not* Mr *Jones but* Dr *Jones*); to bring out a semantic contrast not present in the immediate context and possibly missed under the normal intonation (e.g. *I'm véry busy*, excluding *quite busy, rather busy*, etc.); to clarify after misunderstanding (*I said increase, not décrease*); to affirm belief, purpose, etc., transcending statement of fact (*he will come*). The mechanism for achieving these effects is commonly extra-heavy stress or shifting of the nucleus of an intonation contour. The dependence on phonetic signal in this 'marked' state obviously means a lower degree of predictability than with the syntactically determined phonetic contours. Yet often the need for the application of rule III is clear in a written text.

IV. Most usually coterminous with the syntactic unit clause (though often ignoring the boundaries of embedded [subordinate] clauses), and with some types of phrase (especially phrases in apposition and parallel) is the intonation contour. This is a patterned sequence of pitch levels with a neutral beginning, a linear progress determined often by dialect features (e.g. the gradually falling levels in the body of 'Tune 1' in British RP) and one or more[33] nuclei. The nucleus is a critical point in an intonation contour where, on or including the final prominent syllable, the direction of pitch-change alters or is steepened rather sharply. The rule is central to any discussion of caesura and enjambment, and for our present purpose is useful in reinforcing our predictions of prominence in some syllables, especially where rule II does not help.

Little more than this is necessary to signal the positions of ictus in a line. The 'more' is usually metrical set, the natural tendency to follow verse design wherever syntax does not clearly signal ictus. Verse which we recognize as simple to scan is so by virtue of a syntax which is efficient in signalling prominences and of a powerfully realized verse design. Here is an example of such simple verse, with ictic syllables italicized. It is followed by an annotation of the reasons for these assignments of ictus.

1 4 6 8 10
Know then thy*self*, pre*sume* not *God* to *scan*;

12 14 16 18 20
The *pro*per *stu*dy *of* man*kind* is *Man.*

21 24 26 28 30
Plac'd on this *isth*mus *of* a *midd*le *state,*

32 34 36 38 40
A *being* *dark*ly *wise,* and *rude*ly *great*:

42 44 46 48 50
With *too* much *know*ledge *for* the *Scep*tic *side,*

52 54 56 58 60
With *too* much *weak*ness *for* the *Sto*ic's *pride,*

62 64 66 68 70
He *hangs* be*tween*; in *doubt* to *act,* or *rest*;

72 74 76 78 80
In *doubt* to *deem* him*self* a *God,* or *Beast*;

82 84 86 88 90
In *doubt* his *Mind* or *Body* *to* pre*fer*;

91 94 96 98 100
Born but to *die,* and *reas*'ning *but* to *err*;

Syllables 4, 6, 12, 14, 18,[34] 24, 28, 32, 34, 38, 44, 48, 54, 58, 64, 76, 86, 90, and 96 are ictic by rule I.

Syllables 10, 62, 66, 68, 70, 72, 74, 78, 80, 82, 84, 94, and 100 are ictic under rule II. Less clear examples of the operation of rule II are syllables 1, 21, 42, 52, and 91. Their weight is reinforced by rhetorical, and partly negative, factors. If we did not make 1, *Know*, ictic, we would be forced to confer prominence on 2, *then*. This could be justified only if rule III operated; however, *then* does not specify any particular prior-noticed time, but means 'therefore' or some similar loosely continuative sense. Ictic 21 (rather than 22) has a similar justification. As for *too* (42 and 52), this is justified by similar, though less compelling, negative reasoning: ictic 43 (*much*) would, at least for anyone who knew Pope's manner well, demand a contrast at syllable 53(–54): *little*. *With* (41, 51) makes no sense at all if realized as ictic. The metrical stress on 91 cannot be justified under rule II because *Born but* is not a viable linguistic segment; here we invoke the word-class super-ordination of *Born* over *but* and the rhetorical pointlessness of making *but* prominent within its intonation contour.

8, *God*, bears metrical stress by being prominent under rule III. The contrast *thyself/God* has to be brought out, most likely by making *God* pitch-prominent.

Syllables 20, 30, 36, 40, 50, and 60 are ictic under rule IV: these syllables are all nuclear. Note also that rule IV confirms ictus on some syllables marked under I or II: e.g. 70, 80, 94, 100.

We are left with syllables 16, 26, 46, 56, 88, and 98; to put it more accurately, metrical set (five ictuses per line) suggests that ictus falls on one syllable from each of the stretches 15–17, 26–7, 45–7, 55–7, 87–9, 97–9. At face value, the syllables marked (16, 26, 46, 56, 88, 98) are poor candidates. None is picked out by any of the basic rules I–IV; all are functional items, lexically unimportant; all have reducible vowels, the most probable pronunciation being [ə]. Yet there are good reasons against marking the surrounding syllables as ictic: 15, 17, 25, 45, 55, 87, 89, and 97 are parts of two-syllable words of which the other syllable is unequivocally ictic under rule I; and the monosyllables 27, 47, 57, and 99 could be ictic only by a pitch-prominence which would be difficult to justify rhetorically and semantically. The syllables chosen are ictic for negative reasons and because of the fact of this verse design that it is generally alternate syllables which are ictic. I do not want to suggest that these ictuses are on a par with the other 44 marked in this text; simply, that they can be accommodated to the general pattern without doing too much violence to the language. The important fact is that in this very short sample 88 per cent of ictuses can be predicted on definite linguistic grounds— this dimension of verse-instance (placement of ictus) is unquestionably derived from language itself.

Some ictuses in the Pope extract for which a skeletal metrical structure has been provided appear to be of interest as far as 'weight of ictus' is concerned. Syllable 8 looks as if it might be especially prominent (appropriately), 16, 26, 46, 88, and 98 especially unprominent. The next eight lines contain several syllables of similar interest. I have italicized syllables which are ictic by rules I–IV and numbered those which need further discussion:

A*like* in *ig*norance, his *reason such*,
106

*Wheth*er he *thinks* too *litt*le, or too *much*:
118

*Cha*os of *thought* and *passion*, *all* con*fus'd*

Still by him*self* a*bus'd*, or *dis*abus'd;
140

Created *half* to *rise*, and *half* to *fall*;

Great lord of *all* things, yet a *prey* to *all*;
151 152   156

Sole ju¹⁶¹dge of *Truth*, in *end*less *err*or *hurl'd*:

The *glory, jest* and *ridd*le of the *world*;

Syllables 118, 156,³⁵ and 178 have the same status as 16, 26, etc.; calling these syllables ictic invites us to enquire into the nature of ictus as a generalization. These syllables stretch it to the limit of its tolerance; and yet we must remember that here is not a case of a performer taking liberties with metrical stress by lightening it to an extreme degree—in fact, if a performer made 118 or 178 as prominent as, say, 120 *much* or 180 *world* he would be distorting the contour appropriate to these phrases.

The final syllables of *ignorance* (106) and *disabused* (140) are in positions where ictus is expected. Under rule I the first syllable of *ignorance* is most prominent, the third less, the second least. In *disabused* the final syllable is normally prominent here; however, the first syllable gains main prominence through the parallelism with *abused*. The resistance to heavy stress on syllables 106 and 140 comes from the principle that English words (other than double-barrelled words like *organ-grinder*) can receive only one 'main stress': here, on syllables 104 and 138. Thus the status of 106 and 140 is not unlike that of 16, 26, etc.: ictus is 'weakly realized'—though 106 and 140 are realized by ∧ (secondary) as against ∖ (tertiary) for the monosyllables: the absence of word-juncture before the syllables in question makes the difference. A further difference of weight, this time between 106 and 140, lies in the difference of vowel quality: 106's [ə] against 140's [u]. It is details like these which make metrical texture so various.

In 151–2 and 161–2 the possibilities are ∪ –, – ∪, or – –. Metrical considerations apart, phrases of this structure may occur as *great lórd* or *gréat lórd*, the latter being more characteristic of British English. *Gréat lord* (*sóle judge*) would need special justification under rule III. Since *lord* and *prey* form a clear antithesis which would be destroyed if *great* were ictic, the metrical analysis – ∪ seems insupportable. As for *Sole judge*, there seems no reason to analyse it as – ∪: the uniqueness of man's wisdom and folly is not at issue so much as the paradox of his perplexed rationality. There is no good syntactic reason to choose between – – and ∪ – in either case, and the semantic arguments, though interesting, are inconclusive. Note that the inconclusive debate would be about the interpretation of the language under rule III, not about the performance of these lines.

In such cases, where the language is permissive on stress-placement, alternative judgments of the position of ictus must be allowed—sometimes large numbers of alternatives (cf. Chatman's discussion of *Who would not weep for Lycidas?, Theory*, pp. 151–2). Scansions here can be debated, and we might follow Chatman's useful practice of incorporating in the visual display all alternative scansions based on reasonable interpretations of meaning; e.g.

$$\overset{\cup\quad-}{-}\ -\ \cup\ -\ \cup\ -\ \cup\ -\ \cup\ -$$

Great lord of all things, yet a prey to all;

$$\overset{\cup\quad-}{-}\ -\ \cup\ -\ \cup\ -\ \cup\ -\ \cup\ -$$

Sole judge of truth, in endless error hurl'd.

After one determines as far as possible which syllables of a line are ictic, knowing how (in the above terms) one has made the decisions, a whole area of descriptive metrics—the patterns of verse instances against the norm of verse design—becomes fairly straightforward. One might then, with Robert Bridges, decide to follow this programme:

> . . . English blank verse may conveniently be regarded as a
> decasyllabic line on a disyllabic basis and in rising rhythm
> (i.e. with accents or stresses on the alternate even syllables);
> and the disyllabic units may be called *feet* . . .
>   In the following chapters we will examine the exceptions to
> these conditions, namely:
>   I Exceptions to the number of syllables being ten,
>   II Exceptions to the number of stresses being five,
>   III Exceptions in the position of the stresses . . .[36]

Discussion of III, utilizing such categories as 'reversed' and 'level' feet, is simple and has traditionally been carried on efficiently by metrists. One word of caution is that these categories cover segments of verse which are linguistically more or less artificial; they are not subject to consistent phonetic definition. A foot which is judged $-\cup$ at the level of verse instance may be realized in a delivery instance with a second syllable of greater intensity than the first, but it is perceived as a sequence $-\cup$. Likewise, spondees and pyrrhic feet rarely (perhaps never) consist of pairs of syllables of equal phonetic prominence. II, 'exceptions to the number of stresses being five', invites an answer to the question already implied (of the 'unprominent' ictic syllables in Pope): 'when is an ictus not an ictus?' I, variation in syllable-count, is from the linguist's point of view not an entirely simple matter. The syllable is not a unit which can be taken for granted. It may be defined by appeal to any of several very different criteria, and its acoustic and articulatory boundaries are far from clear-cut.[37] However, as Chatman says, metrics is 'concerned mostly with the number of syllables-as-events; syllables are easily recognized, and the problem of identifying their boundaries rarely matters' (*Theory*, p. 39). The crest of a syllable has enough reality as a perceptual unit for one to recognize it as a clear event in a delivery instance, and in a written text one can determine whether an orthographic sequence contains a syllabic (vowel or syllabic consonant) which has to be realized at peril of distortion of phonological convention.

Extra-metrical syllables are an important source of variation in the texture of instances in several verse designs—in the classical French Alexandrine in distich- and hemistich-final positions, and in English blank verse, for example. They are variable as to frequency, distribution, and phonetic and syntactic constituency. Thus we have a feature potentially profound in effect and available for many highly distinctive manipulations.

The most celebrated extensive use of extra-metrical syllables is in *Paradise Lost*. The existence of large numbers of excess syllables is not in doubt: when Bridges discussed 'Supernumerary syllables accounted for by Elision' he did not intend 'accounted for' to mean 'physically removed':

> In English verse where there is poetic elision of the terminal vowel of one word before the initial vowel of the next word, *the sound of it is not lost*, the two vowels are glided together, and the conditions may be called synaloepha.
> For instance the first example of terminal synaloepha in *P.L.* is
>> Above th'Aonian Mount, while it pursues. i.15
> where the final vowel of *the* is glided into the A of Aonian, it is still *heard* in the glide, though *prosodically asyllabic* . . . [T]he first of two such vowels is *theoretically 'cut out'* of the prosody or scansion.[38]

The intention is to provide for lines which are linguistically of eleven (or more) syllables but which are decasyllabic as far as scansion is concerned. For Bridges 'elision' is a historically more satisfactory explanation than 'equivalence', which admits extra-metrical syllables into the scansional scheme by marking trisyllabic feet as substitutions for disyllabic ($\cup \cup - = \cup -$).

Under the present approach, a syllable which is in the language counts in verse instance. Bridges' data[37] reveal a device which,

far from doing away with extra syllables, points to their presence
as an important characteristic of verse texture. Milton underscores
this device (intentionally or not) by his spelling. In Book III of
Paradise Lost (which is 742 lines long) there are about 230[40] places
where metrical set suggests the loss of a syllable. Many of these are
indicated also by the Miltonic apostrophe (*Heav'n, th'Almighty*);
sometimes the apostrophe is used where no elision is required:
e.g. 171 *spok'n* /spoʊkən/, 329 *hast'n* /heɪsən/ (or/spoʊkn̩/, /heɪsn̩/).
About half of these elisions necessary to yield decasyllabic lines
are, in one way or another, 'unpronounceable'. By this I do not
mean phonetically impossible; the syllable-reduced word or words
do not conform to the rules governing the orders in which one can
juxtapose phonemes in English. For example, *effluence* (6) rendered disyllabic is /eflwəns/, *heav'nly* (19, 213, 217, 298) /hevnli/.
The repeated *heav'n* suggests an unlawful English monosyllable
/hevn/, which is conceivable only where the word *heaven* (and
Ev'n 42, *driv'n* 677) is followed by a vowel, as in *Heav'n and Earth*,
133, 146, etc.: blends such as /hevnənd/ and /drɪvnaʊt/ are phonologically achievable, but the resulting lexical peculiarities (by the
loss of word-juncture) make them surely unacceptable. Similar
objections apply to taking Milton's *th'* at its face value (/ði +
V/ → /ðjV/, /ðV/, 27 times). Unless one can convince oneself that
pronunciations like /ðetənəl, ðjəθ/ are, through frequency, acceptably Miltonic and do not mask recognition of the lexical items
concerned, pronunciation of the article as a full syllable is likely
to be preferred.

   The remaining 110 or so of the 230 suggested elisions are, by
contrast, 'pronounceable'. There are 62 cases where metrical set
invites us to cut a syllable from words like *obedience, chariot,
dominions, Proteus* by substituting a glide /j/ for the medial
syllabic /i/. 18 words like *utterance, deliv'rance, blust'ring* lose a
medial syllabic /ə/. Another common reduction involves words
such as *flower, power* (easily monosyllabic in my version of RP
but less so for some other speakers). Now it must be emphasized
that the characteristic of the 'pronounceable' set is that the syllables concerned are only optionally deletable; they are readily
available for realization in any delivery instance. Indeed, it is
likely that a common stylistic choice (a 'sonorous', 'measured',
'weighty' delivery design) will be to preserve the reducible syllables. It can be said with some confidence that a reading of Book
III of *P. L.* will have over 100, possibly 200, eleven-syllabled lines,
despite Milton's directions by verse design and orthography.

   The distribution of extra-metrical syllables in *P.L.* is note-
worthy. Milton does not allow them to form a regular pattern.

but disposes them evenly, apparently casually, through the line: no part of the line is exceptionally favoured—in Book II extra syllables are approximately equally distributed in the positions between the first and second, third and fourth, and fourth and fifth ictuses, with only slightly more between the second and third and slightly fewer after the fifth. And just as the extra-metrical syllables do not fall predictably in set positions within the line, so also the lines affected by them are spread apparently randomly through the Book, with no bunching. In the long text the rhythmical effect is not striking, but it is constant, and perhaps contributes to the undramatic, non-lyrical, and slightly relaxed style of serious narrative discourse.

The blank verse of Shakespeare's late plays also is saturated with extra-metrical syllables, but the conventions are different. The 'feminine ending' (extra non-ictic syllable(s) after the fifth ictus) appears very frequently: for example, in Act I, Scene ii of *The Tempest* (480 lines of blank verse) there are over 170 lines with feminine endings. It may be thought that, with the feature so thoroughly institutionalized, Shakespeare has made himself subject to the law of diminishing returns: if we should say that this is an aspect of verse design, the 'surprise' element is lost. Daringly, use of the final extrametrical syllable is extended to the centre of the line:

At least/ two glasses./ The time 'twixt six and now. . . .
Have I in such/ a prison./ It works. Come on. . . .
So dear the love my peo/ple bore me;/ nor set. . . .[41]
(/ = foot-division; marked only where relevant in these examples).

The blank verse of this late period is full of extra syllables at all points in the line. Often there is no possibility of omitting these syllables: they are an essential part of the language:

The foul witch Sycorax,/ who with age/ and envy . . .
To whom I am subdued,/ are but light/ to me . . .
(*The Tempest* I. ii. 258, 489)

Elisions, where indicated, are usually even less pronounceable than Milton's:

But that the sea, mounting/ to th'wel/kin's cheek . . . .
And here was left/ by th'sail/ors. Thou, my slave. . . .
(I. ii. 4, 270)

or, if pronounceable, potentially ridiculous:

Where should this music be?/ I'th'air/ or th'earth?/
(I. ii. 387)

Large numbers of extra-metrical syllables, at all points of the line,
produce the 'rhythms of speech' of this late Shakespearean period:

Of off/icer/ and office, /set all hearts/ i'the state . . .
Go make/ thyself/ like a nymph/ o'the sea. /Be subject. . .
(I. ii. 84, 301)

Lines like this are neither fully syllabic nor fully accentual: this
relaxation in the restriction of number of syllables between ictuses
is just sufficient to bring the verse convincingly close to colloquial
language.

Bridges discusses 'Variety in the number of stresses' very briefly
but interestingly (*Milton's Prosody*, pp. 37–40). The examples he
takes from *P.L.* indicate that his subject-matter here is extremely
important for metrics, since the 'omission' of different 'stresses' produces very distinctive lines:[42]

As from the Cénter thríse to th'útmost Póle
And in luxúrious Cíties where the nóyse

Serv'd ónly to discóver síghts of wóe
Nor sérv'd it to reláx their sérried files

A Dúngeon hórrible on áll sides róund

Sole réigning hólds the Tyranny of Héav'n

No líght, but ráther dárkness vísible

His Mínisters of véngeance and pursúit
The Sójourners of Góshen, who behéld
Transfíx us to the bóttom of this Gúlfe[43]

Let us add these exhibits from the Pope passage already discussed:

The próper stúdy of Mankind is Mán
Plác'd on this ísthmus of a míddle státe
With tóo much knówledge for the Scéptic síde
With tóo much wéakness for the Stóic's príde
In dóubt his Mínd or bódy to prefér
Bórn but to díe, and réas'ning but to érr
Alíke in ígnorance, his réason súch
Whéther he thínks too líttle, or too múch
The glóry, jést, and ríddle of the wórld.

By Bridges' criteria, if I infer them correctly, that is nine four-stress lines out of our original sample of eighteen. The criteria seem to be that a syllable is not ictic if it is an unstressed syllable in a word of more than two syllables, or a preposition, conjunction, article or pronoun unless singled out for emphasis under Rule III. On these conditions, about 60 per cent of the lines in Book I of *P.L.* have less than five ictuses. But since these 'omissions' fall into no insistent pattern, the high proportion is not really alarming: the five-stress norm which Bridges assumes seems well established.

Although it would be possible to examine the 'suppressed ictus' as a separate matter,[44] it is best seen as but one manifestation of a general and inevitable tendency for the language of poetry not to fit verse design exactly. The metrical set for the iambic pentameter design has an expectation (reflected in the di-DAH, di-DAH, di-DAH, di-DAH, di-DAH formula commonly used to express an iambic line without actually quoting) of an intonation pattern

That is to say, five separate intonation contours of two syllables each, with the even-numbered syllables perceived as 'heavier', mainly through pitch-change but reinforced by difference of loudness and of vowel and, less powerfully, consonant quality. There are only two degrees of prominence; the odd syllables are all of one weight, the even syllables all of one weight. Such a phonetic contour is possible in English, but in only two constructions. The first, a multiple-branching construction with five units of parallel function and identical internal structure, is illustrated perfectly by the line from *Troilus and Cressida* quoted by Jespersen:[45]

> Her eyes, her haire, her cheeke, her gate, her voice.

The great contrast between ictus and non-ictus established by intonation is strengthened by the contrast of vowels: /ə/ in the odd syllables and diphthongs in the even. For the pronoun *her* we could substitute an article, preposition or conjunction. Compare the first three phrases of Spenser's

> Faire shields, gay steedes, bright armes be my delight
> (*F.Q.* II. vii, 10, 8)

where the distance between the paired syllables is by no means as great because the adjectives need to be more prominent than the function words in the previous example. In addition to noun and prepositional phrases, constructions of auxiliary plus verb (e.g. *will come*) can be accommodated to this fundamental iambic pattern.

But a line consisting of five such structures is extremely unlikely, and if one mixes constructions a line which is only superficially 'purely iambic' results:

> Black rain, and fire, and hail, will burst: oh hear!
> (Shelley, *Ode to the West Wind*, 28)

The second possibility for a 'perfect' iambic pentameter is a line of five disyllabic words with stress on the second syllable, strung together in an additive, listing construction:

> Before, behind, between, above, below
> (Donne, *Elegy XIX*, 'Going to Bed', 25)

The same phonetic conditions apply here as with the phrases: the line will satisfy metrical set most neatly if there is a considerable difference of fullness between the vowels of odd and even syllables.

This is an elusive norm. Very clearly, this 'ideal' iambic line can utilize only a minute portion of the syntactic and lexical selections available in English. But the norm need never be realized in a poem: it is sufficient that enough lines occur with the required number of syllables and ictic sequence, so raising continual expectation that the norm will be realized. Thus we have a poem cumulatively reinforcing verse design in metrical set, more or less strongly according to the 'regularity' of the verse; and at the same time each individual line being measured against the norm. In practice, a poet's choice of (for example) a two-syllabled word with stress on the second syllable; a word of more than two syllables; a construction of more than two syllables, will automatically result in a segment of verse instance which denies the demands of metrical set—happily.[46]

It is a principle in the present theory that, beyond differences of ictus-placement and syllable-count, linguistically different lines are different verse instances. The principle has been tacitly acknowledged by critics who have, to demonstrate the 'feel' of a line, altered it minutely: the smallest linguistic change does alter the texture of a line noticeably. Since a verse design can accommodate an indefinitely large number of sentences, the metrist has an enormous (perhaps infinite) range of instances to discriminate. It would be impracticable and undesirable to demand a total enumeration of verse instances before analysis. The practice of metrical analysis requires nothing as ambitious or mechanical as this. Having determined the type and design of a poem, it is sufficient to observe those features of lexical constituency and of surface-structure which directly contribute to the characteristic texture of a poem or poet, or which set off parts of a poem from each other. One would want to notice, principally, the length of words and the positions of word-junctures relative to foot-boundaries; the distribution of words of different lengths within the line; the distribution of phrase- and clause-boundaries relative to the foot and the line, especially as repeated or varied in a sequence of lines; the structure of phrases, particularly *NP*s; overall and local frequencies of such features. I would claim that the generalizations yielded by such analysis are based in metre and are themselves valuable for comparative study of texts and for style-based critical commentary. However, I would not be prepared to waste words on a terminological argument about whether this (as opposed to the study of ictic patterning) 'is' metrical analysis.

I will give a brief exemplification of the kinds of statement made in this area of the study of verse instance by partial notes on the first two stanzas of Marvell's *The Garden* and the first two paragraphs (stanzas?) of Wallace Stevens' *The Idea of Order at Key West*:[47]

1 How vain/ly men/ themselves/ amaze
2 To win/ the palm, /the oak,/ or bays,
3 And their/ uncess/ant lab/ours see
4 Crown'd from/ some sing/le herb/ or tree,
5 Whose short/ and narr/ow-verg/ed shade
6 Does prud/ently/ their toils/ upbraid;
7 While all/ flowers and/all trees/ do close
8 To weave/ the gar/lands of/ repose.

9 Fair Qui/et, have/ I found/ thee here,
10 And Inn/ocence/ thy sis/ter dear!
11 Mistak/en long,/ I sought/ you then
12 In bus/y com/panies/ of men:
13 Your sac/red plants,/ if here/ below,
14 Only/ among/ the plants/ will grow:
15 Soci/ety/ is all/ but rude
16 To this/ delic/ious sol/itude.

1 She sang/ beyond/ the gen/ius of/ the sea.
2 The wat/er nev/er formed/ to mind/ or voice,
3 Like a bod/y wholl/y bod/y flutt/ering
4 Its emp/ty sleeves;/ and yet/ its mim/ic motion
5 Made con/stant cry,/ caused con/stantly/ a cry,
6 That was/ not ours/ although/ we un/derstood,
7 Inhum/an, of/ the ver/itab/le ocean.
8 The sea/ was not/ a mask./ No more/ was she.
9 The song/ and wat/er were/ not med/leyed sound,
10 Even/ if what/ she sang/ was what/ she heard,

11 Since what/ she sang/ she utt/ered word/ by word.
12 It may/ be that/ in all/ her phras/es stirred
13 The grind/ing wat/er and/the grasp/ing wind;
14 But it/ was she/ and not/ the sea/ we heard.

Line M2 (Marvell line 2) illustrates well marginal departure from the intonational norms of metrical set. Although each foot neatly contains a phrase which by itself could imply the ideal contour, the structure of the whole line prohibits division into four of these desired contours. As the syntax is continuous through syllables 1–4, so is the phonetic contour: the contrasts of prominence between odd and even syllables are diminished, and one syllable, *palm*, has greater prominence than any of the others, because it is the nucleus of the contour. *Palm* is heavier than *win*, despite verse design, and *win* is not as much heavier than *to* and *the* as design would have it. In the ideal line each even syllable is an intonational nucleus, and the contrast between it and its neighbours is polar. Increase in the number of distinctions, and reduction in the physical distance of contrasts, is a natural consequence of the continuity of syntax and is the pervasive characteristic of verse. Straightforward examples of the effect are S8, 10, and 14. The overlapping of foot-boundaries by polysyllabic words has the same effect. M11, *Mistaken long*, avoids a terminal juncture between the second and third syllables by making -*en* more prominent than the archetypal non-ictic syllable: one might express this by saying that it has tertiary stress (whereas the archetype must have the lowest degree, and even *the* in M2 syllable 3 could be weaker than `without too much distortion) but the phonetic realization is more likely to be intonational: -*en* on much the same (high) level as -*tak*-, while *be*(*hind*) in Donne (see p. 312) starts on a markedly lower pitch than (*Be*)*fore*. The necessity to avoid this drop in pitch, to avoid cutting off a lexically unstressed syllable carried into a second foot, is even more obvious when the syllabic concerned is not /ə/: M1 *vain/ly*, M5 *narr/ow-verg/ed*, M12 *bus/y*, M13 *sac/red*, S3 *bod/y wholl/y bod/y*, S4 *mim/ic*.

In a sense, *win* M2 is a 'weak ictus' compared with *palm, oak, bays* which, as well as having sentence-stress, are pitch nuclei. However, M3 *their*, like the weak ictuses in Pope already discussed, is an entirely clearer case: it does not bear sentence-stress. Cf. M8 *of*, M14 (*a*)*mong*, M16 *this*, S1 (*be*)*yond, of*, S2 *nev*(*er*), S4 *yet*, S7 *of*, S8 *more*, etc. The high proportion and random distribution of these reduced ictuses in *The Idea of Order* are a direct product of the simple statement-making syntax which is such an important feature of its style. A second category of reduced ictus comprises non-primary-stressed syllables in words of three or more syllables: M6 prudent*ly*, M10 Inno*cence*, M12 compan*ies*, M15 Socie*ty*, M16 soli*tude*, S3 flutter*ing*, S5 constant*ly*, S6 *un*derstood, S7 verit*able*. Two characteristics of English polysyllabic words make them assimilable to a disyllabic metre. A word which has fixed strong stress on one syllable has also less strong, but still relatively strong, stress on some other, equally predetermined, non-adjacent syllable, and so on down the scale with positionally fixed gradations of value; these relatively prominent syllables are arranged on a principle of weak-strong alternation. So if syllable 1 is the primary lexical stress, syllable 3 will be the next highest value in the word, with a lighter syllable in between. Hence, barring a reversed foot, concurrence of lexical stress with one ictus guarantees that the preceding or following ictus will fall on the next most prominent syllable in the word. This ensures that polysyllables will not grossly disturb the ictic sequence, but, even so, such words are highly resistant to the insertion of terminal junctures to enforce verse design, and to the promotion of secondary stresses to the level of an ictic primary. Multisyllabic words in general imply a tight-knit continuity in tension with the regular fragmentation of metrical set. And of course possibilities for variation are enormous—not only in the segmental composition of ictuses with secondary stress (soli*tude* v. flutter*ing* /u/: /ɪ/) but also in the length of words and their position in the line:

> Society is all but rude
> To this delicious solitude.

If the term 'tension'[48] is applicable to any particular aspect of this frustration of metrical set by the natural characteristics of the language, it is to the employment of disyllabic words with stress on the first syllable: M1 *vainly*, M3 *labours*, M4 *single*, etc. These can be accommodated either in a reversed foot (M14 *Only*, S10 *Even*) or by overlapping the boundaries of feet. There are obvious limits to the employment of reversed feet in iambic metre, but the other device, if used frequently, easily leads to the suggestion of a falling rhythm syncopated against the rising rhythm of verse design:

> Tired with all these for restful death I cry,
> As to behold desert a beggar born,
> And needy nothing trimmed in jollity,
> And purest faith unhappily forsworn,
> And gilded honour shamefully misplaced,
> And maiden virtue rudely strumpeted,
> And right perfection wrongfully disgraced,

> And strength by limping sway disabled,
> And art made tongue-tied by authority,
> And folly (doctor-like) controlling skill,
> And simple truth miscalled simplicity,
> And captive good attending captain ill.
>   Tired with all these, from these would I be gone,
>   Save that to die, I leave my love alone.
>   (Shakespeare, Sonnet lxvi)

The force of Pope's stricture against monosyllabism (which is of course a condemnation of unpoetic diction too) can be appreciated once the impact of disyllables is understood:

> And ten low words oft creep in one dull line

Compare

> And several words oft creep in every line

which is not claimed to be a better line, but at least two of its syllables (3 and 9) are evidently non-ictic. The means of making a string of monosyllables interesting (as verse) are limited. Intra-line terminal junctures, syntactic parallelism, inversions,[49] exhaust the possibilities. In verse where syllable-count is significant and each word is a monosyllable, the incidence of words without normal sentence-stress (conjunctions, prepositions, auxiliaries, articles, many pronouns) must increase to a point where the lines are dominated by them:

> S8 *The sea was not a* mask. *No* more *was* she.
> S14 *But it was* she *and not the* sea we heard.

Doubtless Pope would not have liked these lines; if a modern reader does not, it is not necessarily because he affects, inappropriately, Augustan tastes. These lines (if we consider them weak) remind us that this verse design rests not only on syllable-count: also, the syntax must be of a kind to enforce the internal metrical structure of the line.

The delivery levels

The theory of verse instance sketched above will not construct a delivery design—a set of precise directions for oral performance—from a written text. Nor do my remarks about 'stress', 'prominence', etc., have any necessary connection with the physical properties of a delivery instance. If one has an adequate metrical set and understanding of the language, one will perceive verse instance. There is ample experimental evidence that people listening to their native

language perceive phonetic contours consistent with their understanding of the structure of the utterances presented, 'mishearing'
the physical signal as required. Thus utterances can be (and are)
phonetically impoverished, or masked by noise, without impediment
to communication. I can see no reason why this should not be true
of the perceptually more complex situation of listening to a poetry
reading. Oral poetry is (two ways, by nature and convention) rather
'noisy' language, but, as in the case of acoustic noise, grammar is
generally powerful enough ('language is redundant') to overcome the
noise. The only prescription this theory of metre provides for delivery instances is 'do not contravene the systematic phonemics of
the language' (i.e. rules such as I–IV above). In other words, verse
instance is preserved in delivery instance so long as a poem written
in a particular language is not read in such a way as to obscure the
grammar of that language. This prescription is both permissive (e.g.
there are many places where some terminal juncture is required but
the performer has a choice of which to use) and relative (i.e. audiences
vary in their tolerance depending on familiarity with the poem,
acceptance of a delivery style, etc.); in general, delivery instances are
only loosely controlled by verse instances.

Finally, a delivery instance has 'expressive' dimensions drawing
on linguistic variables which do not enter the theory of metre. The
voice can do everything a written text can do—indicate the syntax
and choice of lexical items—and much more besides. A speaker can
change tempo, insert pauses, drawl, alter volume, whisper, vary the
pitch in a narrow or wide range, speak falsetto, tremolo, lisp, sing,
etc., etc. None of these voice qualities is a part of systematic phonetics; they belong to the highly unsystematized and poorly understood area of paralanguage.[50] A grammar of paralinguistic phonology might be impossible to construct, because the conventions
vary enormously within a language-community and because it is
difficult to distinguish consistently what is voice set (idiosyncratic)
from what is public convention. But despite the difficulties of
formalization with which the linguist is presented, it is observable
that people respond differentially to paralanguage, so that one 'tone
of voice' may be felt to express boredom, another excitement,
others guile, forthrightness, approval, etc.; though they may not
be patterned consistently through the 'language as a whole', paralinguistic features can still convey meanings between speakers.
Communication is considerably less regular and specific than that of
grammar, somewhat more so than communication by gesture (with
which paralanguage has some affinity).

Oral interpreters draw heavily on the resources of paralinguistic
phonology. Chatman acknowledges in a footnote to his article in

KR, xviii (1956), 431, 'the presence of voice qualifiers and differentiators' including 'voice tremolo (particularly in Frost's reading), overloudness, drawl, tonelessness, openness, and hesitation'. These were noticed by Henry Lee Smith, who considered them 'very characteristic of poetry reading'. Such features may be referred to (*a*) the voice set and mannerisms peculiar to a performer; (*b*) the performer's attempt at some conventionalized delivery style; (*c*) a decision by the performer that a particular kind of reading was appropriate to the tone of that poem. It is not at all clear that these factors are relevant to metrical analysis, unless one rather difficult argument can be rendered usable: if the metre of a poem is not arbitrarily chosen (i.e. it is a *determinate* metre), it bears a necessary relation ('appropriateness', 'expressiveness') to the poem's determinate meaning; recovery of that meaning (which includes 'tone', 'style', etc.) should explain both metre and the required style of delivery. But since metre is easily accessible in the surface structure of the poem, while meaning is recoverable only by total comprehension of the deep syntax and semantics (which, in view of the distance between poet and reader, may be impossible), the recovery of tone and of the appropriate paralinguistic phonology is likely to remain much less certain than the discovery of verse instance. It seems necessary and practical to assert and preserve the independence of metre from the realization of a poem in oral form.

Notes to Paper Ten

1 This paper was stimulated by a graduate seminar in metrics which I gave at the University of California, Berkeley, in 1966. My thanks go to the students involved, and also to Seymour Chatman, Lee S. Hultzén, and Geoffrey Leech, who made extensive and valuable suggestions on an early draft.
2 Harold Whitehall, 'From Linguistics to Criticism', *Kenyon Review*, xviii (1956), 412–21; Seymour Chatman, 'Robert Frost's "Mowing": an inquiry into Prosodic Structure', ibid., 421–38; Arnold Stein, 'Donne's Prosody', ibid., 439–43; Chatman, 'Mr Stein on Donne', ibid., 443–51; Stein, 'A Note on Meter', ibid., 451–60; John Crowe Ransom, 'The Strange Music of English Verse', ibid., 460–77; Edmund L. Epstein and Terence Hawkes, *Linguistics and English Prosody*, Studies in Linguistics, Occasional Paper No. 7 (Buffalo, 1959); Henry Lee Smith, Jr., 'Towards Redefining English Prosody', *Studies in Linguistics*, xiv (1959), 68–75; W. K. Wimsatt, Jr., and Monroe C. Beardsley, 'The Concept of Meter; an Exercise in Abstraction', *PMLA*, lxxiv (1959), 585–98; John Lotz, 'Metric Typology', in T. A. Sebeok (ed.), *Style in Language* (Cambridge, Mass., 1960), 135–48; Chatman, 'Comparing Metrical Styles', ibid.,

149–72; Rulon Wells, 'Comments to Part Five [Metrics]', ibid.,
197–200; John Thompson, *The Founding of English Metre* (London,
1961); Terence Hawkes, 'The Problems of Prosody', *A Review of
English Literature*, iii (1962), 32–49; S. R. Levin, 'Suprasegmentals
and the Performance of Poetry', *QJS*, xlviii (1962), 366–72;
Chatman, *A Theory of Meter*, Janua Linguarum, 36 (The Hague,
1965); Fowler, ' "Prose Rhythm " and Metre', *Essays on Style and
Language* (London, 1966), 82–99; Fowler, 'Structural Metrics',
Linguistics, xxvii (1966), 49–64, reprinted in Chatman and Levin,
Essays on the Language of Literature (Boston, 1967), 156–69. For
much of the earlier work cited here the linguistic basis was derived
from George L. Trager and Henry Lee Smith, Jr., *An Outline of
English Structure* (Norman, 1951). A different phonetic approach
is suggested by David Abercrombie, 'Syllable Quantity and
Enclitics in English', *In Honour of Daniel Jones* (London, 1964),
216–22, and 'A Phonetician's View of Verse Structure', *Linguistics*,
vi (1964), 5–13. The framework of generative phonology is adopted
in Morris Halle and S. Jay Keyser, 'Chaucer and the Study of
Prosody', *College English*, xxviii (1966), 187–219.
3 The recent decline of taxonomic phonology in general and Trager–
Smith phonology in particular has contributed to the passing of
this approach.
4 *Grundzüge der englischen Verswissenschaft* (Marburg, 1929). See also
Wilbur Schramm, *Approaches to a Science of English Verse* (Iowa
City, 1935). For further references and discussion, see Chatman,
Theory, 82 ff.
5 In Sebeok, op. cit., 364, 365–6, 366–7.
6 According to Chomsky; for a lucid summary, see his 'The Formal
Nature of Language', Appendix A in E. H. Lenneberg, *Biological
Foundations of Language* (New York, 1967), 406–8.
7 Ibid., 419 ff.
8 Ibid., 411.
9 Ibid., 411–16, for an illustration of how this works.
10 See Lotz, op. cit. (note 2 above).
11 R. H. Robins, *General Linguistics, an Introductory Survey* (London,
1964), 112.
12 See 'The Author's Preface' [to *Poems 1876–1889*] and the letter of
5 October 1878 to R. W. Dixon: *Poems and Prose of Gerard
Manley Hopkins*, ed. W. H. Gardner (Penguin Books, 1953 and
subsequent editions), 7–11, 187–9.
13 On Anglo-Saxon metre see E. Sievers, 'Zur Rhythmik des
Germanischen Alliterationsverses I', *Beiträge zur Geschichte der
Deutschen Sprache und Literatur*, x (1885), 209–314; *Altgermanische
Metrik* (Halle, 1893); J. C. Pope, *The Rhythm of Beowulf*, 2nd ed.
(New Haven and London, 1966); A. J. Bliss, *The Metre of Beowulf*
(Oxford, 1958).
14 For the distinction between rhythm and metre, see Chatman,
Theory, Ch. 2.

15 B. J. Timmer, 'Expanded Lines in Old English Poetry',
    Neophilologus, xxxv (1951), 226–30.
16 In the first 100 lines of the B-text of *Piers Plowman* the average
    is 2·56 unstressed syllables between the first and second stresses –
    much nearer Hopkins' limit.
17 John Hollander in Sebeok, op. cit., 202–3.
18 Line-measurement in unrhymed decasyllabic verse requires
    syntactic rules of some complexity, and there is variation in
    end-stopping from instance to instance. Also, measurement by
    number of ictuses becomes more important.
19 Chatman, *Theory*, 117, in a section on the foot, 114–19.
20 I owe the term to Chatman; cf. his definition, *Theory*, 121: 'the
    running disposition of ictus and non-ictus established by preceding
    sequences, particularly where these were linguistically unequivocal.'
    The qualification 'preceding' may not be necessary—cf. my
    remarks above on the reader's 'cumulative' perception of verse
    design. Chatman's 'linguistically unequivocal' relates to my
    '*efficient* line of poetry'.
21 Though design systematization of contrasts more complex than
    binary is conceivable.
22 These 'categories of verse design' cover much the same ground as
    Chatman's 'Components of English Meter', *Theory*, Ch. 5.
23 E.g. Chatman, *Kenyon Review*, xviii (1956), 422, 424, Whitehall,
    ibid., 418.
24 John Crowe Ransom, 'Wanted: an Ontological Critic', in *The New
    Criticism* (Norfolk, Conn., 1941); the relevant pages are reprinted
    in Chatman and Levin, op. cit. (see note 2), 269–82.
25 My reduction of 'ambiguous' lines to a state of alternativity may
    deny a suggestion which to some critics is highly attractive: the
    possibility of simultaneous recognition, in verse instance and in
    delivery instance, of the co-presence of meanings. I do not take
    'ambiguity' in the Empsonian sense to be defining for poetry:
    viewed with detachment this must be seen as a value promoted by
    one critical persuasion ('tension' has cognate origins). Language is
    ambiguous, on the whole; poetic language, because of such factors
    as compression, preservation and study of texts of alien linguistic
    eras, especially so. But ambiguities can be stated as reasoned
    alternatives, and their statement should be attended with a
    humility concerning our ability to interpret. I cannot begin to
    imagine how to account for the perceptual psychology of a reader
    actively engaged in the experience of an ambiguous verse instance.
    On the whole I agree with Chatman that a delivery instance must,
    if it is to observe the rules of the language, disambiguate; and even
    if one says that often phonology does not mark one interpretation
    rather than another, this is very far from saying that phonology
    simultaneously marks both more than one structure and the fact
    of more than one structure. Even where phonology is ambiguous,
    it does not advertise the separate components of its ambiguity.

For some discussion, see Levin, 'Suprasegmentals' (cited in note 2 above); Katherine T. Loesch, 'Literary Ambiguity and Oral Performance', *QJS*, li (1965), 258–67; reply by Chatman, *QJS*, lii (1966), 283–6; rejoinder by Mrs Loesch, ibid., 286–9.

26 'The Concept of Meter', 596.

27 J. R. Firth, 'Synopsis of Linguistic Theory, 1930–1955', in *Studies in Linguistic Analysis*, Special Volume of the Philological Society (Oxford, 1957), 32.

28 N. Chomsky, M. Halle, and F. Lukoff, 'On Accent and Juncture in English', in *For Roman Jakobson*, ed. Halle *et al.* (The Hague, 1956), 79–80.

29 Review of Maria Schubiger, *English Intonation, its Form and Function* (Tübingen, 1958) in *Language*, xxxvi (1960), 546. (This statement of Chomsky's position no longer holds good today.) The details of Stockwell's proposal can be understood by reference to his 'The Place of Intonation in a Generative Grammar of English', *Language*, xxxvi (1960), 360–7. He suggests that the starting-point for the phrase-structure component of a grammar of English should be, not

$S \rightarrow NP + VP$, but
$S \rightarrow Nuc + IP$ [=Nucleus + Intonation Pattern]
$Nuc \rightarrow NP + VP$
$IP \rightarrow C + JP$ [= Contour + Juncture Point]

The subsequent rewritings of *IP* and its components are in terms of fundamentally structuralist categories. It seems to me that this is a formulation of traditional material which has nothing to do with generative processes. The phonological basis is that of (for example) A. A. Hill, *Introduction to Linguistic Structures: From Sound to Sentence in English* (New York, 1958), where a linguistic form 'consists of' appropriately combined selections from syntactic and suprasegmental systems.

30 Hultzén, 'Information Points in Intonation', *Phonetica*, iv (1959), 107, 108, 119.

31 Chomsky, *Current Issues in Linguistic Theory*, Janua Linguarum, 38 (The Hague, 1964), 65–96; for 'input' and 'output' see Chomsky, *Topics in the Theory of Generative Grammar*, Janua Linguarum, 56 (The Hague, 1966), 77; other rules in systematic phonemics are illustrated in *Current Issues*, and cf. Chomsky and Halle, 'Some Controversial Questions in Phonological Theory', *Journal of Linguistics*, i (1965), 98: 'The systematic phonemic representation includes in addition to purely phonological elements also information about the morphological and syntactic structure of the utterance.'

32 A *prominent* syllable may be so by reason of any or all of the following phonetic characteristics: quality of the syllabic vowel, length, stress, pitch. See Daniel Jones, *An Outline of English Phonetics*, 9th ed. (Cambridge, 1964), 24, 55. The term, which is extremely useful for a notion more inclusive than 'stress' (the

perceptual correlate of intensity, amplitude), is also employed by A. C. Gimson, *An Introduction to the Pronunciation of English* (London, 1962). Both of these books, especially Jones, Chs. 29 and 31, provide much supporting detail for the four rules.

33 On multi-nuclear contours, see Gimson, op. cit., 259–60.

34 *Mankínd* seems right for this word, although several speakers (chiefly American) have suggested *mánkind* or *mánkínd*.

35 I assume that *yet* does not mean 'still'; if it did, it would be prominent under rule II.

36 Robert Bridges, *Milton's Prosody*, rev. final ed. (London, 1921), 1.

37 Gimson, op. cit., 50–2; K. L. Pike, *Phonetics* (Ann Arbor, 1943), 53–5, 116; Chatman, *Theory*, 40–1.

38 *Milton's Prosody*, 9; my italics; discussed by Chatman, *Theory*, 106–12.

39 *Milton's Prosody*, 19–37.

40 All such counts, in discussions like this where there is no space to give criteria in full, must be presented as approximations.

41 *The Tempest*, ed. Morton Luce, 3rd ed. (London, 1926), I. ii. 240, 493, 141. This 'feminine caesura' may be made acceptable by Shakespeare's insistent patterning of the mid-line break: see Fowler, ' "Prose Rhythm" and Metre', 90–1.

42 The point is that repeated suppression of metrical stress at one or more (numerically defined) place(s) in the line rather than any other leads to a distinctive rhythmical character: for example, Marlowe's lines modelled on the types

> Still clímbing after knówledge ínfinite
> > (*Tamburlaine I*, II. vii. 25)

and

> A mínd courágeous and invíncible
> > (*Tamburlaine II*, I. iv. 73)

and Pope's two-part structure:

> Or stáin her Hónour, or her néw Brocáde
> Be stópp'd in *Víals*, or transfíxt with Píns
> > (*Rape*, ii, 107, 126)

43 i. 74, i. 498, i. 64, vi. 599, i. 61, i. 124, i. 63, i. 170, i. 309, i. 329. I have supplied a few stress-marks which Bridges omits; it is obvious that he wanted the lines scanned this way.

44 In ' "Prose Rhythm" and Metre' (p. 97) I implied that the pentameter with apparently less than five ictuses can be explained as a line in which not all of the even-numbered syllables have primary stress. Cf. Whitehall, *KR*, xviii (1956), 418, Whitehall and Hill, 'A Report on the Language–Literature Seminar' [at Indiana University in 1953], in H. B. Allen, ed., *Readings in Applied English Linguistics*. 2nd ed. (New York, 1964), 489–90, and Rulon Wells, art. cit. (note 2), 199, all of whom have the rule that, in Trager–Smith terms, stresses ╱ ∧ ╲ count as 'accented' in verse,

∧\◡ 'unaccented'. Thus a 'pentameter with three stresses' has five ictic syllables stressed variously /∧\, but only three /.

45 *Troilus and Cressida*, I. i. 54. Quoted in 'Notes on Metre' in *Linguistica* (Copenhagen, 1933), which is reprinted in Chatman and Levin, op. cit., 71–90.

46 Cf. ' "Prose Rhythm" and Metre', 99.

47 The texts got chosen simply because, in two different contexts, I happened to be reading them at the time I reached this stage of the first draft of this article.

48 This may be an appropriate point to comment on the notion of 'tension' which has so preoccupied recent metrical theory. (For more detailed comment see my ' "Prose Rhythm" and Metre' cited in note 2 above, and Wimsatt and Beardsley, op. cit.) 'Tension', or Hopkins' 'counterpoint', or more appropriately 'syncopation' as I have suggested (' "Prose Rhythm" ', 95), is a generalized aesthetic effect derived from the inevitable tendency for the phonological realization of the language of a line not to fulfil the expectations of metrical set for some verse designs (' "Prose Rhythm" ', 99). Typical descriptions are: 'tension between the ictus and the usual word stress . . .' (Jakobson, Sebeok, 366); 'the tension, the "counterpoint", between the metrical pattern and the prose rhythm' (Wellek and Warren, *Theory of Literature*, 3rd ed. (Penguin Books, 1963), 169); 'tension between *two* systems: the abstract metrical pattern, as historical product of the English verse tradition, and the ordinary stress-pitch-juncture system of spoken English, determined as it is by requirements of meaning and emphasis' (Chatman, *KR*, xviii (1956), 422). The difficulties attending tension as described in these terms were inadequate definition of 'abstract metrical pattern' (=metrical set), overreliance on Trager and Smith's account of English suprasegmentals, and appeal to delivery instance as the primary source of phonetic information. I now take the position that exact determination of verse instances and generalization to the texture of poems and poets have priority over generalization to the common aesthetic character of a given verse design in a given language.

49 Syntactic inversions sometimes have the opposite effect, that of making the phonetic contour less clear. Because the normal rules of word-order are in abeyance, one is not sure how to stress *themselves* (M1) to make it clear that it is part of *VP*, not *NP*; or what contour to give *have I found* (M9) to prevent the suggestion of an interrogative.

50 Much the best treatment of paralanguage (with a survey of earlier research) is D. Crystal and R. Quirk, *Systems of Prosodic and Paralinguistic Features in English*, Janua Linguarum, 39 (The Hague, 1964).

Eleven

The Rhythm of Beowulf [1]—A Review

The Rhythm of Beowulf was first published in 1942, and has been and remains a stimulus for comment and research: Pope's thesis is attractive and persuasively argued. He acknowledges the usefulness of Sievers' classification of types of syllabic sequence, and this forms an indispensable basis for his own work. But he points out that Sievers' notation cannot be taken as a set of directions for a reading. Though Sievers' symbols represent accurately certain facts about the language of the verse—number of syllables, relation of light and heavy stresses—they are not efficient in implying what the verse sounds like. For example, the notation ´ × | ´ × happens to indicate how a verse like *sīdra sorga* may be read if it is to fit the prevailing rhythm and at the same time not do injury to the syntax of the phrase. The notation × ´ | × ´, on the other hand, is adequate for *on sīdne sǣ* only in indicating that there are four syllables alternating light and heavy: it cannot tell us anything about the rhythm. Worse still, this notation does grave offence to both rhythm and syntax, since the bar is meaningless (it is fortuitously significant in *sīdra sorga*), suggests a rising rhythm in a poem which is obviously in falling rhythm, and implies an erroneous phrase-structure analysis for this sequence of words. Pope claims that the imputation of strict metrical values to Sievers' symbols has led to 'many an infelicitous, clumsily rhythmized performance that could yet call itself faithful to the original' (p. 7).

Pope's proposal is that the metre of Old English poetry—or at least of the normal unexpanded lines in *Beowulf*—is built from units one verse (half-line) long, each verse consisting of a variable number of syllables plus a silent pulse when necessary; these syllables (plus silent pulse) are gathered into two isochronous measures of quadruple time ($^4/_8$). Each measure starts with a stressed syllable or a pulse, and these 'downbeats' are spaced evenly in time, four to a long line. Since the number of syllables in each verse (and therefore measure) varies, there are no absolute lengths for syllables. Varying lengths, number of syllables, and prominence of syllables, are shown in Pope's notation thus:

gomban gyldan   þær me wið laðum

Anacrusis is accommodated in the previous measure:

Ða wit ætsomne   on sæ   wæron

Pope explains what kind of rhythm his theory seeks to establish:

> The verses of *Beowulf* about which there is general agreement—those of types A, D, and E—have what we might loosely describe as a marching rhythm. The primary and secondary accents alternate like left foot and right, and are in general rather strong because of the high concentration of meaning that accompanies the elaborate inflections and the frequent composition of words (p. 52).

An insistent falling rhythm with the statistically dominant type AI as the pattern. Types B and C, at least as represented by Sievers, cannot fit this pattern. For example, line 6, as seen by Sievers (ignoring 'resolution') requires an awkward transition from a falling to a rising rhythm:

egsode | eorlas, | syððan ær|est wearð

Pope's solution is to introduce a half-note rest to begin the first measure of the b-verse:

egsode eorlas,   syððan ærest wearð

By this device he achieves a continuous falling rhythm in which the third down beat is a silent pulse; to symbolize it crudely:

| / × × | / × | / × × | / × × |

Although Pope was not the first to postulate rests in Old English poetry, he was the first to use them consistently and determinedly to achieve a stated metrical aim affecting the rhythm of the whole poem.

But note what happens to the alliteration: instead of the regular AAAB which Sievers' analysis of this line would have produced, we

N

now have AAØA, with the third alliterating syllable transferred to the fourth measure. Similar treatment of line 4, *Oft Scyld Scefing sceapena preatum*, gives ØAAAB with double alliteration within the second measure. Pope discusses this problem (pp. 44–5) and claims that such patterns are valid since the alliterating syllables remain the most prominent in the line, whatever their position; but this claim would have to be supported by a complete restatement of the design rules for *Beowulf* and a very sophisticated account of syntactically-determined gradations in syllabic prominence: Pope gives us neither.

The cornerstone of Pope's theory is, he believes, provided by the harp. By a beautiful strategy, he conducts his argument for initial rests as a regularization of the rhythm of *Beowulf* without reference to the harp, and only later (pp. 88–95) announces that the harp filling the initial rests makes sense of the whole theory. Since initial rests in opening positions (e.g. before the first line of *Beowulf*) cannot be produced (or, more accurately, perceived) some audible non-linguistic device must be proposed to fill the gap. As there are numerous references to the harp in connection with the recitation of Anglo-Saxon poetry, and to this recitation as 'song', it is natural to regard the harp as, in Pope's phrase, the 'vital clue' to the nature of the metre. Indeed, he goes further and imputes the decline of this poetry to the death of the oral tradition of recitation: as the form of the poetry depends on the harp, the form must disappear with the growth of a manuscript culture and with the displacement of the society which cultivated this poetry. This hypothesis is self-evidently impossible to substantiate: it is pure speculation and Professor Pope knows it. The suggestion is merely that a stroke of the harp fills the rests, and this is a reasonable guess; we are never likely to have any information which could support a fuller role for the instrument in the recitation of Anglo-Saxon poetry. Pope's musical notation has no real relation to his guess about the harp—it is not a notation for a musical performance; and, consequently, his theory as expressed in this notation must be judged on linguistic and poetic grounds, not musical.

The second edition of this book makes no change in Pope's thesis—it could not, without becoming a quite different book. The bulk of the new edition is a photographic reproduction of the first, with a few new footnotes inserted, chiefly corrections. More substantial additions are a line-index to the catalogue of rhythmic variations and a new preface of 26 pages. The preface begins by surveying (dismissing) some accounts of Anglo-Saxon metre published subsequent to the first edition of this book. (The remainder of the new preface is devoted to corrections, qualifications, and clarifications of points of detail.) It is a pity that R. P. Creed's excellent article 'A New Approach to the

Rhythm of *Beowulf'*, *PMLA*, lxxxi (1966), 23–33, appeared too late for Pope's comment, for this—as Bliss from Sievers—takes its inspiration directly from *The Rhythm of Beowulf*. Creed simplifies Pope's classification and (valuably) his notation, and in the process offers a classification of *measures* which further liberates the Pope system from Sievers and is thus even more in touch with the rhythm. Creed also makes gestures towards a metatheoretical perspective on the subject which is totally lacking in Pope: 'Pope's catalogue is, it seems to me, parallel to what linguists would call a narrow phonetic transcription (or perhaps a narrow "rhythmetic" transcription), and my schematization an attempt at a kind of "phonemic" ("rhythmemic") restatement' (p. 23).

The motive for Creed's restatement is a very apt criticism of Pope: the demonstration of Pope's thesis 'suffers . . . from its very attempt at inclusiveness and final precision, or, rather, from its failure to generalize' (p. 23). We may connect this with a remark in Seymour Chatman's *Theory of Meter* (The Hague, 1965) that 'the metrist's function is not to find out how many kinds of feet there are, but rather to insure that there aren't any more kinds than necessary' (p. 14).

Pope's classification is *too* delicate. Though his central proposal is doubtless correct—that the verse type is based on an isochronous ordering of pulses rather than only on linear but timeless sequences of syllabic patterns—he undermines its simplicity by attaching metrical autonomy to hundreds of syllabic patterns within the matrix of stress-timing. Elsewhere ('What is Metrical Analysis?', this book, Paper 10) I have presented the arguments against such an extreme of sub-categorization. Any particular segment of verse ('verse instance') is a linguistic realization of an abstract 'verse design' which is one adaptation of a broad 'verse type'. The Germanic verse type was based on stress-timing, isochronous sequence of linguistically prominent syllables. Anglo-Saxon verse design is a limitation of this type in terms of number of prominent syllables, alliterative patterning and loose establishment of a range of intervening light syllables. At a more particular level, the verse design varies in sequence of light and heavy syllables, on the lines of Sievers' scheme. The verse design when understood by a reader or listener induces a perceptual disposition which Chatman and I have discussed as 'metrical set': an expectation that the phonology of the verse design will be continuously implemented by the phonetic contour natural to the syntactic surface-structure of the sentences of the poem. Because of the phonetic variousness of natural language and the 'phonetic' simplicity of verse design (verse has to give an impression of absolute regularity), this expectation will almost never be exactly

satisfied. There is thus an essential disjunction between the categories of verse design (a Sievers-type classification) and the varieties
of verse instance. Pope commits the metrist's usual error of suggesting that the rhythms of actual lines are submembers of classes of
rhythms established in verse design, whereas actually these verse-
instance rhythms are in tension with the norms of verse design.
Moreover, as Pope's 'narrow rhythmetic' notation unwittingly suggests, verse instances are as various as there are sentences in the
language: and their variety is a fact of language which should not be
presented as a fact of metrical design.

In short, although Pope's thesis is successful in establishing the
general character of Old English metre, the attempt to extend it to
every particularity of verse instance seems misguided. It would, however, be possible now to overhaul the whole theory and make it more
powerful without destroying the spirit of the original reading. Many
developments since 1942, none of them alluded to in Pope's 1966
preface, make this a realistic proposal. Advances in the theory of
phonology, and in our understanding of its relation to syntax, would
allow us to abandon Pope's complicated, quasi-musical notation for
stress and length, and to treat the rhythmical phenomena he deals
with as regularly derived products of the surface structure of the
poem. There is now an extensive literature devoted to the application of the phonological methods of modern linguistics to metre—
from the now discarded phonology of Trager and Smith (see *Kenyon
Review*, xviii (1956)) to the generative phonology of Halle and
Chomsky, applied persuasively to Chaucer by Halle and Keyser
(*College English* (December 1966)). Especially interesting for Pope's
thesis are two stimulating short articles by David Abercrombie,
'A Phonetician's View of Verse Structure' and 'Syllable Quantity and
Enclitics in English' (both reprinted in his *Studies in Phonetics and
Linguistics*, London, 1965). Abercrombie, apparently independently
of Pope, explores the implications of isochrony, variable syllable-
quantity and silent pulses (after Stetson) for English rhythm; but
he makes no reference to Old English.

A second area of research which must have significance for metrics
is the study of Anglo-Saxon verse as selection from a stock of memorized formulae for oral composition. The 'oral-formulaic' approach is
obviously not without problems, especially as Anglo-Saxon poetry is
extant only in a written corpus: see the critical survey by R. F. Law-
rence in R. Fowler (ed.), *Essays on Style and Language* (London,
1966). Nevertheless, the materials presented by the proponents of
this approach are suggestive enough—suggestive that the skeleton
of Anglo-Saxon poetry is an ordered structure of syntactic frames
with a non-casual relation to metrical organization. As metre is de-

termined by syntax, analysis on these lines (without commitment to the genetic hypothesis of the strict oral-formulaic school) ought to be metrically revealing: most probably, some linguistic basis for Sievers' typology of half-lines could be established. Ideally, a syntactic description of the structure of half-lines should be integrated with a fuller statement of the 'grammetrics' of the patterns which very obviously extend over longer-ranging stretches of text.

The second edition of *The Rhythm of Beowulf* is extremely welcome. There is no doubt that it has an old-fashioned air: that progress in the study of language between 1942 and 1966 is not really reflected in this new edition. But this is in no sense an absolute criticism. What is important is the republication of a basically sound and exciting theory at a time of renewed activity in the field of metrics and of rapid progress in English linguistics.

Note to Paper Eleven

1 J. C. Pope, *The Rhythm of Beowulf: An Interpretation of the Normal and Hypermetric Verse-Forms in Old English Poetry*. Second edition (New Haven and London: Yale University Press, 1966), xxxvi + 409 pp.

Twelve

Three blank verse textures

As is well known, conventional prosodic analysis is derived from classical quantitative metrics. Although the terms of this form of analysis are inherently unsuitable for a language like English— where 'stress' rather than 'length' has been chosen as the basic principle of metrical organization—they have become firmly established as a descriptive apparatus for English verse. Generations of literary historians persuaded themselves that iambs and anapaests are applicable to English verse, and doubtless many of our more academic poets came to think in these terms. To conceptualize English verse in the jargon of long syllables, trochees, and the rest demands continuous translation into linguistically more appropriate notions, a controlled use of metaphors which could easily become misleading. Some metrical theorists have, apparently, achieved this translation, and found it possible to describe English verse designs efficiently in the old terms.

The limitation on this technique is that it can do little more than establish *verse designs*—that is to say, identify the general mould in which a particular piece of verse is cast, within the framework of the set of verse designs traditional to the English poetic corpus. It is an extremely blunt instrument as far as the identification of verse instances is concerned, and so can display few of the most important distinctions between particular pieces of verse. The literary critic usually responds to this problem by concentrating on the licences poets take with their verse designs: the assumption is that the individuality of verse passages stems from the distinctive ways in which poets break the rules. Robert Bridges' classic study of Milton's prosody, based largely on the study of his use of elision and extra-metrical syllables, draws its value from building on this assumption. In a similar way, critics have paid attention to feminine endings, reversed feet, substitutions of one kind of foot for another, and so on. For a representative example I shall refer to John Bakeless' account of Marlowe's 'mighty line'.[1] Mr Bakeless lists fourteen devices which, allegedly, were more frequently and skilfully used as Marlowe gradually freed himself from the restrictions of the mechanical blank verse of his predecessors:

1 Enjambement of the normally end-stopped line.
2 The introduction of occasional alexandrines.
3 The use of 'tumbling' endings, which have much the effect of alexandrines, and may have been meant as such.
4 Feminine endings.
5 A more artful use of both epic and lyric caesura.
6 A freer substitution of other feet for the basic iambus, including trochees, dactyls, anapaests, spondees, and a characteristic use of pyrrhics.
7 The nine-syllable line.
8 Interpolated and extra-metrical syllables.
9 Tetrameters and even shorter lines.
10 Breaking of lines between characters to give a livelier, more conversational pitch to certain passages.
11 Occasional alliteration.
12 A very sparing use of rhyme.
13 A careful choice of vowel sounds.
14 The development of the 'verse paragraph'.

(Bakeless, pp. 183–4)

These devices are either infractions of the unrhymed iambic penta-meter verse design, or are not provided for by that design. Two comments must be made on this approach. First, the 'versifier's progress' described by Mr Bakeless—from a rigid to a relaxed use of this verse design—is characteristic of most of the other English poets who have written extensively in blank verse: in particular, the metrical freedom of Shakespeare's last plays, in contrast to the greater regularity of the verse of his early comedies and histories, has usually been explained in just those terms. This progress is quite predictable, given the straitness of the design and a productive poet. Second, the devices for varying and breaking up the pentameter are routine licences: some of them—for instance the reversed first foot and the feminine ending—are so frequently used, by so many poets who are in other respects quite different from each other, that one would be justified in treating them as regular alternatives available within the verse design itself. On that analysis, these departures from the basic framework of the pentameter would be hardly more than background features of the line, unless specially frequently manipulated into very distinctive configurations. In fact, we can appeal only to 'special' uses of such features to characterize verse instances: a more delicate analytic apparatus—used in conjunction with the exposition of 'irregularities'—is needed to describe the texture of particular pieces of verse.

By 'texture' I refer to what some critics might call 'metrical style'. It is a generalization of the character of verse instances, the 'feel' of a poem or passage given by a distinctive organization of linguistic details repeated in many lines. Like all stylistic concepts, it is relativistic, quantitative. A feature is neutral in itself: but if repeated a certain number of times it leads the reader to experience some particular tone or quasi-physical perception, to which he may attach an impressionistic label: 'lyrical', 'ponderous', 'rapid', 'halting', 'majestic', or whatever. Critics are ready enough to apply such descriptions; they are less confident about the linguistic sources of their responses to metrical texture. There is usually a wide gap between the descriptive-evaluative labels and the analytic process (if any). This is, unfortunately, true of Mr Bakeless' account of Marlowe: his responses to the mighty line lead him to use phrases like 'barbaric violence', 'lyric quality', 'majesty', 'piercing melody', 'lyric grace', and so forth. Such terms may or may not be objectionable in themselves; they are certainly of little use unsubstantiated by any display of analysis. All that Mr Bakeless does is attempt to show that Marlowe's metre develops into a flexible enough medium to accommodate all these qualities—he does not try to demonstrate the linguistic determinants of the particular qualities which he mentions.

A range of linguistic organizations is available for establishing metrical style. Some of these—the most important, but usually the least noticed—are adjustments of language which entail no disturbance of the verse design. Others break rules of the verse design. In the latter class are extra syllables in the middle or at the end of the line, omitted syllables, reversed feet, equal-stressed feet ('spondees' and 'pyrrhic feet'). If these devices are repeated often enough, they become 'institutionalized' and thus change the verse design, losing their potential for rhetorical force. In the present analysis we are concerned with such infractions employed more moderately and in conjunction with other, non-irregular, devices. These are variations of which no mention is made in the rules of the verse design: for instance, the verse design does not prescribe that there should—or should not—be a syntactic break in the centre of the line (caesura); nor does it specify what treatment the end of the line should receive —whether the syntax should end with the line or run on. Nor does the verse design dictate the relationship between morphology or phrase-structure and the structure of the line, beyond prescribing

that words and phrases should be arranged to give a rising pattern of
alternate light and heavy stresses. I have argued elsewhere that
adjustments of surface-structure syntax affect significantly the
character of verse instances, without disturbing the character of the
verse design. Where patterns of syntax and morphology are inter-
woven with patterns of minor metrical irregularities, and the scheme
so established is repeated to give a cumulative effect, a distinctive
verse texture or metrical style is created. To illustrate this achievement, I will compare three quite different metrical styles in blank
verse. They are exemplified in the following three passages:

Tamburlaine Ah, fair Zenocrate, divine Zenocrate,
    Fair is too foul an epithet for thee,
    That in thy passion for thy country's love,
    And fear to see thy kingly father's harm,
    With hair dishevelled wip'st thy watery cheeks;   5
    And like to Flora in her morning's pride,
    Shaking her silver tresses in the air,
    Rain'st on the earth resolved pearl in showers,
    And sprinklest sapphires on thy shining face,
    Where Beauty, mother to the Muses, sits,   10
    And comments volumes with her ivory pen,
    Taking instructions from thy flowing eyes,
    Eyes, when that Ebena steps to heaven,
    In silence of thy solemn evening's walk,
    Making the mantle of the richest night,   15
    The moon, the planets, and the meteors, light,
    There angels in their crystal armours fight
    A doubtful battle with my tempted thoughts
    For Egypt's freedom and the Soldan's life,
    His life that so consumes Zenocrate;   20
    Whose sorrows lay more siege unto my soul
    Than all my army to Damascus' walls;
    And neither Persia's sovereign nor the Turk
    Troubled my senses with conceit of foil
    So much by much as doth Zenocrate.   25
    What is beauty, saith my sufferings, then?
    If all the pens that ever poets held
    Had fed the feeling of their masters' thoughts,
    And every sweetness that inspir'd their hearts,
    Their minds and muses on admired themes;   30
    If all the heavenly quintessence they still
    From their immortal flowers of poesy,
    Wherein as in a mirror we perceive

The highest reaches of a human wit—
If these had made one poem's period,   35
And all combin'd in beauty's worthiness,
Yet should there hover in their restless heads
One thought, one grace, one wonder, at the least,
Which into words no virtue can digest.
But how unseemly is it for my sex,   40
My discipline of arms and chivalry,
My nature, and the terror of my name,
To harbour thoughts effeminate and faint!
Save only that in beauty's just applause,
With whose instinct the soul of man is touched,   45
And every warrior that is rapt with love
Of fame, of valour, and of victory,
Must needs have beauty beat on his conceits,
I thus conceiving, and subduing both,
That which hath stopt the tempest of the gods,   50
Even from the fiery spangled vein of heaven,
To feel the lovely warmth of shepherds' flames,
And march in cottages of strowed weeds,
Shall give the world to note, for all my birth,
That virtue solely is the sum of glory,   55
And fashions men in true nobility.
                (Marlowe, *Tamburlaine the Great I*. V. ii. 72–127)

Prospero My brother, and thy uncle, call'd Antonio,—
        I pray thee, mark me, that a brother should
        Be so perfidious!—he whom next thyself
        Of all the world I lov'd, and to him put   60
        The manage of my state; as at that time
        Through all the signories it was the first,
        And Prospero the prime duke, being so reputed
        In dignity, and for the liberal Arts
        Without a parallel; those being all my study,   65
        The government I cast upon my brother,
        And to my state grew stranger, being transported
        And rapt in secret studies. Thy false uncle—
        Dost thou attend me?
Miranda   Sir, most heedfully.
Pros. Being once perfected how to grant suits,   70
        How to deny then, who t'advance, and who
        To trash for over-topping, new created
        The creatures that were mine, I say, or chang'd 'em,
        Or else new form'd 'em; having both the key

Of officer and office, set all hearts i' th' state   75
To what tune pleas'd his ear, that now he was
The ivy which had hid my princely trunk,
And suck'd my verdure out on 't. Thou attend'st not?
Mir. O, good sir, I do.
Pros.   I pray thee, mark me.
    I, thus neglecting worldly ends, all dedicated   80
To closeness and the bettering of my mind
With that which, but by being so retir'd,
O'erprized all popular rate, in my false brother
Awak'd an evil nature; and my trust,
Like a good parent, did beget of him   85
A falsehood in its contrary, as great
As my trust was; which had indeed no limit,
A confidence sans bound. He being thus lorded,
Not only with what my revenue yielded,
But what my power might else exact, like one   90
Who having into truth, by telling of it,
Made such a sinner of his memory,
To credit his own lie, he did believe
He was indeed the duke; out o' th' substitution,
And executing th' outward face of royalty,   95
With all prerogative;—hence his ambition growing,—
Dost thou hear?
Mir.   Your tale, sir, would cure deafness.
Pros. To have no screen between this part he play'd
And him he play'd it for, he needs will be
Absolute Milan. Me, poor man, my library   100
Was dukedom large enough: of temporal royalties
He thinks me now incapable; confederates,
So dry he was for sway, wi' th' King of Naples
To give him annual tribute, do him homage,
Subject his coronet to his crown, and bend   105
The dukedom, yet unbow'd,—alas, poor Milan!—
To most ignoble stooping.
                    (Shakespeare, *The Tempest*, I. ii. 66–116)

                    From early days,
Beginning not long after that first time
In which, a Babe, by intercourse of touch   110
I held mute dialogues with my Mother's heart,
I have endeavoured to display the means
Whereby this infant sensibility,
Great birthright of our being, was in me

Augmented and sustained. Yet is a path   115
More difficult before me; and I fear
That in its broken windings we shall need
The chamois' sinews, and the eagle's wing:
For now a trouble came into my mind
From unknown causes. I was left alone   120
Seeking the visible world, nor knowing why.
The props of my affections were removed,
And yet the building stood, as if sustained
By its own spirit! All that I beheld
Was dear, and hence to finer influxes   125
The mind lay open, to a more exact
And close communion. Many are our joys
In youth, but oh! what happiness to live
When every hour brings palpable access
Of knowledge, when all knowledge is delight,   130
And sorrow is not there! The seasons came,
And every season wheresoe'er I moved
Unfolded transitory qualities,
Which, but for this most watchful power of love,
Had been neglected; left a register   135
Of permanent relations, else unknown,
Hence life, and change, and beauty, solitudē
More active even than 'best society'—
Society made sweet as solitude
By gentle inobtrusive sympathies,   140
And gentle agitations of the mind
From manifold distinctions, difference
Perceived in things, where, to the unwatchful eye,
No difference is, and hence, from the same source,
Sublimer joy; for I would walk alone,   145
Under the quiet stars, and at that time
Have felt whate'er there is of power in sound
To breathe an elevated mood, by form
Or image unprofaned; and I would stand,
If the night blackened with a coming storm,   150
Beneath some rock, listening to notes that are
The ghostly language of the ancient earth,
Or make their dim abode in distant winds.
Thence did I drink the visionary power;
And deem not profitless those fleeting moods   155
Of shadowy exultation: not for this,
That they are kindred to our purer mind
And intellectual life; but that the soul,

Remembering how she felt, but what she felt
Remembering not, retains an obscure sense   160
Of possible sublimity, whereto
With growing faculties she doth aspire,
With faculties still growing, feeling still
That whatsoever point they gain, they yet
Have something to pursue.

(Wordsworth, The Prelude [1850], ii, 265–322)

No one can fail to see that, although these passages are all of the same verse design—unrhymed iambic decasyllabic verse—there are striking stylistic, or 'textural', differences between them. Each passage has a quite distinctive style, to the extent that they are all ready subjects for parody. Furthermore, the verse texture reflects intrinsic features of the syntactic organization of the text, and is independent of any style of delivery which an actor or reader might choose: that is to say, in each case the language closely restricts the range of possible delivery styles. This fact may be tested by working out an adequate reading of one passage, holding the distinctive rhythm in one's head and then attempting to transfer it to one of the other extracts: Prospero in the manner of Tamburlaine is just not on—and the failure arises from linguistic, not dramatic, causes. In the Tamburlaine speech the language is inescapably melodic, even incantatory; the syntax is divided up into units of highly predictable length (one verse-line long), and these units are very repetitive in their internal structure. The distinctive phonetic character of Marlowe's lines (there are several kinds of Marlovian line) quite obviously results from the repetitiveness of the syntax: the commonplace of Marlowe criticism is that he achieves an architecture of the line, a grand fabric of phonetic pattern—through syntax and, perhaps, ultimately destroying syntax as a vehicle of meaning. One does not have to (or cannot) maintain alertness to Marlowe's syntax, for finally it is doing non-semantic things. It is a way of enforcing an overarching secondary rhythm built on predictability. Those who are familiar with Information Theory will know that there is an inverse correlation between predictability and informativeness. Response to the sonorousness of Marlowe's verse (a response which is obviously invited) wars against recovery of its meaning.

Late Shakespearean blank verse, though equally parodiable, is, locally, much less predictable. Prospero's account of his and Miranda's exile from Milan is both complicated and emotionally difficult. A lot of information of quite a detailed kind has to be taken in by the audience; Prospero's schoolmasterly demands of Miranda—'Dost thou attend me?'—are really addressed to the audience, for

it is *our* attention which is enjoined. The emotional difficulty is
Prospero's: what he reveals to Miranda here, for the first time, he
knows will contribute to the loss of her innocence, to her growing
away from him. Under these communicative and emotional pressures, Prospero's language is disjointed, hesitant. The dramatic
appropriateness of his style of speech in relation to his anxiety about
Miranda's response is obvious. What does need pointing out, perhaps, is that this lack of fluency in Prospero is an aid to audience
concentration. This fact is not so strange if we remember the connection between linguistic predictability and informativeness.
Tamburlaine's language can lull one into a feeling that he is thinking
fine and grand thoughts. Often—the last ten lines of his speech are a
case in point—one can hardly work out the precise content of these
thoughts unless one quite consciously breaks out of the 'grammetric'
matrix which straitjackets the language and which deadens one's
semantic response. But Prospero's language enforces alertness:
since you can never tell what twists of sentence-structure will
occur next, you have to pay attention very carefully. When a
speaker has something important to say, inarticulacy is forgiven—
the audience is happy to jerk along with the speaker from one fragment of thought to the next. In fact, the audience has no choice:
the broken syntax makes attentiveness obligatory.

The disjointed character of Prospero's language is obviously the
chief influence on the texture of the verse. But if we show that it is
fractured in this way locally, we must also show its underlying
regularity: how it avoids breaking up completely, in a word, how
the verse design escapes being destroyed by the apparently random
metrical texture.

I have included the extract from *The Prelude* principally as a foil
to the other two pieces. Wordsworth here attempts a relaxed, dis-
cursive style, serious and—except around lines 120–30—unexcited.
The flat style of narration and exposition, with its ostentatiously
damped passion, might well be found tedious, and certainly some
details are audaciously near to prose: *I have endeavoured to display
the means whereby this infant sensibility* . . . This is a confident and
technically superb poet writing for, and within, a literary culture
which has assimilated the achievements of Shakespeare and Milton
in this particular verse design. The fluency of Wordsworth's verse is
to a large extent attributable to the stability of the metrical tradition in which he writes. From his own point of view, as a practising
poet, the example of tens of thousands of lines of extant blank verse,
written by the two most influential poets in the language, had to be
enormously valuable. But the significance of this tradition for the
audience of *The Prelude* is even greater. The existence of a well-

established tradition of blank verse allows Wordsworth to allude to the norms of the design without stating them in his own composition. It is this facility which makes it possible for him to steer so close to un-metered language in safety. He can assume that educated readers will impose a generalized blank verse rhythm on his poem, if only they are reminded of the heritage by an occasional reference to it: stock inversions, as *in me | Augmented and sustained*, ll. 114–15, *to finer influxes | The mind lay open*, ll. 125–6; ellipses, e.g. *Yet is a path*, l. 115, *No difference is*, l. 144; the Shakespearean trick of reversing the stresses on certain words, e.g. *óbscure*, l. 160; Miltonic enjambments, as for instance *our joys | In youth*, ll. 127–8, *register | Of permanent relations*, ll. 135–6, *by form | Or image unprofaned*, ll. 148–9; traditional elisions, as *the unwatchful eye*, l. 143. Such allusions, though discreetly and sparingly used, are potent signals to the experienced reader of Shakespeare and Milton, and they allow Wordsworth to relax the verse design to his own level of rhythmic fluidity.

One *tour de force* of classical English blank verse is the accommodation of many-syllabled words. The iambic pentameter line has an internal structure based on two-stress units, but these units are reflected accurately in the stress patterns of only a small range of morphological and syntactic arrangements in English: two-syllabled words with the stress on the second syllable, such as *above, beyond, away, pursue*, and two-word phrases in which the first word is a lightly-stressed item such as a preposition, auxiliary verb, pronoun —*he went, in debt, to go, my hat*, etc. In the unlikely event that pentameter verse could be composed entirely of such units, the natural stress-pattern of the syntax would exactly realize the idealized stress-pattern of the verse design: alternating light and heavy stresses with only one contrast of *level* of stress: light versus heavy. In fact, the stress-patterns associated with English syntax and morphology are much more complicated and diverse, and the phonetic contours of English sentences require several rather subtle differentiations of stress-level. That is to say, stress-contrasts in English are more finely distinguished, and more various, than the simple two-level, up-and-down di-DAH-di-DAH pattern of the iambic verse design. Now polysyllabic words are a particular challenge because, to speak impressionistically, they level out the stress-contrasts and smooth the transitions between syllables. The impact of many polysyllabic words on the verse instance is to soften and relax it (and also speed it up). If a poet can accommodate a large number of polysyllabic words, and can distribute them in a rather informal way relative to the verse line, then his verse may assume a general character of easy expository statement. The learned quality of most English polysyllables guarantees the seriousness of the exposition.

But the catch is that this blank verse style requires enormous technical skill. The use of predominantly polysyllabic words compounds the difficulty of adjusting the stresses of the word to the metrical stresses of the line, and also reduces the latitude available to the poet for arranging the 'functional' parts of his sentence-structure (pronouns, conjunctions, articles, copulas, etc.). From this point of view, lines like Wordsworth's *Unfolded transitory qualities*, l. 133, are impressive feats of virtuosity. However, there is little point admiring Wordsworth's technical achievement in lines like this: the long words do not stand out splendidly as do the magnificent exotic proper names in Marlowe (*Usumcasane and Techelles both*) or in *Paradise Lost* (*In Vallombrosa, where th' Etrurian shades*). In Wordsworth the polysyllables produce a kind of metered academic language, a continuous expository tone rather than points of spectacular decoration. The stress-distinctions are levelled out, as we have seen, and the relationship with iambic verse appears tenuous until we realize that, even in this language of reduced accentual prominences, relatively heavy and relatively light stresses alternate regularly as the verse design demands. The metre is 'backgrounded' with great care so that it is quite unobtrusive but at the same time a stable and faultless foundation.

In both of the earlier passages, the metre might be said to be more 'active' than it is in this extract from *The Prelude*—particularly so in Tamburlaine's speech. In Marlowe, the verse instances are phonologically repetitive—because of formalized syntactic patterning—and so build a metrical superstructure on top of sentence-structure. To show the mechanics of this process would require a longer analysis than there is space for here. In general terms, the details of syntactic patterning in units smaller than the sentence are repetitive, in that phrases of similar type recur at similar points within the verse line. The effect of this is to assert a phonetic pattern which is (*a*) ten syllables long; (*b*) of determinate internal structure but *not* the up-and-down $| \times / | \times / | \times / | \times / | \times / |$ implied by the verse design, with its two degrees of stress only; (*c*) not coterminous with the larger-scale syntactic units. The line-endings, and hence the line as a unit, are emphasized by phrases of similar syntactic or morphological type occurring at the end of the line, reiterating a cadence; in fact, there is more than one type of cadence. Phrases and polysyllabic words fall into groups as follows:

> thy country's love, thy watery cheeks, her morning's pride, thy shining face, her ivory pen, thy flowing eyes, the richest night,

my tempted thoughts, the Soldan's life, their masters' thoughts, their restless heads.

thy kingly father's harm, thy solemn evening's walk.

period, worthiness, chivalry, victory, nobility.

The matching of phrases in the first group particularly is especially striking. The syntactic parallelism is attended by phonological repetition (though not rhyme): of the four syllables in this cadence, the first is always a lightly-stressed, but not necessarily reduced, syllable constituting a monosyllabic function word, usually a possessive pronoun; the third syllable always the second in a two-syllable word, and always the vowel [ɪ] or [ə]. The word-boundaries always occur in the same positions relative to the foot. The effect is a kind of 'syntactic rhyme', which can be perceived as pure pattern and at the same time 'arrests' the syntax at the line end. Thus the overall syntax is interrupted, and a powerful expectation of end-stopping is produced. A particularly noticeable case of what I have called the 'non-semantic' effect is the transition between lines 46 and 47: it is all too easy to misinterpret the predicate attending 'every warrior' as simply 'rapt with love'—quite the wrong meaning, for Tamburlaine goes on to qualify 'love' ('Of fame,' etc.). If the Marlovian verse-texture is well established by this time, the reader/audience should experience a strong expectation of syntactic pause after 'love'. This is a good illustration of the tendency, in this form of verse, for syntactic segmentations to be determined by an induced 'set' towards the stress-and-intonation patterns.

I will return to this question of prosodic 'interference' with syntax in a moment. It is unnecessary to stress, perhaps, the direct phonetic value of Marlowe's patterning. At the end of the line, the verse texture works not only as an influence on syntactic interpretation, but also as a pattern in itself: it is, after all, a cadence—a definite sequence of phonetic shapes. Such phonetic patterns occur in other parts of the line too. For example, one repeated structure embraces syllables 2–5 of several lines: *sprinklest sapphires, comments volumes, doubtful battle, highest reaches*, etc. In places where this pattern of the first half of the line accompanies the cadence pattern, a very characteristic Marlovian line emerges:

For Ég/ȳpt's frée/dŏm and the Sól/dăn's lífe

I have marked only relevant stresses and foot-divisions. Notice that both of the patterns—that in the first half of the line and that at the

o

end—superimpose a falling rhythm on the rising rhythm of the verse design: this is a consequence of the morphology of the lexical items which have been selected. Notice also that the two patterns within the line parallel each other, and are interconnected; sometimes this connection is emphasized by alliteration or near-alliteration:

> And sprinklest sapphires on thy shining face.

In later verse (classically, Pope's) this particular whole-line pattern is used extensively in relation to a balanced or antithetical syntax: in this way, the phonetic contour is justified by the meaning, since it serves to point up the semantic organization of the line. In Marlowe, as we have seen, the line as a phonetic unit is strongly emphasized, and the line boundaries are often arbitrary as far as the long-term syntax is concerned. The syntactic arbitrariness of the line is reinforced by the satisfaction of the phonetic contour within it. Balance is constantly suggested in lines where it is gratuitous or inappropriate:

> A doubtful battle with my tempted thoughts . . .
> Their minds and muses on admired themes . . .

A doubtful battle is related to *my tempted thoughts* by the secondary rhythm, although it has a more basic relation to *fight* in the previous line, and *my tempted thoughts* to *For Egypt's freedom*, etc., in the next. In the second example, an even stronger version of this phonetic pattern (it is reinforced by alliteration and internal rhyme) severely disturbs the syntax. The sequence *their hearts, their minds and muses* is broken up; the prepositional phrase *on admired themes* appears, quite pointlessly, to modify *their minds and muses* rather than *inspir'd*. These effects are very characteristic of Marlowe, and illustrate well the way a powerfully articulated verse texture can distract from meaning.

Marlowe's distinctive verse texture is achieved within the normal regularities of the verse design. The only infringements of the design are two lines with a missing syllable each (13 and 26) and one with an extra syllable (55); these have no effect on the overall style. The predominant rhythm brings a refinement, not replacement, of the 'metrical set' induced by the regularity of the design.

But in the *Tempest* extract there is a marked discord between the metrical set proper to the design and the texture of verse instances. This tension is guaranteed by conspicuous variation in the length of line. Only half of the lines in this extract are ten syllables long. The rest are eleven, twelve, or thirteen syllables long. In most cases, the extra syllables are accommodated at the ends of lines (feminine endings), but sometimes they appear in the body of the line, causing a much more severe disturbance to one's metrical expectations:

Of officer and office, set all hearts i'th'state

(ᵕ · · · ᵕ shows sequences of light syllables occupying the place of one metrically unstressed syllable ˣ in the verse design.) Elsewhere, the length of the line is controlled by conventional elisions and pseudo-elisions (see 'What is Metrical Analysis?' pp. 161–4): *per-fidious* (59), *Prospero* (63), *being* (63), *liberal* (64), *parallel* (65), etc. These extra-metrical syllables and pseudo-elisions, coming at random points within the line, serve a very important function: they help to frustrate a harmful predictability in the recurrent structure of verse instances which might threaten the liveliness of the verse texture (as the extract from *Tamburlaine* is dulled by its repetitiveness). In this case, the danger is that the feminine endings will, through over-use, defeat their own object: rather than simply securing occasional independence of the pentameter verse design, they may fall into a stylized pattern which comes to be accepted as the norm. But the presence of extra-metrical syllables earlier in the line disturbs the reader's anticipatory metrical set so that the acceptance of extra syllables later in the line is de-automatized. In this way, the reader is discouraged from regarding the feminine ending as part of the verse design, so he can still experience the tension between a ten-syllabled design and an instance of more than ten syllables. But this is a precarious experience, for the reader is kept uncertain about the regularity of the verse—or rather, about *which* regularity to trust. This very uncertainty is, of course, a positive feature of the verse style.

Line-length is only one of several variables which Shakespeare arranges so as to produce the nervous, unstable style of this passage. Another important factor is the disposition of the caesura. The extract is perfectly typical of late Shakespearean blank verse in the frequency of strong syntactic breaks within the line coupled with close syntactic transitions between the end of one line and the beginning of the next. Since the caesura tends to occur at more or less the same place in the line (usually after the fourth, fifth, or sixth syllable), a relatively constant secondary metrical unit may appear between one caesura and the next. This is the 'straddled line', a pentameter within two normal pentameters: *and to him put | The manage of my state*, ll. 60–1, *and for the liberal Arts | Without a parallel*, ll. 64–5, *he did believe | He was indeed the duke*, ll. 93–4; there are several other examples in this passage, but these are the most perfect ones. I have shown elsewhere[2] the way in which constant employment of straddled lines can set up a 'counterpoint' between the movement of the basic lines and that of the secondary lines, and there is a tendency towards this dual movement in the passage under discussion. But as with the feminine endings, stylization is avoided: straddled lines do not appear continuously, and their length varies, producing an uncertainty about syllable-count in the centre of the line (i.e. at the end of the straddled unit) like that felt at the line ending. Appropriately, the audience will be as hesitant in perceiving the structure of the verse as Prospero is in articulating it. But this does not mean that the verse will be perceived as unstructured: the various sources of metrical irregularity are themselves too diverse, and too controlled, to submerge the basic verse design. The delicate suggestions of competing verse designs provide a satisfying tension in the texture of the passage, but these are *only* delicate suggestions.

Finally, a metrical analysis which set out to do full justice to the verse style of this extract from *The Tempest*—as of any piece of verse—would need to include a complete exposition of the syntactic surface-structure of the passage. The real key to the verse style exemplified by our extract from *The Tempest* is its syntactic versatility: as I have already mentioned, the relationship between syntax and metre is quite unpredictable because of the syntactic range of the passage. We know that sentence- and clause-boundaries tend to occur in the middle of lines, but beyond that there is no certainty. Inevitably, this syntactic diversity makes it impossible for an analysis to be offered in the space of this short essay, but I can give some hints towards a crude do-it-yourself analysis. In the analysis, we have to ask 'What syntactic segments are matched to what metrical units?' The relationship between the phonological implications of surface-structure syntax, which are in theory infinitely variable, and the phonological expectation of the verse design, which is in theory fixed, is the chief influence on the texture of the verse as it extends continuously through a poem. This relationship can be studied 'from either end': we could start with a description of the syntax or with a statement of the verse design. Whichever starting-point is chosen, we have to select certain kinds of unit for our initial segmentation. Supposing we began with syntax, we could, for instance, notice the length of words in the text, determining whether there was any tendency for words of a certain length to occur with any particular frequency. We saw that the incidence of polysyllabic words is of great importance to the style of the Wordsworth passage: the high density of such words, in reducing the accentual contrasts between metrically stressed and unstressed syllables, and in generally smoothing out phonological transitions and increasing the fluidity of the verse; and the random distribution of such words relative to the line, in avoiding gratuitous phonetic patterning. In Marlowe, on the other hand, many-syllabled words are not particularly prominent, but there is a decided preference for two-syllable words with primary stress on the first syllable: *passion, kingly, father, wat(e)ry, Flora, morning's*, etc. What is more, these disyllables tend to fall in regular places in the line; I have commented above on the phonetic consequences of this regularity. Shakespeare's lexical choices are different again. No one type of word is favoured, and certainly polysyllables do not predominate. There are, on the contrary, many monosyllabic words, and a few lines which consist entirely or almost entirely of monosyllables (e.g. 60, 76, 99). I do not know whether the frequency of monosyllables could be said to be exceptional—the subjective impression is that this is not the case. Rather, the monosyllabic sequences seem to be natural to the colloquialism of the piece, and indeed are a cause of the audience's perception of this colloquialism.

Finally, we might consider the 'grammetrics' of *The Tempest* from the other direction: starting with a metrical segmentation and seeing how the syntax is adjusted to it. How this might be done was suggested when I discussed Marlowe: take any metrical segment and study what occurs within its boundaries. In the case of Marlowe, if we take the last four, or five, or six syllables in the line we find that the syntactic units contained within that syllabic span are remarkably consistent: a prepositional phrase, or a particular kind of noun phrase, in a large proportion of cases. This syntactic consistency ensures that the metrical units with which we began are not arbitrary segments: Marlowe's lines are divided systematically into units intermediate in size between the foot and the line. The syntax defines these units. But in the *Tempest* extract, there are no intra-line units picked out by syntactic repetition. If we select any constant sequence of syllables relative to the line as a whole, we will find that the syntactic arrangements within that sequence are quite capricious. This assertion can be very easily tested; I invite the reader to make this observation for himself—understanding the syntactic arbitrariness of Shakespeare's metre is an excellent way of coming to understand the general thesis of this paper.

Notes to Paper Twelve

1 *The Tragicall History of Christopher Marlowe* (first published 1942, reprinted Archon Books, Hamden, Conn.), ii, 173–204.
2 ' "Prose Rhythm" and Metre', *Essays on Style and Language* (London, 1966), 90–2.

Thirteen

Some stylistic features of the *Sermo Lupi*

It may be thought that Wulfstan's style has been described often enough to make further treatment unnecessary.[1] We are familiar with his lexical and morphological peculiarities, intensifying adverbs and adverbial tags, and rhetorical devices, which include alliteration, two-stress rhythmical patterns, word-lists, repetition. The features have been enumerated by critics and editors through the last eighty years. They have been the special concern of editors because the doctrine has grown up that the Archbishop's style is so idiosyncratic that its detection in a text can provide a basis for attribution. It is not the purpose of this article to consider the validity of this use of stylistic description, but to suggest that the selection of stylistic features for description, largely conditioned by the needs of authorship tests, has failed to provide a general literary description of the stylistic qualities.[2]

Two scholars have written recently on the subject of Wulfstan's style: Professors McIntosh and Bethurum.[3] Professor Bethurum's approach is summed up in the first sentence of her section on style: 'Wulfstan's homilies are the work of a skilled rhetorician and illustrate the teachings of the manuals of rhetoric which he must have studied.' Professor McIntosh is concerned with Wulfstan's rhythm, and the core of his argument is found in a much-quoted sentence: 'Wulfstan's prose consists of a continuous series of two-stress phrases related in structure to the classical half-line, and severely restricted in somewhat the same fashion to certain rhythmical patterns' (p. 114). He continues:

> these phrases are always *small syntactic units*. They are not
> mere metrical motifs torn from the text by wilfully or arbitrarily
> cutting between two adjacent elements in a sentence which
> have an intimate syntactic connexion, for example, preposition
> and noun, or pronoun and verb. Some phrases are more

obviously separable than others, as is true of half-lines in the classical verse, but on the whole Wulfstan's prose is easier to split up on the basis of natural speech-pauses which delimit these small syntactic units, than the verse is . . . (p. 116).

Two things are implied here: first, that there is in Wulfstan a constant relation between rhythmical and grammatical units in terms of coincidence of boundaries between pairs of each of these types of unit; second, that Wulfstan's style differs in this respect from that of other writers of rhythmical Old English. Professor McIntosh does not expand these implications. The first, the relationship between grammar and rhythm, underlies much of what follows in this article.

An investigation of the types of grammatical unit which are contained in Wulfstan's rhythmical units suggested these observations on the style of the *Sermo Lupi*. What follows is, of necessity, a partial and non-statistical description. Although a full study of the styles of Old English, or of Wulfstan alone, would require an extended treatment, nevertheless the requirements of such a description may be here indicated:

First, a complete GRAMMATICAL analysis of the texts in question, using the methods of modern descriptive linguistics. The most significant grammatical features, for the literary critic, are not those which have been given most attention by the grammarians of Old English. Whereas the arrangement of words into classes and paradigms has been exhaustively covered, there have been few studies [4] of what is called 'word-order' and what is in reality the structure of sentences in terms of clauses, clauses in terms of phrases, [5] phrases in terms of words. It is the structure of the larger units which is most variable and therefore stylistically most significant: a writer can alter word-structures, or his language's inventory of morphemes, only at the risk of failing to communicate.

Second, a RHYTHMICAL analysis. Here the approach of Professor McIntosh can be adopted and modified. A two-stress rhythmical unit of the type discussed by him will be called a *foot*: it merits a special term because it appears to be the minimal rhythmical unit which is basic to much Old English. Units larger than the foot may be predicted. For example, a series of three identical feet $/\times\times/\times$, $/\times\times/\times$, $/\times\times/\times$ might be said to constitute a type of non-minimal rhythmical unit, as against $/\times\times/\times$ by itself, or a series of feet of a different type: $/\times/\times$, $/\times/\times$, $/\times/\times$. Clearly, rhythmical units larger than the foot will have to be recognized in the poetry or in those parts of Ælfric where alliteration is used to link 'half-lines' into pairs. Again, a foot with internal alliteration, e.g. *w*ide on *w*orolde, has to be regarded as phonologically different from one without such alliteration but with an identical rhythm, e.g. *ealles to swyðe*.

Third, the VOCABULARY must be described on a much broader basis than has been attempted hitherto. It is immediately obvious that the *Sermo Lupi* has a distinctive vocabulary: but this needs to be explained by wider statements than those involving minute vocabulary contrasts, e.g. between *lagu* and *æ* or *gesælig* and *eadig*.[6] Briefly, it may be suggested that a start might be made by listing words which are unique in, or rare outside, Wulfstan; by stating how great is the concentration of unusual lexical items in a particular text. (One suspects that part of the force of the *Sermo Lupi* comes from the frequency with which the author bombards his audience with strange and powerful words.) Finally, unusual or striking collocations should be examined. Wulfstan, with his quantities of co-ordinated pairs, is a very suitable subject for such study.

I am advocating the study of Old English style, and especially that of Wulfstan, from a broader viewpoint than has been customary. Instead of picking out specific, prominent, features, without reference to their wider contexts, we should take into account the whole of grammar, or phonology (not only rhythm), or lexis. The description is to be, at the outset, a linguistic description which deals with a text at each of these three separate levels, making possible a study of the relationship between sets of data revealed at these levels. We might investigate the correspondence between grammatical and rhythmical segments, or the effect that co-ordination in nominal groups has on the size of the vocabulary. Our ideal approach is a complete analysis at each of these levels before any attempt is made to characterize the style, and before using any grammatical, phonological, or lexical information as a basis for judgment on Wulfstan's authorship. We need to penetrate into the linguistic character of his writing, and to survey all his authenticated work. Before using any stylistic evidence in a test of authorship, we must examine not only Wulfstan; we must accumulate a large body of comparative data from other authors. In the scope of this article I shall limit myself to discussing a set of related stylistic features of the *Sermo Lupi*, merely as examples of the types of stylistic information revealed by a linguistic attitude, not as end-products of a comprehensive analysis. These features are not isolated fragments picked out at random, but aspects related to each other and to the general linguistic framework within which Wulfstan writes.

i *Variety of sentence-structure*

At first it might seem that Wulfstan does not use a large variety of types of sentence, but this is not the case. There is, it is true, no great use of bound[7] clauses, and there is a preference for direct over inverted order. To add to an impression of lack of variety, frequently two or three sentences of the same structure will tend to follow one another.[8] The monotonous rhythm further supports this impression. But the normal range of Old English sentence-types is found. Some varieties may be noted: Imperative structures (PC):[9] *gecnawað þæt soð is* (l. 7),[10] *Understandað . . . spæcan* (ll. 11–13); structures with indirect object: *7 us unwedera foroft weoldan unwæstma* (l. 59); predicatorless sentences: *Wala þære yrmðe 7 wala þære woroldscame . . . yrre!* (ll. 119–20); subjectless sentences: *Ac worhtan lust us to lage . . . scoldan* (two sentences, ll. 65–7), *Utan . . .* (many examples, ll. 186–end); questions: *And la, hu mæg mare scamu . . . for agenum gewyrhtum?* (ll. 100–1); simple SPC sentences: *7 huru hit wyrð þænne egeslic 7 grimlic wide on worolde* (ll. 10–11), *And þæs we habbað . . . bysmor gelome* (ll. 49–50).

In addition to these examples of the variety of separate types of sentence, three other features diversify sentence-structure: variety in the types of subordinate clauses used (e.g. adjectival, *þe smeade . . .*, ll. 14–15, nominal, *þæt deofol . . .*, ll. 11–12, adverbial, *þeah hy . . .*, l. 13); variety in the orders of subordinate and main clause; variety of length of sentence, ranging from two clauses packed into one foot (*gecnawað þæt soð is*, l. 7) to sentences extending over many lines (*7 egeslic . . . deore gebohte*, ll. 86–91). It is impossible here to exemplify all the different structures which come under the above headings, since the variety is considerable.

ii *Use of direct rather than inverted order*

Inversion of subject and predicator is a characteristic of earlier styles of Old English, particularly of the *Chronicle*. Wulfstan's preference is for direct order. For example, in the opening lines of the *Sermo Lupi* we find the following clauses, subordinate as well as main, beginning with the direct order SP:

> ðeos worold is . . .; hit nealæcð . . .; hit is . . .; hit sceal . . .
> yfelian . . .; hit wyrð . . .; deofol (þas þeode) . . . dwelode . . .;
> lytle getreowþa wæran . . .; hy . . . spæcan . . .; unrihta to fela
> ricsode. . . .

Then there is an inversion, *næs . . . fela manna*,[11] followed by another string of direct-order sentences. The main clauses which begin sentences employ direct order frequently; Wulfstan's 'rhetorical' use of inversion is by and large limited to expanded clauses.

iii *Use of parenthesis*

Parenthetical clauses interrupting other clauses or sentences are common. They are always one foot in length, and the effect they give

of discontinuity in the main clause may be compared with that
achieved by Wulfstan's placing of adverbial phrases, similarly one
foot in length, between subject and predicator. The effect is rhythmical rather than grammatical:

Ac soð is þæt ic secge (l. 37); hrædest is to cweþenne (l. 48);
gecnawe se þe cunne (l. 99); swa hit þincan mæg (l. 160); etc.

iv *Expanded clauses*

An important means of achieving variety in grammar is found below
the rank[12] of the sentence, within the clause. Wulfstan displays
much subtlety in the ways in which he expands simple clauses. A
clause is expanded by repeating one or two of its primary elements of
structure (S, P, C, or IO), leaving the expansion dependent upon, and
therefore linked to, the opening clause. Wulfstan varies this practice
by repeating different elements of clause-structure in different orders,
and by taking this procedure to different lengths. The first instance
we meet in the *Sermo Lupi* (ll. 15–17) is:

$$\overset{S}{}\ \overset{P}{}\ \overset{C}{}\ \overset{C}{}\ \overset{P}{}$$

(ac dæghwamlice)[13] man ihte yfel æfter oðrum (7) unriht rærde

(7) unlaga manege (ealles to wide gynd ealle þas þeode).

The letters above: man ihte = S P, yfel æfter oðrum = C, unriht = C, rærde = P, unlaga manege = C.

The basic clause, SPC, is *man . . . oðrum*; the first expansion, CP,
unriht rærde, depends on *man* for its S; the second, C, *unlaga manege*,
depends on *man* for its S and *rærde* for its P. A particularly common
type of expansion involves the repetition of S or P only, many
times:

(And) us stalu (7) cwalu, stric (7) steorfa, orfcwealm (7) uncoðu,
hol (7) hete (7) rypera reaflac derede (swyþe þearle). (ll. 56–8)

With element labels: us = C, stalu = S, cwalu = S, stric = S, steorfa = S, orfcwealm = S, uncoðu = S; hol = S, hete = S, rypera = S.

Eadweard man forræde (7 syððan) acwealde (7 æfter þam)
forbærnde. (ll. 77–8)

With element labels: Eadweard = C, man = S, forræde = P, acwealde = P, forbærnde = P.

Hy hergiað (7) hy bærnað, rypað (7) reafiað (7 to scipe) lædað.
(ll. 126–7)

With element labels: Hy = S, hergiað = P, hy = S, bærnað = P, rypað = S, reafiað = P, lædað = P.

Non-primary elements of clause-structure (in effect, adverbial
phrases) may be repeated at length in a similar way. We should note
the extraordinary series in ll. 132–8, where twenty adverbial phrases
are attached to one past participle, *forsyngod*; here (as in the
example quoted above from ll. 56–8) we have instances of what are

called Wulfstan's 'word-lists': in grammatical terms, lists of groups
or phrases rather than words.

It is impossible here to illustrate all the types of expansion used in
the *Sermo Lupi*: I shall pass on to two of the more complex examples,
asking the reader to find instances of different arrangements of elements in the shorter expanded clauses. One expansion is not particularly effective because it is obscured in a rambling sentence which
starts in a subordinate clause in line 87:

'S'   P   C   P
þæt sceotað (togædere) (7) ane cwenan (gemænum ceape) bicgað
                                        C   P
(gemæne) (7 wið þa ane) fylþe adreogað, (an after anum 7 ælc

æfter oðrum, hundum gelicost þe for fylþe ne scrifað,) (7 syððan
                    P
wið weorðe) syllað (of lande feondum to gewealde)
   C   C
Godes gesceafte (7) his agenne ceap. . . .[14]

A frequent and much more successful type involves repetition of only
one part of the predicator, usually the participle of an auxiliary+
participle group. Our example is a series of such clauses in lines 40–9.
The auxiliary part of the predicator is symbolized P^i, the repeated
participle P^{ii}; the sentences are marked off by oblique strokes; once
again, elements other than S, P, and C are enclosed in parentheses,
and it will be noticed that here these non-primary elements occupy a
much smaller part of the sentences than they did in the previous
quotation:

                  S P^i P^{ii}
(7) Godes hus syndan (to clæne) berypte (ealdra gerihta) (7 innan)
P^{ii} S P^i P^{ii}
bestrypte (ælcra gerisena), / (7) wydewan syndan fornydde (on
                  S P^{ii} P^{ii}
unriht to ceorle), / (7) to mænege foryrmde (7) gehynede (swyþe) /
      S P^{ii} P^{ii} P^{ii}
(7) earme men syndan (sare) beswicene (7 hreowlice) besyrwde
                              P^{ii}
(7 ut of þysan earde wide) gesealde (swyþe unforworhte,
                              S P^{ii}
fremdum to gewealde) (7) cradolcild geþeowede (þurh

wælhreowe unlaga for lytelre þyfþe wide gynd þas þeode) (7)
  S P^{ii} S P^{ii} S P^{ii}
freoriht fornumene (7) þrælriht genyrwde (7) ælmesriht gewanode
                              S   "P^{ii}"   S P^{ii}
(7, hrædest is to cweþenne,) Godes laga laðe (7) lara forsawene.
(ll. 41–9)

This lengthy series of expansions is successfully sustained; an in-
tolerable extreme of expansion is avoided by occasionally supplying

a P^i (*syndan*); but towards the end seven P^{ii}'s are allowed to build up tension uninterrupted by a P^i. After this crescendo, the orator gathers breath in the parenthesis *hrædest is to cweþenne* before a final restatement of the pattern: S, *Godes laga*, is accompanied by the alternative P^{ii}, the adjective-as-complement *laðe*. Finally, the standard expansion SP^{ii}, *lara forsawene*,[15] brings the set of clauses to a close.

v *Discontinuity, and the treatment of adverbs*

Discontinuous verbal groups (i.e. groups with auxiliary and participle or infinitive separated) are very common in Old English. A common type, the structure P^{i}S(C)P^{ii}, is illustrated from the *Chronicle*: *Hæfde se cyning his fierd on tu tonumen* (894, Sweet VIII, ll. 30–1). In the *Chronicle*, discontinuity in the verbal group can be attended by inversion: that is to say, the split in the predicator is filled by the subject, and sometimes, as in the clause just quoted, by the complement too. Wulfstan sometimes preserves direct order, and fills the gap in another way, as in the first example of discontinuity which we meet in the *Sermo Lupi* (ll. 9–10):

S   P^i P^{ii}

7 swa hit sceal nyde for folces synnan   yfelian swyþe.

fram dæge to dæge[16]

ær Antecristes tocyme

Here the gap is filled by three adverbial phrases, each one foot long, of a type exceedingly frequent in Wulfstan. Three of the five feet in the clause are taken up in this way, and in the remaining two the rhythm is completed by the adverbs *nyde* and *swyþe*.

A discontinuous predicator may be interrupted by a parenthetical clause, as in lines 131–2 and 160–1:

P^i S   P^{ii}

ac wearð þes þeodscipe, swa hit þincan mæg, swyþe forsyngod. . . .

P^i P^{ii}

Her syndan þurh synleawa, swa hit þincan mæg, sare gelewede

S

to manege on earde.

Both adverbs and parenthesis interrupt the predicator in one case (ll. 138–40):

P^i

And eac syndan wide, swa we ær cwædan, þurh aðbricas 7

                                   P^{ii} P^{ii}

þurh wedbrycas 7 þurh mistlice leasunga forloren 7 forlogen

S

ma þonne scolde.

Two uses of the adverb are illustrated in the above quotations, both linked to the rhythmical pattern. The first, and the simplest, is the employment of a single adverb, usually a noun or adjective in an oblique case,[17] to fill out a rhythmical unit which contains P, P^i, or P^{ii}. In the quotations just given: 7 swa hit sceal *nyde*, yfelian *swyþe*, *swyþe* forsyngod, *sare* gelewede. This list could be extended to illustrate simple adverbs, exocentric one-member adverbs, and exocentric two-member adverbs (preposition+noun) filling first or second position of strong stress, before or after P, P^i, and P^{ii}. We may make a short list, starting from near the beginning of the *Sermo Lupi*:[18]

7 huru hit wyrð *þænne*, Understandað eac *georne*, dwelode *to swyðe*, wæran *mid mannum*, ricsode *on lande*, ac *dæghwamlice* man ihte.

The second prominent use of the adverb (again conditioned by the rhythm) embraces adverbial groups (endocentric, as *ealles to swyþe*) and longer phrases (exocentric, prepositional, as *gynd ealle þas þeode*). These longer units correspond in length to the foot, and are extremely mobile in their placing within the clause; Wulfstan exploits all the possible positions—before S, between S and P, between P and C, after C, or between P^i and P^{ii} in direct-order clauses, elsewhere in inverted clauses. We have already illustrated one use (within P^i . . . P^{ii}) and may note three more of the several other possibilities:

before S (ll. 20–1, cf. 21–2);

Forþam *mid miclan earnungan* we geearnedan þa yrmða. . . .

after P (ll. 97–8);

7 wed synd tobrocene *oft 7 gelome*.

after C (ll. 29–30);

7 we forhealdað æghwær Godes gerihta *ealles to gelome*.[19]

Adverbial groups and phrases occupying one foot are not only mobile in Wulfstan but extremely numerous. There is over 0·5 of such a unit for every clause in the text (counting rank-shifted clauses but not expansions). These grammatical-rhythmical units are frequently accumulated in series (ll. 9–10, 30–1, 56, 121–2, 132–8, 180–2, etc.). This favourite unit of Wulfstan's carries his typical lexical tags (*ealles to swyþe*, etc.). Professor McIntosh remarks (pp. 118–19), 'Furthermore, the common tags that Wulfstan uses have this same rhythmical characteristic; they either form a two-stress phrase in themselves (for example, *ealles to gelome*) or else they serve to fill out a phrase which would otherwise be too light rhythmically (for example, *georne* in *and beorgan us georne*).' In such idioms as *for Gode and for worolde, ealles to swyþe*, we must note the convergence of Wulfstan's favourite lexical items, his standard rhythm, and a much-used grammatical structure. It is not enough to list them as 'catch-phrases'. They are best understood as a natural product of the concurrence of grammar, lexis, and rhythm, not merely as tags scattered randomly through his writings.

vi *Symmetry* v. *syncopation*

Since the last device discussed involved a consideration of grammar and rhythm together, we may now conveniently examine another stylistic effect produced by the interplay of grammar and phonology.

An earlier quotation from Professor McIntosh's 'Wulfstan's Prose' should be recalled: 'these [rhythmical] phrases are always *small syntactic units*' (p. 116). I wish to explore the implications of this with regard to (1) the size of syntactic units contained within one foot and (2) the coincidence of boundaries between rhythmical units and between syntactic units (sentence, clause group, phrase, word, morpheme) or elements of structure (S, P, C,IO, etc.).

(1) The first may be dealt with quickly. Professor McIntosh's 'always' ought to be modified, for grammatical units of widely different sizes (ranks) can be contained within the two-stress rhythmical segments. The smallest units, morphemes, do not occur, as in Old English they are almost exclusively monosyllabic. Words also may be excluded: the nearest approach to one word coinciding neatly with one foot is in cases where a preposition and a noun fill one foot, the noun taking both main stresses:[20] *þurh siblegeru*;[21] *7 woroldstruderas*. Groups and phrases, of all grammatical units, are the most frequent carriers of the two-stress rhythmical pattern, and these are presumably the units Professor McIntosh had in mind:

| apóstatan abróþene |, | órfcwealm 7 úncoðu |, | rýpera réaflac |,

| éalles to swýþe |, | þurh rícra réaflac |.

However, the largest grammatical units, sentences and clauses, occur within the boundaries of the foot, although sentences very infrequently:

| gecnáwað þæt sóð is |, | ðeos wórold is on ófste |,

| hwær seo ýrmð gewéarð |, | And utan Gód lúfian |.

Because grammatical units of different ranks can occupy the same size of rhythmical segment, one can have clauses crushed into one

foot or spread out over many: this is too obvious to need illustration.
Less obvious is that one can—and Wulfstan does—'stretch out' a
clause in a variety of directions, by confining P and extending S, for
example:

| And éac her syn on éarde | apóstatan abróþene |
7 cýrichatan hétole | 7 léodhatan grímme | . . . . (ll. 141-2)

(2) The coincidence of the boundaries between rhythmical units
and those between grammatical units is not an invariable rule. In
fact, about a third of all feet in the *Sermo Lupi* contain major syntactic boundaries within them, not coinciding with their own limits.
In the examples below, syntactic boundaries are marked with an
oblique stroke:

| 7 býsmara / gebíden |, | we / þa bóte / mótan |, | 7 óðrum /
derede |, | 7 béarn / his módor |, | drífað / þa dráfe |.

Correspondence *v.* non-correspondence of rhythmical and grammatical boundaries, especially boundaries between elements of
clause-structure, is manipulated by Wulfstan to produce the effects I
have called *symmetry* and *syncopation*. Symmetry is revealed in the
opening lines:

| / ðeos woróld is on ófste / | | / 7 hit néalæcð þam énde / |.

Clause-boundaries correspond exactly to rhythm-boundaries. Again:

| / We him gýldað síngallice / | | / 7 hy us hýnað dǽghwamlice / |
(ll. 125-6)
| / Hy hérgiað ; hy bǽrnað / | | / rýpað / 7 réafiað / | /
7 to scípe lǽdað / |. (ll. 126-7)

Although major grammatical divisions occur inside the rhythmical
units, yet no element of clause-structure overruns[22] the rhythm-
boundaries in this example. In the next example, the effect of mild
syncopation in the first foot is overcome by the symmetry of correspondence of group and rhythmical unit boundaries in the ensuing
eight feet:

| / And utan / wórd 7 wéorc / | | / ríhtlice fádian / | | / 7 úre
íngeþanc / | | / clǽnsian geórne / | | / 7 áð 7 wed / | | / wǽrlice

héaldan / | | / 7 súme getrýwða / | / hábban us betwéonan / | |
bútan uncræftan / |. (ll. 195–7)

But some of Wulfstan's most striking sentences achieve their effect
by a violent use of syncopation. A particularly fine sentence is
dominated by an alternation of syncopation and symmetry:

| / Ne béarh nu foróft / | | / gésib / gesíbban / | | / þe má þe
frémdan / | | / ne fǽder his béarne / | | / ne hwílum béarn / | | / his
ágenum fǽder / | | / ne bróþor / óþrum / |. (ll. 61–3)

This is echoed in lines 92–4:

| / þæt fǽder / geséalde / | | / béarn wið weórþe / | | / 7 béarn / his
módor / | | / 7 bróþor / séalde / óþerne / | | / frémdum to gewéalde / |.

The unnaturalness described by Wulfstan in these two passages
seems echoed in the violent syncopation, where the syntax is played
against the rhythm. In *gesib gesibban, ne fæder his bearne, ne broþor
oþrum,* and *7 bearn his modor,* S and C are yoked together by the
stress in a way underlined as abnormal by the symmetry of the
alternate units. In the second quotation, a clause (*7 broþor sealde
oþerne*) is telescoped into one foot; as the earlier part of the sentence
has required that a main stress be placed on every element of
clause-structure, one is forced to acknowledge the inhumanity of the
thought by offending against the rhythm, by suddenly introducing
a foot with three strong stresses.

vii *Parallelism*

This has, of course, been pointed out by other writers.[23] It consists
basically of the repetition of grammatical structures of the same
type, and in this respect is dealt with in viii (1), below. But this basis
of grammatical repetition is accompanied by a second linking
feature, the use of lexically related words. We may thus distinguish
between simple grammatical repetition with no lexical connexion
between the repeated structures, and parallelism (including antithesis) with lexical connection or contrast. Illustrations of parallelism
are:

      ⎧ We him gyldað singallice
   7 ⎨
      ⎩ hy us hynað dæghwamlice (ll. 125–6)

Here there is repetition of every part of the clause-structure, and the
contrast is aided by phonological correspondence.

$$\left\{\begin{array}{l}\text{Forþam mid miclan}\\\text{earnungan}\\\text{7 mid swyþe micelan}\\\text{earnungan}\end{array}\right.\left\{\begin{array}{l}\text{we geearnedan}\\\text{þa yrmða}\\\text{we þa bote}\\\text{motan æt Gode}\\\text{geræcan}\end{array}\right.\left\{\begin{array}{l}\text{þe us onsittað,}\\\text{gif hit sceal}\\\text{heonanforð}\\\text{godiende weorðan.}\end{array}\right.$$

(ll. 20–3)

Here there is no word-for-word grammatical repetition; only the broad outline (adverbial phrase+main clause+subordinate clause) is repeated. The lexical repetition at the beginning is a clue that a parallel structure is to follow, and the contrast *þa yrmða: þa bote* is quite clear. Lines 27–35 provide an example of extended antithesis:

> On hæþenum þeodum ne dear man forhealdan lytel ne micel þæs þe gelagod is to gedwolgoda weorðunge,
>
> 7 we forhealdað æghwær Godes gerihta ealles to gelome.
>
> And ne dear man gewanian on hæþenum þeodum inne ne ute ænig þæra þinga þe gedwolgodan broht bið 7 to lacum betæht bið,
>
> 7 we habbað Godes hus inne 7 ute clæne berypte.
>
> And Godes þeowas syndan mæþe 7 munde gewelhwær bedælde,
>
> 7 gedwolgoda þenan ne dear man misbeodan on ænige wisan mid hæþenum leodum. . . .

Notice the reversal in order of statement in the last pair, and the unifying of the whole set of clauses by the repetition of key lexical items.

Parallelism in sentence- and clause-structure is found everywhere, and inside the larger antithetical or parallel structures are pairings of words, linked or contrasting in meaning, within the group:

> inne ne ute, stalu 7 cwalu, stric 7 steorfa, swutol 7 gesene, ne lare ne lage, tyne oððe twelfe, þegene 7 þræle.

viii *Rhetorical structures larger than the sentence*

Most clauses in the *Sermo Lupi* begin with a word which conventionally would be called a 'conjunction': *and, ac, forþam, þæt, þeah, þær, gif* are the most common. If one paid attention to the rule of prescriptive grammar that a sentence must not start with a conjunction, one would have to segment much of the *Sermo Lupi* into extremely long sentences consisting of, in some cases, dozens of loosely linked free clauses. Fortunately, this rule is meaningless for the grammar of Old English. The words are best treated as a class of

P

initiators, i.e. units which begin, not link, sentences and clauses. The seven members of this class given above fall into two subclasses, sentence-initiators (*and, ac, forþam*) and clause-initiators or binding conjunctions. Divisions between sentences are marked before sentence-initiators if they are followed by a full clause-structure SP(C)(IO); within sentences, divisions between clauses are marked before clause-initiators, if they are followed by a full clause-structure. Sentence-boundaries are placed before those occurrences of *and* which are followed by both P^i and P^{ii}, but not before those which are followed by P^{ii} only or by no part of P. It is evident that segmentation into sentences on these principles yields a very large number of short sentences, just as Professor McIntosh's rhythmical segmentation yields a very large number of short rhythmical units. Yet one has a strong impression of the existence of formal units longer than these—the impression that fairly long passages of the *Sermo Lupi* cohere very closely. What is the nature of these large rhetorical units?

(1) *Units composed of repeated identical or similar structures.* It was mentioned above that similar grammatical and rhythmical patterns tend to repeat themselves in series. The repetition, or echoing, of one grammatical structure is a common device in very formally organized prose in periods other than Old English. Like Lyly, Wulfstan (e.g. *Sermo Lupi*, ll. 27–37) uses series of two-part sentences, or structures arranged in multiples of two. Bacon's essay 'Of Studies' is dominated by a tripartite structure, established in the opening sentence by the three phrases *for delight, for ornament*, and *for ability*, and repeated many times using combinations of three sentences, clauses, and groups. Wulfstan's most usual and simple way of establishing units larger than the sentence is by assembling sets of sentences based on the same grammatical structure. Both the beginning and the end of the *Sermo Lupi* have passages of this nature. The homily opens with a series of short [24] sentences mostly of the structure SP(C); it ends, as is usual with Wulfstan, with fifteen lines of sentences based on *utan*. Lines 160–6 are unified by five sentences beginning *Her syndan* and having the common structure PS, with expansions by repetition of S; cf. ll. 96–9. This means of linking sentences together by accumulating similar structures is reinforced by repetition of groups and phrases.

(2) *Other means of linking sentences.* These are various and unclassifiable, often turning on a combination of grammatical, lexical, and rhythmical aids to unity. Our first example involves the repetition of lexical items and grammatical units smaller than the clause to link a number of sentences together in what might be called a 'paragraph'. It is ll. 25–50, a set of sentences already unified in parts by parallelism (27–35) and by repetition and expansion (37–49):

And micel is nydþearf manna gehwilcum þæt he Godes lage
gyme heonanforð georne 7 Godes gerihta mid rihte gelæste. On
hæþenum þeodum ne dear man forhealdan lytel ne micel þæs þe
gelagod is to gedwolgoda weorðunge, 7 we forhealdað æghwær
Godes gerihta ealles to gelome. And ne dear man gewanian
on hæþenum þeodum inne ne ute ænig þæra þinga þe gedwolgodan
broht bið 7 to lacum betæht bið, 7 we habbað Godes hus inne
7 ute clæne berypte. And Godes þeowas syndan mæþe 7 munde
gewelhwær bedælde; 7 gedwolgoda þenan ne dear man
misbeodan on ænige wisan mid hæþenum leodum, swa swa man
Godes þeowum nu deð to wide þær cristene scoldan Godes lage
healdan 7 Godes þeowas griðian. Ac soð is þæt ic secge, þearf
is þære bote, forþam Godes gerihta wandean to lange innan
þysse þeode on æghwylcan ende, 7 folclaga wyrsedan ealles to
swyþe, 7 halignessa syndan to griðlease wide, 7 Godes hus
syndan to clæne berypte ealdra gerihta. . . .[25] 7, hrædest is to
cweþenne, Godes laga laðe 7 lara forsawene. And þæs we habbað
ealle þurh Godes yrre bysmor gelome. . . .

Sets of lexical items recur whose relationship is easier to show
diagrammatically than by italics in the text (read from left to right
and downwards to follow the sets as they are patterned in the text):

Godes lage
   Godes gerihta
      On hæþenum þeodum
         gedwolgoda
   Godes gerihta
      on hæþenum þeodum
         gedwolgodan
            Godes hus
               Godes þeowas
         gedwelgoda
     (mid hæþenum leodum)
              Godes þeowum
Godes lage
              Godes þeowas
  Godes gerihta
           Godes hus
  (ealdra gerihta)
Godes laga

Five of these six sets of identical or closely related lexical items contain three or more members each. As the diagram shows, the members of the sets are spread evenly through the text: *Godes lage* runs

right through, and the others are well distributed. Stylistic coherence would not have been achieved if the members had been bunched together, with the sets following one another and not interlocking. Our diagram might have shown:

Godes lage
Godes lage
Godes lage /
Godes gerihta
Godes gerihta
Godes gerihta /
On hæþenum þeodum
on hæþenum þeodum
mid hæþenum leodum / etc.,

with strong 'lexical breaks', marked by oblique strokes, destroying the effect of unity.

Unity is also achieved by restricting the grammatical patterns which carry these lexical items. Eleven have the nominal group structure noun in genitive+noun,[26] three the adverbial phrase structure preposition+(adjective+noun), three are simple nouns, and one is an adjective+noun nominal group.

One final example, ll. 55–9, illustrates a further method of linking sentences together (the sentences are labelled (*a*)–(*d*) to facilitate discussion):

(*a*) ac wæs here 7 hunger, bryne 7 blodgyte, on gewelhwylcan ende oft 7 gelome.

(*b*) And us stalu 7 cwalu, stric 7 steorfa, orfcwealm 7 uncoðu, hol 7 hete 7 rypera reaflac derede swyþe þearle.

(*c*) 7 us ungylda swyþe gedrehtan.

(*d*) 7 us unwedera foroft weoldan unwæstma.

Here we have four sentences arranged in a sequence which shows a gradual transforming of one structure to another, completely different. The first sentence is extremely simple, with the structure PS(S) followed by two adverbs, phrase and group, respectively, of the standard type. The second has a curious inversion and a long series of 'internal' expansions of the subject: CS(SSSS)P. Although it is very different from its predecessor as far as clause-structure is concerned, it is clearly linked in other respects: not by parallelism, or lexical features, but by two aspects of the expansion of clause-structure. In both (*a*) and (*b*) it is S which is repeated; and six instances of the seven subjects found in the two sentences have the group-structure noun+noun co-ordinated, and the seventh the variant of noun+noun linked by a genitive. Perhaps Wulfstan expands S so extensively in the second sentence in order to underline the fact that it is this feature which connects the two sentences. The connection between (*b*) and (*c*), however, needs no special clue: both have the same elements of clause-structure in the same order—CS(SSSS)P in (*b*) and the unexpanded CSP in (*c*). (*d*), like (*c*), is a very short sentence, so the two are immediately associated by their common length (one clause, two feet, in each case). But the clause structures themselves are dissimilar: (*c*) has CSP, (*d*) IO SPC. The link consists of the position of *us*, which is identical in each clause although it is an exponent of two different elements of clause-structure (C and IO respectively), and the position of *ungylda* and *unwedera*, lexically and phonologically similar and exponents of the same element of clause-structure, S. It is by such steps as these that the sequence of sentences PS(S)—CS(SSSS)P—CSP—IO SPC is linked together into a unit larger than the sentence.

This article has attempted to demonstrate the process which can lead to a penetrating analysis of the linguistic character of Wulfstan's style. This approach has made use of a type of descriptive statement perhaps unfamiliar to students of Old English, but which, it is hoped, goes some way towards explaining the distinct stylistic impression of one writer. Scholars have been so confident of their knowledge of Wulfstan's style that they have been ready to base attributions on the detection of its salient features. Within the very limited field of Wulfstan studies, this attitude is perhaps harmless. But the fact remains that a more fundamental and searching approach to Old English style reveals features which, under the old approach, have gone unnoticed. It may be thought that the old approach does less than justice to Wulfstan as a stylist. But the two attitudes are not contradictory: my approach has often touched on features which have been pointed out by other writers—for example, the adverbial phrases and the rhythm. Such points of detail, however, are best seen in the context of a wider linguistic framework, through an analysis which is conscious of the whole vocabulary, grammar, and phonology. It is hoped that, in the future, thorough lexical, grammatical, and phonological studies of Old English texts will be made, so that our present subjective and partially expressed feelings about the qualities of Old English style may be rationalized.[27]

Notes to Paper Thirteen

1 See A. S. Napier, *Über die Werke des altenglischen Erzbishofs Wulfstan* (Weimar, 1882), 11–19; J. P. Kinard, *A Study of Wulfstan's Homilies; Their Style and Sources* (Baltimore, 1897),

19–32; K. Jost, 'Wulfstan und die angelsächsische Chronik', *Anglia*, xlvii (1923), 105–23; K. Jost, 'Einige Wulfstantexte und ihre Quellen', *Anglia*, lvi (1932), 265–315; Angus McIntosh, 'Wulfstan's Prose', *Proceedings of the British Academy*, xxxv (1949), 109–42; K. Jost, *Wulfstanstudien*, Schweizer anglistische Arbeiten, xxiii (Bern, 1950), 155–68; D. Whitelock, *Sermo Lupi ad Anglos*, 2nd ed. (London, 1952), 26–7; D. Bethurum, *The Homilies of Wulfstan* (Oxford, 1957), 87–98; James M. Ure, *The Benedictine Office*, Edinburgh University Publications, Language and Literature, No. 11 (Edinburgh, 1957), 30–4.

2 On stylistic analysis and authorship tests, it may be noted in passing that (*a*) the stylistic features selected have been either surface features (e.g. *ealles to swype*, easily noticed by an imitator) or linguistically minute (e.g. *deofol* without the article). If one believes that an author has 'linguistic fingerprints' these are better revealed by full linguistic description. (*b*) Stylistic arguments have, quite properly, always been backed up by non-linguistic evidence: provenance of the MS, content of the text, literary inferences from Wulfstan's known biography.

3 See note 1 for references.

4 See, e.g., C. A. Smith, 'The Order of Words in Anglo-Saxon Prose', *PMLA*, viii (1893), 210–44; S. O. Andrew, 'Some Principles of Old English Word Order', *Medium Ævum*, iii (1934), 167–88; S. O. Andrew, *Syntax and Style in Old English* (Cambridge, 1940); C. R. Barrett, *Studies in the Word-Order of Ælfric's Catholic Homilies and Lives of the Saints* (Cambridge, 1953).

5 Here the traditional term is retained, but a distinction between *group* and *phrase* is made when this becomes necessary below. The grammatical theory implied is that set out by M. A. K. Halliday, 'Categories of the Theory of Grammar', *Word*, xvii (1961), 241–92; the terminology is largely that current [*ca*. 1962, R.F.] among my colleagues of the Linguistics Association (Great Britain).

6 K. Jost, *Wulfstanstudien*, 155–7.

7 I.e. 'subordinate': bound clauses are those which can serve only as parts of sentences, not as whole sentences.

8 Cf. Professor McIntosh's comment on this tendency in the rhythm: 'It may be noted that a particular pattern tends to be followed by itself more frequently than would be the case in a succession of patterns which formed a purely random series . . .' ('Wulfstan's Prose', 136, note 6).

9 The symbolization for elements of clause-structure is S=subject, P = predicator, C = complement, IO = indirect object. 'Predicator' is that part of the clause which contains the verbal element plus adverbs, if any; the term is used to preserve 'verb' for a class of words (like 'noun'), not an element of clause-structure. 'Predicator' must not be confused with 'predicate', a traditional term not used in this type of analysis. Note that my definition of P is unorthodox in including adverbs within it

(although, for ease of presentation, adverbs are set off in parentheses from P in some examples below).

10 Quotations from the *Sermo Lupi* are taken from Professor Bethurum's edition from Nero A.i and Hatton 113, pp. 267–75 of *The Homilies of Wulfstan*. Division into sentences does not follow Miss Bethurum's punctuation. All clauses which start with a subordinating conjunction (*þæt, þeah, gif,* etc.) are treated as clauses, but clauses beginning with a co-ordinating conjunction (*and, ac, forþam,* etc.) are treated as sentences; this is intended as a means of segmenting the text into units of a manageable size, not as a rule for Old English.

11 This could alternatively be explained as a subjectless clause.

12 Cf. Halliday; the units sentence, clause, group/phrase, word, morpheme, are *ranked* in that descending order of 'magnitude'.

13 Non-primary elements of clause-structure are enclosed in parentheses.

14 This is one of the few sentences (cf. ll. 152–9) in Wulfstan which remind one of some of Ælfred's cumbersome sentences: in both cases we find excessive length and trailing subordination or expansion. The whole Wulfstan sentence (which begins 7 *egeslic,* l. 86) is made difficult by a shift of subject, imperfectly re-established by *þæt* in the part quoted here.

15 This, right at the end, brings in a new subtlety, as *lara* is not a simple member of the long series of S's set up before it, but an expansion of *laga,* dependent on *Godes.*

16 In Hatton 113 only.

17 I.e. an exocentric adverb.

18 *On ofste* and *þam ende* may be left out as they are subject to alternative identifications as C; then follow *nyde* and *swyþe* as above.

19 Note that, as in P^i . . . P^ii, parenthetical clauses are interchangeable with adverbial groups/phrases in the final foot in a clause: 7 eal þæt syndan micle 7 egeslice dæda, *understande se þe wille* (ll. 94–5, cf. 98–9).

20 Readers may feel that this contradicts one of the most useful phonological criteria for the segmentation of the word—the fact that it takes only one primary stress (cf. *bláck bírd* with *bláckbìrd*); but this does not apply in a system which like Professor McIntosh's recognizes only two degrees of stress. Verse is commonly regarded by linguists as having only this one stress contrast. See Harold Whitehall and Archibald A. Hill, 'A Report on the Language–Literature Seminar', *Readings in Applied English Linguistics,* ed. Harold B. Allen (New York, 1958), 394–7. See also note 27.

21 Or |*þurh síblegeru 7 þurh mistlice fórligru*|—which would be an exceptionally long unit. The vertical strokes indicate boundaries of rhythmical units.

22 Here we are approaching the concept of the run-on line, of central

importance to the comparison of the rhythm/grammar
relationship in Wulfstan, Ælfric, and OE poetry.

23 E.g. D. Bethurum, *The Homilies of Wulfstan*, 90: 'In the larger
units may be noted sentence and word parallelism, in the smaller
alliteration and rhyme of both kinds.'

24 Similarity of *length* in consecutive sentences is another way of
obtaining coherence over a long passage.

25 Ll. 41–8 quoted above, p. 205.

26 This structure generates another item not in any of the sets,
Godes yrre.

27 Since this article was written the following have become available:
Fowler, 'Sentence and Clause in English', *Linguistics*, xiv (1965),
5–13; Fowler, *Essays on Style and Language* (London, 1966),
especially Chs. 1 and 5. These may help to explain further the
general orientation and details of my approach.

Fourteen

Linguistics and the analysis of poetry

Probably all of us have antipathies to 'mere form' and to merely formal description. How can we avoid those feelings, with this stricture of I. A. Richards ringing in our ears?

> This trick of judging the whole by the detail, instead of the other way about, of mistaking the means for the end, the technique for the value, is in fact much the most successful of the snares which waylay the critic . . . We pay attention to externals when we do not know what else to do with a poem.[1]

But modern criticism, which in nine out of ten of its manifestations claims descent from Richards, is preoccupied with the form, the means, of poetry. The paradox is puzzling only when we have in mind a too-simple dichotomy between form and meaning, means and end, expression and content.[2] Richards' 'technique and value' is the most dangerous wording of this false distinction; it leads into the inevitable 'mere technique' and the like. Of course, mechanical formal description deserves all the scorn it gets, especially when it imputes value exclusively to material virtuosity. But poetic form cannot be refined away, treated as an attractive way of communicating something which is distinct from form and transcends it. The foundation of excellent practical criticism is the refusal to believe that the only meaning that there is is meaning as distinct from form and that value unquestionably resides in an immaterial heaven to which form is dross. We must believe that formal description not only leads to, but *is*, a statement of meaning—that we are making significant, valuable statements when we describe the form of poetry. If we do not, then our descriptions are bound to be merely technical: we make a reality of that fiction the 'externals' of poetry.

My objection is, in fact, to two aspects of critical sterility. One, 'The Heresy of Paraphrase', has been condemned repeatedly with that distaste for 'statement' which in this century springs from Richards' distinction between the language of science and the language of poetry. The most eloquent preacher against it is Cleanth Brooks, who protests most relevantly against 'the implication that the poem constitutes a "statement" of some sort, the statement being true or false . . .'[3] The second heresy is that, if you set aside content, you are left with form as a mere vessel or means which can invite only sub-critical judgments of efficiency or of prettiness. Brooks' denial of paraphrasable content does not leave him with just poetic technique as a focus of attention, metre, syntax and imagery as 'a kind of envelope which "contains" the content' (p. 178). The fusion of form and content which his model of poetry—a popular and probably enlightening model—urges gives us a pattern or structure as the valuable and revealable core of a poem. His language is, of necessity, highly figurative as he discusses this. The pattern is evidently of a high degree of abstraction, more abstract than the patterns of linguistic form: this is made evident by such terms as 'inner', 'internal', 'core'. 'Unity' is another concept he introduces: the reconcilement of discordant elements and the resolution of stresses. We recognize here that common discussion of the undiscussible which has been carried on ever since Coleridge launched Imagination on the world.

Whatever this pattern is which results from and reflects all the components of a poem, it is acknowledged by most New, Practical and Linguistic critics to be discoverable through verbal analysis. This attitude makes respectable the study of form. It is, however, a difficult respectability to uphold, for one is constantly open to the charge of excessive formalism, of neglecting the 'critical' for the 'technical' part of literary study. Such an accusation must be based on the same false distinction which underlies all these pairs of terms so adroitly and persuasively handled by Richards. But the possibility of having this charge levelled at them should in any case make practical critics careful to use verbal analysis with tact and sensitivity.

If we believe that verbal analysis should be conducted with a due regard for 'value', just how technical should we allow it to be? Are precision, detail, and completeness of formal description desirable ideals? Objectivity, commonsense, and the use of a readily communicating terminology obviously are. Close reading still has some distance to go before it can fulfil its original anti-impressionistic aim. Wellek is right to complain of the deplorable gulf between linguistics and criticism; that split is, happily, mending.[4] But it is arguable that the verbal analysis of literature, if it is designed to be not merely technical, must not approximate too closely to the scientific precision of modern linguistics.[5] One linguist has condemned 'linguistic stylistics' tainted by a 'preformulated literary thesis';[6] others view the process of verbal criticism as analogous to the testing of a hypothesis—and are probably nearer the mark.[7] If we attempt to refine our practical criticism to the state of an infallibly all-revealing procedure, we ensure that criticism remains just technical. All features of the text assume equal significance. The preformulated literary thesis, or hunch, or the critic's perceptive preliminary reading, is essential to a healthy practical criticism.

I have chosen to analyse a poem which points up these issues very clearly: 'anyone lived in a pretty how town' by by e. e. cummings; the analysis does not pretend to be complete—no analysis could.

> anyone lived in a pretty how town
> (with up so floating many bells down)
> spring summer autumn winter
> he sang his didn't he danced his did.
>
> Women and men (both little and small)
> cared for anyone not at all
> they sowed their isn't they reaped their same
> sun moon stars rain
>
> children guessed (but only a few
> and down they forgot as up they grew
> autumn winter spring summer)
> that noone loved him more by more
>
> when by now and tree by leaf
> she laughed his joy she cried his grief
> bird by snow and stir by still
> anyone's any was all to her
>
> someones married their everyones
> laughed their cryings and did their dance
> (sleep wake hope and then) they
> said their nevers they slept their dream
>
> stars rain sun moon
> (and only the snow can begin to explain
> how children are apt to forget to remember
> with up so floating many bells down)

> one day anyone died i guess
> (and noone stooped to kiss his face)
> busy folk buried them side by side
> little by little and was by was
>
> all by all and deep by deep
> and more by more they dream their sleep
> noone and anyone earth by april
> wish by spirit and if by yes.
>
> Women and men (both dong and ding)
> summer autumn winter spring
> reaped their sowing and went their came
> sun moon stars rain.

Here, I shall argue, the paraphrasable content, if one cares to extract it, is so explicit and overtly trivial as to throw out of court the view which puts value all on that side. What is left for us to admire? Superficially, the 'cleverness' of the form, the linguistic expertise: but this is an imperfect response, like valuing a good-looking but un-functioning machine. Either way (and both ways are possible on the form/meaning model of poetry) is critically disreputable and mani-festly inadequate as a commentary on our responses or their pre-sumed causes.

The heresy of paraphrase is not, of course, the belief that content exists. It is that it is separable from other sorts of meaning, and the sole repository of value and object for critical attention. Reading poetry involves the discovery of contextual meaning; we cannot feel secure in our response until we think we know what the poem is about. This is especially true of a poem like 'anyone lived': it is, for-mally, so extraordinary that we feel we must uncover the narrative skeleton before we can understand what sort of a creature it is. Once the contextual meaning of *anyone* and *noone* is grasped (a man and a woman) we can soon piece together at least this:

> anyone lived in a . . . town; noone loved him; someones married
> their everyones; one day anyone died; busy folk buried them.

And, bringing in some of the less directly communicated contextual meanings, we arrive at:

> Once upon a time there was a man living in a certain place
> where people went about their ordinary duties in an ordinary
> way; one woman grew to love him, although few noticed this;
> she shared his passions; they married; time passed; he died,

she died subsequently or consequently, and they were buried together; they were dead, but life went on.

Perhaps one would be tempted to pursue this line of enquiry and comment upon a 'theme' generously hinted at in the poem's treatment of the background happenings around this couple's story: the continuity of life and human activities unaffected by the central narrative, with almost certainly a note of censure in the word *busy*. Then there are those perceptive children in the great Romantic tradition. Clearly, following this line can lead us to a view of the poem as sentimental and possibly trite. Whether we like this, or whether this is expected from cummings, is not at issue here. I would say that it is manifestly inadequate as an account of the poem's total meaning or our response to it.

Let us imagine that the poem's reader has reached the stage that my analysis has at the moment. He feels that, in a way, he 'understands' the poem; he may feel he likes it, but knows that this cannot be because of that portion of its meanings which he understands so far. There is much in the formal detail that puzzles him still, but certain patterns are beginning to emerge. Now the challenge of the form is sufficient incentive for him to re-read, if only formalistically ('Is *didn't* a noun?'). But there is another incentive, something in the shape of the narrative; not narrative structure in conventional terms, but symmetry in other dimensions: [8] the highlighting of a precise and stylized story against a steady, hardly differentiated, movement in the background; the almost mathematical abstractness of the characters; the persistent balance in events and style. So the reader may go on speculating, and perhaps determine that there is emerging a significance to the narrative more satisfying than the sentimental and quasi-moral one he has already discovered. I hope that he will go on to suspect that this is Brooks' 'pattern' or 'structure', which will turn out to be in the formal meaning as well as the content. We shall be on firmer ground if we approach this pattern from the direction of form, not content, and I now wish to indicate how this may be done.

Here a brief linguistic excursus is necessary.[9] The primary distinction is between two types of linguistic meaning, formal and contextual. Contextual meaning is roughly 'meaning' in the ordinary sense—the relation of linguistic symbols to features of the world outside language. Formal meaning in poetry is the level at which stylistic patterns occur, but these patterns are at the same time part of a design which goes beyond form. That is to say, the analysis of form can have critical uses beyond mere descriptive stylistics. Formal patterns are found on three levels: grammar, phonology and lexis.[10] Lexis may be understood as vocabulary, if it is a matter of the inventory of available dictionary items in a language; as diction, if it is a selection from that inventory for a particular purpose (e.g. 'poetic diction'); as collocation, if it is the relations between lexical items in a text which are under discussion. A piece of language can be described in three ways, on three different levels of abstraction:

Phonology /mæn/, a pattern of phonemes (distinctive speech-sounds) with no meaning except that of being a permitted and common sequence of English phonemes.

Lexis   *man*, one of the hundreds of thousands of English lexical items, less specific or material than /mæn/ and more specific than

Grammar N (noun), one of a number of grammatical labels which can be applied not only to *man* but also to thousands of lexical items in the same category.

Let us first look at the lexical patterns found in 'anyone lived'.

It must be emphasized that the scholarly study of lexis is at a very tentative stage. Whereas one can at least struggle along in semantics and lexicography, there are very few guides and principles for the study of the *relationships* between lexical items. The best that we can do is arrive at some prominent sets of items, and in doing so detect some patterns and relationships. These patterns, perhaps independent of grammar and narrative, are called *collocations*. Some are unexpected and yield metaphor: the effect of 'badged with blood' is not produced by the grammatical structure of the phrase, nor by the contextual meaning, for *badged* has not its 'literal' meaning here. On the other hand, 'the grass was green' establishes a sort of homogeneous lexis by juxtaposing items which collocate habitually; 'spring summer autumn winter' is an example of this second case. However, collocation works not only through bright points of detail, but also through the building-up of collocational sets over a larger area.[11]

In 'anyone lived' there is first a very homogeneous list of nouns and verbs which habitually go together, chiefly in texts which describe ordinary human behaviour or make a survey of human life (Jaques avoids them because his survey is totally metaphorical):

> lived, sang, danced, cared for, sowed, reaped, grew, loved, laughed, joy, cried, grief, married, laughed, cryings, did, dance, sleep, wake, hope, said, slept, dream, died, kiss, buried, dream, sleep, reaped.

The most important thing about their relationship is simply their occurrence all together; the order of occurrence is that determined by the progress of the narrative. They provide a concentrated and consistent focus on the human behaviour in the poem: collectively, they enforce a sense of what the poem is about.

Actual details of lexical juxtaposition are also important. Here there are lexical items conveying a scheme of progression, specifically temporal progression. I thus list sequences rather than individual lexical items:

> up . . . floating . . . down; spring summer autumn winter; sun moon stars rain; autumn winter spring summer; more by more; when by now; tree by leaf; bird by snow; stir by still; sleep wake hope and then; stars rain sun moon; up . . . floating . . . down; little by little; was by was; all by all; deep by deep; more by more; earth by april; wish by spirit; if by yes; summer autumn winter spring; sun moon stars rain.

These fragments are a prime cause of the poem's appearance of 'ungrammaticalness' (others are the almost complete lack of punctuation, a merely superficial matter, and the use of a few lexical items in the 'wrong' word-classes). Yet almost all of them are grammatical units (adverbs) with a clear relation to the sentences in which they occur; they do not interfere with the large-scale grammatical organization. Internally, however, they are agrammatical: they are lexical strings, not structured phrases. The chief forms of order, all implying temporal progression or alternation, are:

(1) *Linear progression.* Clearest in the three lists of seasons; in each case the natural order is preserved, with a change in starting-point. The twice-repeated *up . . . floating . . . down*, interleaved with *with . . . so . . . many bells*, has the three movements of a ringing bell (a natural time-marker) in proper sequence.

(2) *Patterned list.* Several different responses to *sun moon stars rain* are possible: AAAB with *sun*, *moon* and *stars* as heavenly bodies, *rain* as a feature of climate; ABBA with *sun* and *rain* classed together (climate) and *moon* and *stars* (night). At the same time, *sun* and *rain* are opposites, so another notation (with lower-case acknowledging the similarity that still remains) could be offered: aBBz. One would perhaps hesitate to specify a basic pattern, for all have the same suggestion of a succession of days and nights and indifferent weather. *Sleep wake hope and then* is basically ABCD, but perhaps also ABAB, with the implication of *sleep-hope* (dream) and *wake-then* (reality).

(3) *Binary replacement.* Of the thirteen 'x by y' phrases in the list above, only one (*little by little*) is an accepted idiom and used 'liter-

ally'. The others use *by* ungrammatically, as a link or pivot to signal the replacement of complementary, or opposite, or naturally succeeding, states or objects. Classification may be unimportant; the pattern and the items juxtaposed more so. The pattern derives from *day by day* (temporal measurement) and *little by little* (spatial measurement). *Day by day* could not unreasonably be said to be present among the meanings in the poem, evoked by suggestive analogy in a manner much exploited by Dylan Thomas: *once below (upon) a time, all the sun (day) long.*

It is evident that these two lexical groups involve very different sorts of linguistic operation—accumulation and juxtaposition respectively—and function very differently in the total pattern of the poem. There is a kind of constancy and solidity in the first, a firm and enduring background. The second has a more localized movement, most powerful in the 'x by y' series. This is not a grammatical pattern: *was by was* could hardly be said to be grammatical. To generalize it still further, it is something like 'x *link* y'. x and y are sometimes the same (*more by more*, AA), sometimes complementary or opposed within the same class (*stir by still*, az). Of course, the pattern is present in other, and grammatical, phases which I have not mentioned so far: for example, *women and men* (az), *little and small* (AA), *dong and ding* (phonologically az). The 'link' here is *and*, used with grammatical propriety. The pattern is also in the balance, sometimes multidimensional, found in almost every line in the poem; and it is in the metre, with its insistent two-stress beat. I would maintain that it is in the contextual meaning also: man and woman are certainly az; *noone and anyone* semantically az; and the narrative is the link. But the most specific clue to all this is the second lexical set I have discussed, or, more accurately, the collocational, flagrantly ungrammatical, structure of the items in that set.

A characteristic of the grammar has been hinted at already: the poem appears ungrammatical, but is in fact simple in its large-scale movement, and only difficult in details.[12] Our first task (only briefly hindered by the almost complete lack of punctuation) is to separate the high-ranking grammatical units. One unit emerges clearly: the type of clause consisting of a subject (S), predicator (P)[13] and complement (C), usually with an adverbial phrase (A) attached to the predicator:

	S.	P.	C.	A.
1	anyone	lived	—	in a pretty how town with up so floating many bells down
2	he	sang	his didn't	spring summer autumn winter
3	he	danced	his did	

	S.	P.	C.	A.
4	Women and men both little and small	cared for	anyone	not at all
5	they	sowed	their isn't	} sun moon stars rain
6	they	reaped	their same	
7	children but only a few }	guessed	*that noone loved him more by more*	——
8	*(that) noone*	*loved*	*him*	*more by more*
9	(and) they	forgot	——	down / *as up they grew autumn / winter spring summer*
10	*(as) they*	*grew*	——	up / *autumn winter spring / summer*
11	she	laughed	his joy	} when by now and tree by leaf
12	she	cried	his grief	
13	anyone's any	was	all	to her / bird by snow and stir by still
14	someones	⌐married	their everyones	
15		{ laughed	their cryings	} sleep wake hope and then
16	(and)	⌐did	their dance	
17	they	said	their nevers	} stars rain sun moon
18	they	slept	their dream	
19	(and) only the snow	can begin to explain	*how children are apt to forget to remember with . . . down*	
20	*(how) children*	*are*	*apt to forget to remember*	*with up so floating many bells down*
21	anyone	died	——	one day
22	if	guess	——	——
23	(and) noone	stooped to kiss his face	——	——
24	busy folk	buried	them	side by side
25	they	dream	their sleep	⌐little by little and was by / was all by all and deep by / deep and more by more
	noone and anyone			earth by april / wish by spirit / and if by yes
26	Women and men	⌐reaped	their sowing	} both dong and ding / summer autumn / winter spring
27	(and)	⌐went	their came	sun moon stars rain

Despite the perhaps formidable appearance of this table, it demonstrates the simplicity of the sentence- and clause-structure of the

Q

poem. There are no difficulties in accounting for it wholly in terms of one construction, SP(C)(A). (Brackets here indicate optional elements.) As far as the order of the elements of clause-structure is concerned, this is invariably SP(C), with only A varying in position (coming before S in 2–3, 9, 10, 11–12, 13, 21 and 25, and between S and P in 26). So the clauses utilize 'direct' order, with 'inversion' coming in only through the position of the normally (and here therefore unstrikingly) mobile A.

One measure of the complexity of sentence-structure in any text is the number and means of relation of *rank-shifted* clauses. These are clauses which are 'demoted', subordinated to the function of an element of structure within another clause. They are shown in italics in the table, and can be seen to be few in number: clause 8, acting as C in clause 7; 10, A in 9; 20, C in 19. Only two sentences are complicated by rank-shift; for the rest, clauses are connected by the simplest possible means. Some very ordinary linking-words are used (shown in the first column) and apart from these, two simple devices link clauses. The special status of A (suggested also by the lexis) is indicated by its application simultaneously to more than one clause (2–3, 5–6, 11–12, 15–16, 17–18, 26–7), thus associating the pairs of clauses with which it keeps company. Another device, clause-linking by expansion, is found in 14–16 and 26–7: a complete SPC clause is expanded by the provision of additional combinations of PC dependent on the original S.

Some of the lexical exponents of the structural position A have already been discussed, with the passing comment that, although they may be agrammatical internally, their external relations (i.e. their relation to P) are quite clear. The residue from the lexical description is:

(1) in a pretty how town with up so floating many bells down;
(2) not at all;
(3) down;
(4) as up they grew;
(5) up;
(6) with up so floating many bells down;
(7) one day;
(8) side by side;
(9) both dong and ding.

2 and 3, 5–8 need no comment. *In a pretty how town*, whatever the puzzles of *pretty how*,[14] is unmistakably a prepositional adverbial phrase based on *in a . . . town*. *With . . . down* is best viewed as a modifier of *town*, not *lived*, so does not come under the heading of exponents of A. 4 is a rank-shifted clause, and its structure is shown as

clause 10 above. 9, *both dong and ding*, qualifies *reaped*, and is under-standable by reference to the ringing of the bells as a symbol of the passing of time: 'women and men reaped while time went by . . .' But there is more to the phrase than that, for it is the first sign we have met so far of a basic grammatical and lexical ambivalence in the details of the poem's form. It is the time-symbolism of the poem which invites us to identify *both dong and ding* as an adverb. If we appealed to line 5 we would interpret it differently, as an adjective phrase modifying *women and men*. In this alternative interpretation the words *dong* and *ding* seem to deny the contextual meaning given them by their association with bells. I would suggest that they pro-vide further reinforcement of the lexical relation of *women* and *men*; *dong* and *ding* are, phonologically, different yet similar, with the same sort of complementary sameness-in-difference as *women* and *men* (there it is semantic, of course); similarly with *little* and *small*—semantically distinguished items of a like semantic kind. At the same time, *both dong and ding* is both adverb and adjective: as adverb, it works for that part of the contextual meaning concerned with the passing of time; as adjective, it is a symbol of a formal pattern of great abstractness (az, x *link* y) already detected.

The agrammatical adverbial phrases have no internal clues to word-class, but are validated by occurring in a clear framework: There is a similar situation with the exponents of C. The following simplification of the first table will show how what is perhaps the poem's oddest grammar is restricted to a very limited part of clause-structure:

2	he sang	his didn't
3	he danced	his did
5	they sowed	their isn't
6	they reaped	their same
(8	noone loved	him)
11	she laughed	his joy
12	she cried	his grief
14	someones married	their everyones
15	laughed	their cryings
16	did	their dance
17	they said	their nevers
18	they slept	their dream
(24	busy folk buried	them)
25	they dream	their sleep
26	women and men reaped	their sowing
27	went	their came

8 and 24 are perfectly normal and co-operate with the other 'normal' (though less simple) clauses to give a firm basis for the analysis of the poem in terms of SPC. For the rest, it could be said that normality is confined to the SP part of the clauses, all of which employ the same order, and all of which except 14–16 have acceptably collocable exponents of S and P. The shock comes when C is added. In establishing the exponents of C in these clauses, the presence throughout of the possessive personal pronouns is of great importance. Besides allowing us to draw the line in front of them (*his*, etc., could hardly end P) they identify what follows them as nouns. In syntactical terms, the status of *didn't, did, isn't, same, everyones, nevers* and *came* is clearly noun, just like *joy, grief*, etc. Now the use of a lexical item in more than one grammatical class is not peculiar to cummings: it has been going on for centuries, and now involves many important items in our vocabulary (*run, hit, cry*, etc.). This background enhances the acceptability of cummings' extension of the usage, as does his actual use of some very familiar items of this sort. Scrutiny of the vocabulary more generally reveals that much of it is of this grammatically dual-purpose nature:

dance(d), care(d), rain, guess(ed), love(d), laugh(ed), (cried), snow, laugh(ed), cry(ings), dance, sleep, hope, (slept), dream, rain, snow, guess, kiss, dream, sleep, wish, rain.

Others are items which can be noun or verb with only slight phonological alteration: *lived* (*life*), *grief* (*grieve*).

The presence in the poem of so many lexical items which can be, according to the circumstances, either noun or verb, tends to make more acceptable extravagant shifts of word-class of the type represented by *didn't*. But the verb-noun shift is not the only one found among the complements, nor do shifts occur among the complements only. *Their same* is an unusual version of *the same*; *his joy, his grief* and *their dream* are made complements of verbs which do not normally have complements; *their everyones* is unusual in its plural inflexion and in the qualification by *their*; *cryings* is an unaccustomed plural; *nevers* involves a shift from adverb to noun; *their sleep* is provided as a new complement to a verb which has a very limited range of complements (*dream a dream, dream that* . . .). These unorthodox complements are just one prominent part of a more widespread indeterminacy of word-class encountered throughout the poem. More examples are to be found highlighted in the adverbial phrases 'x by y' noted earlier. In some cases 'x' and 'y' are filled from an unconventional sub-class of nouns: *tree by leaf, bird by snow, earth by april, wish by spirit*; in the rest there is a more radical unorthodoxy with the selection of the 'wrong' word-class altogether: *more by more, stir by still, was by was, all by all, deep by deep, if by yes.* There are one or two other peculiarities of word-class: e.g. use of *anyone* and *noone* as proper names (in part; there is the possibility of ambivalence every time they occur), *how* as an adjective.

My description, as will have been obvious, was neither a full nor an impartial one: such a description, giving as it must do the same significance to all data, is wholly improper in critical linguistics. I have attempted to persuade the reader that the grammar is, despite appearances, extremely simple and pretty unremarkable. Even those grammatical peculiarities which look most strange can be reduced to rule and class, and all are readily understandable because they are set in a framework (the clause- and phrase-structures) of extreme repetitiveness and clarity. The framework contains lucidly collocated lexical items at points where the narrative could be endangered by incoherence (e.g. *busy folk buried them side by side*) but elsewhere word-patterns function daringly and often submerge the grammar in the interest of conveying the abstract pattern.

A volume could be written on the metre of 'anyone lived': for the very simple reason that we lack any full-scale treatment of the verse-form employed here.[15] Metrics is surely the most lamentably neglected and complacent area of literary studies today, and sprung rhythm—for that is what we have here—particularly so. In this article I have space only to print the scansion I find most attractive of the possible alternatives, and comment upon it:

anyone lived | in a pretty how town
(with up so floating | many bells down)
spring summer | autumn winter
he sang his didn't | he danced his did.

Women and men | (both little and small)
cared for anyone | not at all
they sowed their isn't | they reaped their same
sun moon | stars rain

children guessed | (but only a few

and down they forgot | as up they grew
autumn winter | spring summer)
that noone loved him | more by more

when by now | and tree by leaf
she laughed his joy | she cried his grief
bird by snow | and stir by still
anyone's any | was all to her

someones married | their everyones
laughed their cryings | and did their dance
(sleep wake hope | and then) they
said their nevers | they slept their dream

stars rain | sun moon
(and only the snow | can begin to explain
how children are apt | to forget to remember
with up so floating | many bells down)

one day anyone died | i guess
(and noone stooped | to kiss his face)
busy folk buried them | side by side
little by little | and was by was

all by all | and deep by deep
and more by more | they dream their sleep

noone and anyone | earth by april

wish by spirit | and if by yes.

Women and men | (both dong and ding)

summer autumn | winter spring

reaped their sowing | and went their came

sun moon | stars rain.

(Underlining links words in the same foot; vertical lines mark caesura.) This scansion takes account of the following features and units:

(1) *Stressed and unstressed syllables.* There is no difficulty deciding where stress is to go: the most important words in each line, grammatically and lexically, receive main stress, and receive it on syllables determined by the normal word-stress rules of English. The only place where the metre overrides the expected 'prose rhythm' is in l. 21, where the word *everyones* has to bear two main stresses, contrary to the usual practice whereby one word has only one dominant stress. The lightly-stressed syllables follow readily.

(2) *Foot.* Hopkins employs the term 'foot' in his discussion of sprung rhythm, although it might be questioned whether this unit has the same value as in syllabic verse, where the foot is a numerically-determined segment of the line. Nevertheless, it is evident that the light syllables of sprung rhythm are not without relation to the main stresses between which they are distributed: they can be fitted into a pattern. No more than two occur between main stresses: we do not have (as in *Piers Plowman*) so many that they float unattached. I have attached them to the preceding strong syllable, with some claim that this represents the way one naturally feels about the internal structure of the lines. If this is so, it is a product once again of normal English word- and phrase-stress: main stress tends to fall predominantly at the beginning of a word or phrase: *anyone, pretty how*. So it is with this poem, and by analogy other phrases are accommodated to the foot-pattern without violence: *up they, cried his*. The bracketed light stresses at the beginnings of lines do not count: they are examples of *anacrusis*, familiar in Old English poetry, 'a kind of running start'[16] to the line which makes no difference to the pattern of the first foot.

(3) *Line*. Each line has four main stresses, irrespective of the number of syllables (from four to twelve) it contains. This is the primary factor in line-measurement, reinforced by rhyme (*down*: *town*) and half-rhyme (-*ones*: *dance*). So the break at the end of the line is qualitatively different from that in the middle. Additionally, and despite the punctuation, the poem is fairly firmly end-stopped by the occurrence of major syntactic divisions at the ends of lines.

(4) *Caesura*. Again as in Old English poetry, every line divides into two, more or less on grammatical prompting. Every line except one (25) splits into two equivalent segments. In twenty-four of the thirty-six lines the first half-line runs on into the second. Thus the lines are (usually) grammatically split into two half-lines which are still linked by metre.

Although I have described the formal patterns of this poem on three distinct levels, these distinctions have less significance than the scheme might suggest. We do not respond to a poem in three separate ways, nor even three separate ways at the same time. 'The poem itself' as a formal unit is a composite in which the relationships between its components are more vital than the distinctions, and a composite which is greater than the sum of its parts. For ordinary language, we can talk about grammar, vocabulary, and sounds, add the three levels together, and we have an adequate description. But the language of literature is 'more highly structured'[17] or has extra 'dimensions of meaning'.[18] There is, in fact, a powerful 'inner organization', hardly describable in linguistic or any other precise analytical terms, which is the way linguistic levels are put into relationship—the manifold tensions and/or coherence between them.[19] As Winifred Nowottny says,

> meaning and value in poems are the product of a whole array
> of elements of language, all having a potential of eloquence
> which comes to realization when, and only when, one element
> is set in discernible relation with another . . . (p. 18)

The primary structure, pattern, unity, of poems is produced by the establishment of *significant* relationships: the organization of technicalities to draw value out of technique.

Some of the technicalities which I have picked out as interesting are: the simplicity and lack of prominence of the grammar; the uncertainty of parts of speech; the binary formula in grammar, lexis, and metre, and the simultaneous opposition and equation of distinctions at all levels. The last is the most overt facet of the poem's pattern. There are two people at the centre of the narrative, made one by marriage and death; but they do not stand out totally, for it is made clear that they are only a part of the undifferentiated flow and mass of life as a whole—life which both ignores and acknowledges them; and their nonentity, in contrast to their defined position as the only direct protagonists in the story, is pointed up by their names: *noone* and *anyone*. Linguistic high points, too, both stand out and merge into a steady flow. The strong stresses of the metre are insistent and prominent, but, as we have seen, they are absorbed into feet, the feet into half-lines, and the half-lines themselves are not as separate as at first might appear—linked by the grammar across the caesura quite regularly. The lines, through iteration of the four-stress pattern, and the consistency of their speed, are monotonous, and one notices less than one might the end-stopping which I pointed out. Perhaps the poet intended the lack of punctuation to contribute to that effect. The effect is, of course, like that of an easy and undistinguished ballad rhythm.

I have already noticed the strange co-existence of semantic contrast and equivalence, especially in the agrammatical linked pairs of words: *women and men, little and small, if by yes, when by now, dong and ding*. The components of the last one of these are the same, and yet different, on the phonetic level too. The phrase exemplifies well one of the most striking features of the poem, the close coherence of linguistic patterns at all levels. In this poem, individual structures gain significance through being reflected in and matched with their likes at the same and other levels, so that from them one can abstract a more general pattern which is itself not describable in linguistic terms. But it is, after all, a pattern of monotony: just like life, whatever ballad-makers say.

Notes to Paper Fourteen

1 *Principles of Literary Criticism* (reprint 1963 of 2nd ed., London, 1926), 24.

2 On disclaimers of this false distinction see René Wellek, 'Concepts of Form and Structure in Twentieth-Century Criticism', *Neophilologus*, xlii (1958), 1–11. It may be of interest to note that the same fallacious division (often in identical terms) has bedevilled linguistic theory in the same period of this century, with the views of Leonard Bloomfield at the centre of controversy; it was left to J. R. Firth to state boldly that the description of form *is* the description of meaning.

3 *The Well Wrought Urn* (second impression, London, 1960), 179; see especially Chs. 4 and 11. On the irrelevance of that sneaking criterion of 'truth' see the comments on 'fictionality' in Wellek and Warren, *Theory of Literature* (third edition, Harmondsworth,

1963); and Wellek in T. A. Sebeok (ed.), *Style in Language* (New York, 1960), 101.

4 'The Main Trends of Twentieth-Century Criticism', *Concepts of Criticism*, ed. Stephen G. Nichols, Jr. (New Haven, 1963), 351. The co-operation of linguistics and criticism can be seen in (e.g.) Sebeok's *Style in Language*; W. Nowottny, *The Language Poets Use* (London, 1962); Fowler, *Essays on Style and Language* (London, 1966); S. B. Chatman and S. R. Levin, *Essays on the Language of Literature* (Boston, 1967). For further discussion of the relations of linguists and critics, see Papers 3–6 of this volume.

5 I have so argued in 'Linguistics, Stylistics; Criticism?' *Lingua*, xvi (1966), 153–65 (this volume, Paper 2).

6 M. A. K. Halliday, 'The Linguistic Study of Literary Texts', in H. G. Lunt (ed.), *Proceedings of the Ninth International Congress of Linguists* (The Hague, 1964), 302.

7 John Spencer and Michael J. Gregory, *Linguistics and Style* (London, 1964), 61.

8 Cf. Brooks, op. cit., 178, where, groping towards a definition of 'structure' by negative demonstration, he eliminates couplet, canto arrangement, and mock-epic as aspects of the 'structure' of *The Rape of the Lock*.

9 And a briefer sub-excursus. The argument for using analytic methods and terms derived from modern linguistics is a simple one, but often misunderstood. It is not claimed that linguistics is an infallible and all-powerful key to criticism, but simply that, as an interest in language and language analysis is a central part of modern criticism, and efficiency of analysis is a requirement, it is reasonable to use methods of great proven efficiency. On this and related questions see my 'Linguistic Theory and the Study of Literature', *Essays on Style and Language*, 1–28 and 'Linguistics, Stylistics; Criticism?' *Lingua*, xvi (1966), 153–65.

10 Most of the linguistic terms used here are explained in M. A. K. Halliday, 'Categories of the Theory of Grammar', *Word*, xvii (1961), 241–92; I differ from Halliday in some points, for example in my suggestion here that phonology can for some purposes be regarded as a full and describable level of form. It should be noted that the methods used here are not those of the current generative grammar of Noam Chomsky simply because generative grammar is not well adapted to textual analysis.

11 This is the principle behind the image-hunting approach to Shakespeare, so well known from the writings of Spurgeon and Clemen.

12 J. P. Thorne discusses some features of the poem's grammar in 'Stylistics and Generative Grammars', *Journal of Linguistics*, i (1965), 49–59; see also S. R. Levin, 'Poetry and Grammaticalness' in Lunt, op. cit.

13 'Predicator' is not the same as the traditional 'predicate'. It might be defined as 'the verbal part of a clause'. 'Verb' is retained

for a *class of word* (like 'noun'); 'predicator' is an *element of clause-structure* (like 'subject').

14 'And how are you?' said Winnie-the-Pooh.
Eeyore shook his head from side to side.
'Not very how', he said. 'I don't seem to have felt at all how for a long time.'

15 A linguist's account of syllable-counting metre is S. Chatman, *A Theory of Meter* (The Hague, 1965); but stress-timed or 'sprung' rhythm remains untreated.

16 Kemp Malone in A. C. Baugh (ed.), *A Literary History of England* (London, 1948), 25.

17 Nowottny, op. cit., 72.

18 G. Leech, ' "This Bread I Break"—Language and Interpretation', *A Review of English Literature*, vi (April 1965), 67.

19 This interlevel relationship has been discussed by linguists under the names of 'cohesion' or 'convergence'. See Leech, art. cit., Halliday, 'The Linguistic Study of Literary Texts', M. Riffaterre, 'Criteria for Style Analysis', *Word*, xv (1959), 172.

Fifteen

On the interpretation of 'nonsense strings'

Katz's statement of the core of the problem of ungrammaticalness is worth quoting at length:

> The knowledge that enables a speaker to understand sentences —his knowledge of the rules of the grammar—must be identically the knowledge that enables him to understand semi-sentences, for semi-sentences are understood in terms of their well-formed parts. Moreover, the knowledge a speaker uses to recognize the respects in which a semi-sentence is ungrammatical is also his knowledge of grammaticality: knowledge of the grammatical rules is here employed to discover instances of their violation. . . .
>
> [But] though the knowledge a speaker requires to understand well-formed sentences and the knowledge he requires to understand semi-sentences is one and the same, and though a generative grammar can represent all the grammatical knowledge a speaker has and can account for how he is able to understand sentences, yet such a grammar cannot account for how a speaker is able to understand semi-sentences ((1964), 401–2).

The problem of accounting for this ability is one part of the central problem of understanding the relation between linguistic competence and linguistic performance (see Lyons and Wales (1966), *passim*). The concept of grammar is made more adequate by restricting its functions; so we create an acute and potentially fruitful necessity for resolving the whole question of the place of a grammar in an account of the observed working of language. The force of Katz's limitation of the contribution of grammar in the study of ungrammaticalness is to invite us to investigate yet another aspect of the theory of performance: 'The task a speaker performs when he understands a semi-sentence involves, in addition to his use of grammatical knowledge, THE USE OF KNOWLEDGE OF ANOTHER KIND' (Katz (1964), 402; my emphasis). I have no intention of attempting to set out the nature of this 'knowledge' or of its 'use'. Nor will I summarize previous arguments since the most influential are readily accessible (Chomsky (1961); Katz (1964); Ziff (1964); Miller and Chomsky (1963); Chomsky (1965), 75–9, 148–53: the first three and the relevant extract from the fourth in Fodor and Katz (1964)). The general feeling has been that ungrammatical strings are interpreted if they contain 'sufficient structure' for them to be related to relevant members of the set of grammatical sentences; that these deviant sentences fall into categories reflecting the manner and the closeness of their relation to the sentences generated by the grammar. I agree with Katz that the process of interpretation is a more valuable subject for study than a categorization or hierarchization of ungrammaticalness. But against his requirement of 'jointly exhaustive proper subsets' SS (SEMI-SENTENCES) and NS (NONSENSE STRINGS) of the set of UNGRAMMATICAL STRINGS ((1964), 402) and his condition of incomprehensibility of NS, I argue a unifying interpretative capability for all ungrammatical strings, independent of linguistic competence (i.e. not greatly dependent upon 'sufficient structure'). Thus mature, fluent, native speaker-hearers can interpret utterances of the type Katz labels NS. I believe we can generalize the interpretation of all ungrammatical strings to a performance skill (Chomsky: 'imposing an interpretation') which is a special case of syntactic performance which in turn is part of the overriding 'problem of serial order in behaviour'. Although this skill includes use of vestigial structure in cases where this exists, it has also other, non-grammatical, techniques to employ.

I embrace two rather considerable limitations. One is to make no mention of things semantic. This is partly by way of specific exclusion: I do not want to discuss material of the Jabberwocky type, where interpretation depends solely on an ill-understood aspect of semantic performance, guessing the meaning of unfamiliar lexical items. From the point of view of my approach (as for Fries, apparently) Jabberwocky is grammatical. Less trivially, I exclude semantic matters because, despite discussions of the last few years, the relation between syntax and semantics still needs clarification. I am aware that this limitation leaves parts of my discussion unsatisfactory. The second limitation is one of illustrative material: I examine chiefly some of the examples from the important earlier discussions, including fragments from the poem 'anyone lived in a pretty how town' by e. e. cummings, which Levin (1964) and Thorne (1965) have commented on and which raises the problem of interpretation in the face of lack of 'sufficient structure'[1] in a peculiarly dramatic way.

The question 'Do we understand ungrammatical strings by the application of linguistic competence?' is asked by Levin in the form 'Can we fix the grammar so that it will generate observed yet intuitively ungrammatical sentences?' From his and Thorne's discussion it would seem that the grammar does not explicate ungrammatical strings. This is evident from the lack of mechanical success of such rules as

(1) $N\rightarrow$did (he danced his did)
(2) $NP\rightarrow$did (he danced his did)
(3) $N_{\text{period of time}} \rightarrow N_{\text{state of mind}}$ (a grief ago)

which either generate thousands of unwanted sentences ((1) *the did was late*, (2) *sing was late*, (3) *four happinesses ago*), or, to prevent such 'overgeneration' (Levin's term), require restrictions so complex as to make the grammar fail the criterion of simplicity. Another reason for believing that we do not understand *he danced his did* by referring to a rule (say, (1) above) which is part of our linguistic competence in the same way that, for example, the rules *Pron.→he*, *N→lunch* are, is that this explanation does not acknowledge our feeling that *he ate his lunch* is grammatical whereas *he danced his did* is not. Chomsky mentions that a 'well-chosen deviant utterance may be richer and more effective' ((1961), 234); a fact that every schoolboy poet knows. The richness lies in the demand the deviation makes on one's interpretative ingenuity to recognize its own ingeniousness, to (for example) hold two structures, or formatives (as with puns), in mind simultaneously. 'Imposing an interpretation' on a deviant utterance is a quite different process from interpreting a grammatical sentence. It requires supplementing one's grammatical competence with a performance skill. Adopting Katz's term, let us say that *a year ago* is in the 'comprehension set' ((1964), 411 ff.) for *a grief ago*; any explanation of our response to *a grief ago* must acknowledge that we (*a*) understand *grief* in this context; AND (*b*) understand it by its relation with *year*. Likewise with *he danced his did*: a rule *N→did* carries only the information appropriate to *N→lunch, cat, house, string*, etc. What is immediately peculiar about *he danced his did* is the conflict of the nonce-rule *N→did* and the grammatical rule *V→did*.

Thorne proposes a very sensible solution to this dilemma – the dilemma that a grammar (a representation of competence) cannot explain deviant strings and their interpretation ((1965), 51): 'Given a text, like Cummings' poem, containing sequences which resist inclusion in a grammar of English it might prove more illuminating to regard it as a sample of a different language, or a different dialect, from Standard English.' Such an approach works only if the deviance is rather extensively manifested, and its efficiency depends somewhat on the length of the text in question. Fortunately, the kind of irregularity this poem exhibits 'is regular in the context of the poem' ((1965), 58). Interpreting the sentences of the poem is 'like learning a language' ((1965), 55): one seeks to discover regularities which imply rules which one has not (yet) internalized as part of one's linguistic competence. The better—though still inexact but unimportantly so—analogy is that of understanding an unfamiliar dialect of one's own language, for one is not simply processing new linguistic data as in language acquisition but is at the same time establishing some kind of relation to the grammar one knows. The value of Thorne's analogy is that it suggests that the procedure of interpretation or syntax-detection is not initially bound by one's own grammar, so one is prepared to regard the formal regularities of the text as independent new structure as well as to consider them as deviant exemplars of the grammar one knows. It is not, I grant, fully understood how a hearer interprets even perfectly grammatical sentences.[2] Nevertheless, it seems fairly clear that interpreting an ungrammatical string is a rather special operation. As well as recovering whatever grammar the string has (as proposed by Katz [1964]), i.e. acting on the assumption that the string is a deviant string of his own language, the native interpreter is prepared to scan a deviant utterance for any structure which is NOT dictated by the grammar of his language; in this latter respect he is not behaving as a native speaker-hearer behaves towards a grammatical sentence of his language. These two processes together constitute 'imposing an interpretation' on an ungrammatical string. Though the hearer's competence will tell him whether a string is or is not a grammatical sentence of his language, it will not, unsupplemented by a syntactic performance skill akin to that employed in learning a language, interpret an ungrammatical string for him.

In one respect the analogy of learning a dialect/language may be a little misleading. The chief component of this syntactic performance skill is the capacity TO LOOK FOR NEW STRUCTURE in general, not to look only for whatever new structure is repeated strikingly in a text. Regular irregularity does occur, as Thorne says; sometimes recognizing the repetition of a deviant structure helps interpretation, sometimes not, as we shall see. Essentially, the ability is powerful enough for us to recognize the pattern of an apparently unique deviation without such help. Ziff's distinction between 'variants' and 'inventions' ((1964), 396 ff.) answers to this between regular and unique deviation. Ziff does not succeed in making the distinction rigorous, and it is difficult to see how one could do so, except in some quite arbitrary way. The distinction is trivial and relative: if an interpreter has the skill to cope with unique deviation, he obviously has the skill to cope with deviation which is repeated a few or many times. The point is that the skill may be likened to that of learning a new dialect or language (presumably); it is only sometimes that the deviation is so iterated as itself to be like a new dialect.

Consider a sentence from Milton quoted by Levin ((1962), 26): *Him who disobeys, me disobeys*. From the standpoint of my twentieth-century non-Miltonic linguistic competence it is highly ungrammatical, like the sentence *Them who likes, us likes* offered by Levin, which would be judged grossly deviant if produced by a foreign student or one of my children. Certainly there are Miltonically naïve speakers who would have trouble interpreting the first sentence as *Whoever disobeys him, disobeys me*. Perhaps *Him who disobeys, me disobeys* is really as deviant as the alleged nonsense strings *If go ninth John as* or *Truth a scientists universe the*; I am almost inclined to think so, though I find it very hard to get a clear perspective on the sentence independent of my knowledge of the syntax of Miltonic blank verse. What is evident to me is that I can make good sense of the sentence by using nonce-rules which render *who* as *whoever* and restore the structural order *SVO*. Also it is evident that Milton demands that his reader should carry out such operations very frequently, but that the operations required are not all identical. Note that the sentence in question illustrates two competing orders of structural elements; crudely represented, we have: [*S(OSV)OV*], [(*him who disobeys*) *me disobeys*]. *Paradise Lost* freely uses a variety of structural orders in clauses; in *NP*'s, frequent reversal of the normal order of *Adj* and *N*; adverbial and adjectival phrases apparently randomly positioned relative to nouns and verbs; often lengthy interruptions between *S*, *V*, and *O*. As a consequence, the syntax of the poem is almost continuously both ungrammatical and 'unacceptable' in the technical sense[3] (Chomsky (1965), 10–15). I would suggest that learning this 'dialect' (with whatever help comes from the reader's general familiarity with the syntax of mainstream English poetry) entails not only the detection of regular irregularity but also maintaining a constant state of alertness towards the syntax, a willingness to stop and unravel any difficult sentence on the basis of its own structure.

Let us return to *he danced his did*. One's immediate intuition connects it with grammatical English sentences such as *he ate his lunch*, *he bought a house*, *John owns three houses*. These parallels spotlight the highly deviant use of *did*. But the interpretation is incomplete because it connects *he danced his did* with no comprehension set of sentences, and it thus remains meaningless despite the recovery of a good deal of English structure. Further scrutiny of the text reveals that the sentence belongs to a rather extensive class of relatedly ungrammatical sentences:

> he sang his didn't, he danced his did, they sowed their isn't, they reaped their same, she laughed his joy, she cried his grief, (someones) laughed their cryings, they said their nevers, they slept their dream, they dream their sleep, women and men reaped their sowing, (women and men) went their came.

These replicate the structural peculiarities of *he danced his did* very consistently (and thus strengthen the perception of KIND of ungrammaticalness). There is general anarchy in the word-class exponence of objects, and, at least as striking, use of intransitive and semi-transitive (*dance, sing*, etc.) verbs as full transitives. A third feature affecting these sentences and indeed saturating the whole poem is the presence of so many formatives which, with little or no morphophonemic alteration, could be either noun or verb: *lived, sang, danced, cared, guessed, loved, laughed, cried, grief*, etc. This fact possibly enhances the acceptability of the shift of word-class in which *did* is involved. This is a marginal contribution to the interpretation of *he danced his did*, however. Survey of apparently relevant sentences in the next reveals structural homogeneity in this 'dialect', consistency of relation to the grammar of English, but helps very little with the specific problem of arriving at a meaning for *he danced his did*.[4]

In the poem there is the sentence *someones . . . did their dance*. Does *he danced his did* mean 'he did his dance'? This would give the complete line *he sang his didn't he danced his did*, the interpretation 'he didn't do (sing) his song, he did his dance'. This suggestion of the character 'anyone' as a musical entertainer who performed his dance routine rather than his song routine is quite gratuitous and implausible. 'He didn't sing, he díd dance' seems altogether less objectionable. Here the 'source' is structurally remote from the 'target' and one has to suppose that the interpretation is imposed by constructing a route something like this:

> *he díd dance* (SOURCE)—*he díd do his dance—he díd his dance—he danced his did* (TARGET)

The route is actually a set of 'transfer rules' (to adapt Katz's term, 1964: 411–14) and the above series of sentences is no more than an informal indication of the sequence of their operation. Transfer

R

rules may be like phrase-structure rules or transformational rules. In this case, they have to show a path between the source and the target and at the same time represent distinct intuitions concerning: (1) the linear positional switching of formatives—*did* with *dance* and *didn't* with *sing*—by a rule of the form XY→YX; (2) the unlawful reallocation of a formative of category V to category N; (3) the semi-lawful change of a formative from the subcategory $V_{intr.}$ to the subcategory $V_{tr.}$. These dual demands on the rules raise considerable difficulties with regard to their ordering. The route requires a large number of complex and highly anomalous (for English) rules. I will not attempt to set them out in full. Some manœuvres—for example changing V from $V_{intr.}$ to $V_{tr.}$—seem simple enough but in fact require rather complicated shifts: in this case, *dance* begins and ends as V but appears temporarily as N in order to preserve *did*. Again, it is very difficult to render *did* as *did* (rather than *do*) in the target sentence, since the past morpheme has to be retained in the positional transformation $he + \text{past} + X + his + Y \to he + \text{past} + Y + his + X$ to give *danced* rather than *dance* in the target. In general, the structural changes are simple enough (e.g. the removal of the heavy affirmative stress on *did*) but the combination of these changes and changes affecting lexical items directly introduces great awkwardness in the sequence of rules. However, the interpretation is possible, if cumbersome; similarly, interpretations involving sources such as *he danced, he danced his dance*, etc., are possible but inelegant as far as the necessary transfer rules are concerned. (By 'possible' I mean 'possible'; not 'recommendable' or 'correct' or 'sensible'.)

'He didn't do his song, he did his dance' may be objectionable as an interpretation. But it is not obvious that 'he didn't sing, he díd dance' is particularly appropriate to the context of the opening lines of the poem. What if (to dodge into the inventive chaos of literary semantics for a moment) we were to reject the 'literal' meanings of *sang* and *danced*? Suppose the line is interpreted as 'he rejoiced in (or celebrated) what he didn't do, he rejoiced in what he did do' or 'he took pleasure in what didn't happen to him, he took pleasure in what did happen to him'; he was happy with everything in his life, bad and good, whether his actions, or those of others towards him, were negative or positive in their effect. Here the source sentence(s) must have the surface structure $NP_1 + V + NP_2$ or $NP_1 + V + Adv$ where $Adv \to Prep. + NP_2$, and NP_2 in both cases is a subordinate clause of the type *what he did: he was happy with what he didn't do, he was happy with what he did (do)*. Obviously such a clause can be easily, though irregularly, nominalized. (The regular transformation would yield *his doing(s)*.) Compare and contrast:

he guarded what he possessed/his possessions; she didn't like what he did/his actions/his behaviour; it was sufficient for what I needed/my needs; they treasured what Mao said/Mao's sayings

and in the poem:

Women and men . . . reaped their sowing/what they had sown.

This exercise, though perhaps tedious, is rather revealing. The two interpretations are irreconcilable; one cannot sensibly support both and justify this refusal to choose by invoking the richness of poetic meaning. The incompatibility can be explained once we understand what we do when we impose these interpretations. The two series of transfer rules are totally dissimilar, one route excluding the other—this would not be the case if the alternative sources were *he danced* and *he did his dance*, for example. Again, whereas the first interpretation (source: *he did dance*) is obviously incorrect, the second is not obviously wrong. The great contrast in complexity of the transfer rules may not be unrelated to one's feeling about the wrongness of the first and the plausibility of the second. But these comments are beside the point, which was simply to demonstrate that what goes on when one 'imposes an interpretation' entails syntactic ingenuity which is a performance skill only erratically dependent on fragments of one's grammatical competence.

As a final example, consider *with up so floating many bells down*. This is surely a nonsense string: 'just "word-salad" ' (Katz [1964], 402 of sentences like *truth a scientists universe the*). Is it comprehensible?

anyone lived in a pretty how town
(with up so floating many bells down)

The parentheses are helpful. They suggest that the seven words form one unit. The first word, *with*, almost certainly establishes the unit as a modifier of *lived* or *town* in the preceding sentence; this would be consistent with the general use of phrasal modifiers throughout the poem. *Many bells* is the only structure within the line, and it is peculiarly unhelpful as far as understanding the line as a whole is concerned. To make any sense of the line, one must impose a syntax on it by postulating a nonce-rule which is not a rule of the grammar of English. Here one could propose

floating up and down→floating up down→up floating down

followed by

with so many bells up floating down→with up so floating many bells down.

This interpretation is both plausible and simple; whether it is 'correct' or 'adequate' in a critical way is another matter. I am well aware that it takes no note of other points of interest in the line, for example the rhythmical symmetry of *up* and *down* and the implications of this in relation to the semantic, syntactic and rhythmical play with opposites which goes on throughout the poem. Here I have wanted simply to demonstrate 'imposing an interpretation'.

Chomsky ((1965), 151) illustrates briefly the fact that 'the notion "grammaticalness" cannot be related to "interpretability" (ease, uniqueness, or uniformity of interpretation), in any simple way, at least'. He points out that some ungrammatical sentences are readily interpretable, whereas some grammatical sentences (including, but not consisting entirely of, the class of 'unacceptable' sentences) are difficult to interpret. Katz by implication denies this independence of grammaticalness and interpretability by proposing that some ungrammatical sentences are, by the fact of being ungrammatical to a certain degree, incomprehensible: 'nonsense strings'. We can avoid confusion only by distinguishing between grammaticalness as a condition determined by the characteristics of the grammar as a representation of competence, and interpretation as an activity to be accounted for in a theory of performance. Since observed sentences are produced by the interaction of competence and factors of a non-grammatical kind, then their interpretation depends on the application of skills which are not strictly aspects of 'knowing the language'. A principal skill is the retrieval of the syntax of an utterance.[5] There are many conditions under which this recovery of syntax is difficult; some are grammatical conditions, so we say that some utterances are ungrammatical: there is no conventional route between the syntax of the utterance and the rules the interpreter knows. In this case we say that the hearer, or reader, has to 'impose an interpretation': to make sense of the utterance, he uses not only his regular syntax-recovery procedures (normal performance) and his grammar (competence) but also some other performance skill(s). One of these is to look for new syntax, to postulate that a nonce-rule can be invoked to connect a particular utterance to the grammar. This skill must be akin to the skill used in acquiring a language or understanding a strange dialect—the ability to make and evaluate hypotheses about new linguistic data. A related secondary skill is to compare deviant utterances, to look for regular patterns in the ways grammatical rules are broken. These skills must depend partly on other non-linguistic factors, principally motivation and intelligence. So we study interpretation as part of the study of performance.

I would end by drawing attention again to the announced limitations of this paper, in order to suggest some much more ambitious lines of enquiry which would be necessary to complete the argument. I have tried to show only that the interpretation of highly ungrammatical strings must involve the exercise of a syntactic aptitude which is independent of the knowledge of the syntax of L which a speaker of L possesses. This performance skill must be employed to construct a deviant route from the string to (a) postulated underlying well-formed string(s). Thus although the interpretative skill is itself independent of linguistic competence, it operates partly by appeal to competence in that understanding finally takes place when a hypothesis about covert structure is achieved. (It is in the nature of the case that there is no linguistic test for the correctness of an interpretation.) The problem I have avoided is the nature of the initial prerequisites in an observed ungrammatical string to the process of 'imposing an interpretation' on it. It is obviously untrue that there is no utterance which cannot be interpreted; but it is probably true that there is no ungrammatical string of L which cannot be interpreted. The problem narrows to the fact that we do not have a definition of 'ungrammatical string of L'. In cases of extreme ungrammaticalness, where does 'of L' leave off and 'not of any L' begin? What is the minimal grammar of L which the L-unspecific performance skill needs in order to allow its work to start? The answers to these questions await psycholinguistic investigation of a very delicate kind.

References

Chomsky, N. (1961). 'Some Methodological Remarks on Generative Grammar', *Word*, xvii, 219–39. (Reprinted in Fodor & Katz, 1964: 384–9 under the title 'Degrees of Grammaticalness'.)

Chomsky, N. (1965). *Aspects of the Theory of Syntax*. Cambridge, Mass.: MIT Press.

Fodor, J. A. and Katz, J. J., eds. (1964). *The Structure of Language*. Englewood Cliffs, N.J.: Prentice-Hall.

Fowler, R. (1967). 'Linguistics and the Analysis of Poetry', *Critical Survey*, iii, 78–89 (this volume, Paper 14).

Fries, C. C. (1952). *The Structure of English*. London: Longmans.

Katz, J. J. (1964). 'Semi-sentences', in Fodor & Katz (1964: 400–16).

Levin, S. R. (1962). *Linguistic Structures in Poetry* (Janua Linguarum, No. 23). The Hague: Mouton.

Levin, S. R. (1964). 'Poetry and Grammaticalness', in Lunt, H. G. (ed.), *Proceedings of the Ninth International Congress of Linguists*. The Hague: Mouton.

Lyons, J. and Wales, R. J., eds. (1966). *Psycholinguistics Papers*. Edinburgh University Press.

Miller, G. A. and Chomsky, N. (1963). 'Finitary Models of Language Users', Ch. 13 of Luce, R. D., Bush, R. R. & Galanter, E., *Handbook of Mathematical Psychology*, ii, New York: Wiley.

Thorne, J. P. (1965). 'Stylistics and Generative Grammars', *JL* i, 49–59.

Thorne, J. P. (1966). 'On Hearing Sentences', in Lyons & Wales (1966).

Ziff, P. (1964). 'On Understanding "Understanding utterances" ', in Fodor & Katz (1964: 390–9).

Notes to Paper Fifteen

1 I mean 'lack of structure given by the grammar of English', not 'lack of structure', of course.

2 That is, how we are to relate 'knowing a rule' with 'understanding a sentence which exemplifies that rule'. For discussion see Thorne (1966) and parts of other papers in Lyons and Wales (1966).

3 Any adventurous literary critic who strays into these pages must be prepared to take 'ungrammatical' and 'unacceptable' as neutral descriptive terms designed to indicate the character of the syntax as it must appear to a reader equipped with a grammar of twentieth-century English. No evaluation is intended.

4 For a fuller treatment of the language of this poem, within the neo-Firthian syntactic framework, see Fowler (1967) (this volume, Paper 14).

5 That this is not inevitably a grammatical skill (i.e. part of linguistic competence) is suggested by the failure of analysis-by-synthesis models of interpretation.

Further reading

In the notes to the papers collected in the present work a large number of books and articles have been cited, usually in specific, and often technical, contexts. I have here selected some titles which are of more general interest, and some which I think are of direct relevance to the perspective on language and literature adopted in this book. In the Linguistics list, I have included some elementary textbooks for readers who are new to the discipline.

1 Linguistics

BLOOMFIELD, LEONARD, *Language* (London, 1933).

CHOMSKY, NOAM, *Aspects of the Theory of Syntax* (Cambridge, Mass., 1965).

CHOMSKY, NOAM, *Syntactic Structures* (The Hague, 1957).

FODOR, J. A., and J. J. KATZ (eds.), *The Structure of Language, Readings in the Philosophy of Language* (Englewood Cliffs, N.J., 1964).

FOWLER, ROGER, *Introduction to Transformational Syntax* (London, Routledge & Kegan Paul, 1971).

GLEASON, H. A., JR, *An Introduction to Descriptive Linguistics* (2nd ed., New York, 1961).

JACOBS, RODERICK A., and PETER S. ROSENBAUM, *English Transformational Grammar* (Waltham, Mass., 1968).

KATZ, J. J., and P. M. POSTAL, *An Integrated Theory of Linguistic Descriptions* (Cambridge, Mass., 1964).

LANGENDOEN, D. TERENCE, *Essentials of English Grammar* (New York, 1970).

LYONS, JOHN, *Introduction to Theoretical Linguistics* (London, 1968).

LYONS, JOHN (ed.), *New Horizons in Linguistics* (Harmondsworth, 1970).

REIBEL, DAVID A., and S. A. SCHANE (eds.), *Modern Studies in English, Readings in Transformational Grammar* (Englewood Cliffs, N.J., 1969).

ROBINS, R. H., *General Linguistics, an Introductory Survey* (London, 1964).

ROBINS, R. H., *A Short History of Linguistics* (London, 1967).

SAPIR, EDWARD, *Language* (New York, 1921).

SAUSSURE, FERDINAND DE, trans. Wade Baskin, *Course in General Linguistics* (New York, 1959).

2 Criticism

BOOTH, WAYNE C., *The Rhetoric of Fiction* (Chicago, 1961).
BRADBURY, MALCOLM (ed.), *Contemporary Criticism* (London, Stratford-upon-Avon Studies, 1970).
BROOKS, CLEANTH, *The Well Wrought Urn* (New York, 1947).
CRANE, R. S. (ed.), *Critics and Criticism* (Chicago, 1952).
CRANE, R. S., *The Languages of Criticism and the Structure of Poetry* (Toronto, 1953).
DAVIE, DONALD, *Articulate Energy* (London, 1955).
ELIOT, T. S., *Selected Essays* (3rd ed., London, 1951).
EMPSON, WILLIAM, *Seven Types of Ambiguity* (3rd ed., London, 1953).
EMPSON, WILLIAM, *The Structure of Complex Words* (New York, 1951).
ERLICH, VICTOR, *Russian Formalism—History, Doctrine* (2nd ed., The Hague, 1965).
KERMODE, FRANK, *Romantic Image* (London, 1957).
KERMODE, FRANK, *The Sense of an Ending, Studies in the Theory of Fiction* (London and New York, 1966).
LODGE, DAVID, *Language of Fiction* (London, 1966).
NOWOTTNY, WINIFRED, *The Language Poets Use* (London, 1962).
WARREN, A., and R. WELLEK, *Theory of Literature* (3rd ed., Harmondsworth, 1963).
WIMSATT, W. K., JR, *Hateful Contraries, Studies in Literature and Criticism* (Lexington, Ky., 1965).
WIMSATT, W. K., JR, *The Verbal Icon, Studies in the Meaning of Poetry* (Lexington, Ky., 1954).

3 'Linguistic Criticism'

Notice that I have put 'scare quotes' around the heading of this section of the reading list: they are to warn that, even if Linguistics and Criticism are confidently identifiable methods and fields of study, 'Linguistic Criticism' is not an established mode of scholarly activity—and, according to the Introduction to this book, ought not to be. However, we need a concise label to gather some writings of linguists who have recently interested themselves in the relevance of linguistics to literary studies.

BAILEY, RICHARD W., and DOLORES M. BURTON, S.N.D., *English Stylistics, a Bibliography* (Cambridge, Mass., 1968).
BRONZWAER, W. J. M., *Tense in the Novel, An Investigation of Some Potentialities of Linguistic Criticism* (Groningen, 1970).
CHATMAN, SEYMOUR B., *A Theory of Meter* (The Hague, 1965).

CHATMAN, SEYMOUR B., and S. R. LEVIN (eds.), *Essays on the Language of Literature* (Boston, 1967).

CRYSTAL, DAVID, and DEREK DAVY, *Investigating English Style* (London, 1969).

FOWLER, ROGER (ed.), *Essays on Style and Language* (London, 1966).

FREEMAN, DONALD C. (ed.), *Linguistics and Literary Style* (New York, 1970).

LEECH, GEOFFREY N., *A Linguistic Guide to English Poetry* (London, 1969).

LEVIN, S. R., *Linguistic Structures in Poetry* (The Hague, 1962).

LOVE, GLEN A., and MICHAEL PAYNE (eds.), *Contemporary Essays on Style; Rhetoric, Linguistics, and Criticism* (Glencoe, Ill., 1969).

MCINTOSH, ANGUS, and M. A. K. HALLIDAY, *Patterns of Language, Papers in General, Descriptive and Applied Linguistics* (London, 1966).

'New Attitudes to Style', *Review of English Literature*, vi (1965).

SEBEOK, THOMAS A. (ed.), *Style in Language* (New York, 1960).

SPENCER, JOHN, and MICHAEL GREGORY (eds.), *Linguistics and Style* (London, 1964).

SPITZER, LEO, *Linguistics and Literary History: Essays in Stylistics* (Princeton, 1948).

Index of names

Because of the nature of this collection, some names of authors and editors (e.g. Chatman, Levin, Sebeok) are repeated many times in bibliographical footnotes. It seemed superfluous to index all these repeated references.